STARS, CARS AND CRYSTAL METH

STARS CARS AND

JACK SUTHERLAND

(AS TOLD TO JOHN SUTHERLAND)

FABER & FABER

This edition first published in the UK in 2016 by
Faber & Faber Ltd, Bloomsbury House,
74–77 Great Russell Street,
London WC1B 3DA

Printed in the UK by CPI Group (UK) Ltd, Croydon CR0 4YY

A CIP record for this book is available from the British Library

ISBN 978-0-571-32353-1

2 4 6 8 10 9 7 5 3 1

To Jeison Valencia
My Love, My Saviour

CONTENTS

Everybody hurts.
REM

FOREWORD BY RUPAUL

Jack and I came to know each other back in 2000, when he was the chauffeur who drove me to an appearance for Outfest. We started to casually chat on the trip back home, and we took to each other from that first meeting, on that hot day in Hollywood. My sense that Jack was someone special was confirmed as I saw him, a day or two later, attempting to do a lap round my pool in orange Speedos and high heels. This, I thought, is a man who does not take himself too seriously. The twenty-two marbles – what a surprise. Who would have known!

Over the years we remained close friends and I saw him go up and down. His downs were quite extreme and intense – it's a wonder he ever came back, but fortunately he did and he has. That was very clear to me on our last meeting in London in 2015.

This is a brave book, I think, and one which Jack has put on paper (Jack an author – who would have thought it?). He has decided to open up his eventful and colourful life for all to read for one reason only, as he says: to help others who are struggling to cope with life and addiction.

Love, Ru

PREFACE: DOWN, OUT AND COLD

'You,' the man said, weighing his words thoughtfully, 'are the biggest fuck-up I have ever known in the whole of my life.'

He didn't say it unkindly. But he didn't say it nicely, either. There was no reason he should.

From him, a compliment of a kind. Mickey Rourke had himself, as he often admitted, been washed up more often than the proverbial greasy-spoon breakfast plate. He knew the ups and downs of life: none better.

He'd twice taken his career into the ring and had his face rearranged, beyond the skill of cosmetic surgery, in regular facial encounters with glove and canvas.*

The angelic features which had propelled the young Mickey into world fame with his early cameo in *Body Heat* (two minutes still studied in every screen-acting school) were gone. A certain menace remained, though. Particularly when it was glowering two inches from your face.

Perhaps he was right. About me. Well, the fact is, he was most certainly right. He'd been good to me, and I'd let him down, big time. Fuck-up I was. But then, however often he

* I've just read (November 2014) that he's gone back into the ring, aged sixty-two. In Russia. Putin loves him, apparently.

was counted out, Mickey himself had always come back, hadn't he? Wasn't there hope? Even for fucked-up me?

This was 2010. After his early success, he'd sunk low. But his performance in *The Wrestler* (#1 on ranker.com's list of his movies) and his OTT depiction of gravel-voiced evil in *Iron Man 2* had made him Hollywood's comeback kid.

Mickey Rourke was back where he belonged: on top.* And, at this moment, looking down from that great height on me. A stain on the red carpet. Wrecked by methamphetamine. (The only way I could do the impossible job demanded of a Rourke PA, I told myself. Not true, but it was all I had to hold on to.)

Long and short? I was fired. And if that was all, I was lucky.

Could I, now the certified biggest fuck-up Mickey Rourke had ever known in the whole of his fucking life, come back? Iron Jack 2? It was 2010. Winter. New Mexico. Snow. And I was in a T-shirt.

* He's still on top: *Sin City 2*.

1: DODGING THE SEPTIC TANK

It's not a good start in life to be Irish and illegitimate. Download the movie *Philomena* from iTunes and stock up with Kleenex to see why. I escaped being transported, like Ireland's 'lost generation' of bastardy, to far-off places, to be abused as forced labour or a sex slave. I escaped the septic tank in which, as I happened to read in a recent Buzzfeed article, Irish nuns simplified the disposal of the unwanted bastard babies they'd starved to death. That's how those sisters of mercy regarded children who came into the world like I did. Sewage. Ireland has never loved the children of 'fallen women'. Which is how I started life. Fallen-woman spawn.

My birth mother, as best I've ever been able to find out, was a salesperson in a Dublin shoe store. Young and pretty, I like to fantasise. 'Theresa Hennessy' was the name on the birth certificate – a suspiciously common name in Ireland. Once when I was (temporarily) rich and found myself residing in an Irish castle, I toyed with the idea of going on the hunt for Theresa. But I lost my nerve in the face of being rejected again. On another occasion I employed a private investigator to track her down. No luck. It's like looking for a newsagent called Patel in Birmingham, a busboy called

Hernandez in San Diego – or, come to that, a Jack Sutherland in Scotland. If it was a false name, as I now think, 'Theresa' chose well. Her story will never be told. Perhaps it doesn't need to be. In Ireland it's a common enough story.

This much I do know. My birth mother got into 'trouble' (that uniquely Irish euphemism) with a married man, about whom I know nothing. Divorce was not an option – even if the bastard (the real bastard in this case) was inclined to do the decent thing and make an 'honest woman' of my BM. Which he clearly wasn't. Ireland didn't approve of breaking the sacred vows of marriage.

The above facts are the sum total of what I got from the friendly English obstetrician who treated 'Theresa' in her last weeks of pregnancy. This was 1973. For five years there had been legal abortion in England. Nothing would have been easier for 'Theresa' than to make a first-trimester long-weekend trip, Dublin to Liverpool. Two hours in the family planning clinic, a cup of tea, soothing conversation and a biscuit, then back, free as a bird, to Ireland, an honest woman again.

Instead 'Theresa' managed to keep her 'trouble' secret and came over to England to give birth, not to abort. She had evidently decided she was not going to kill her baby. Nor was she going to pass him/her to the kindness of nuns and their septic-tank solution. She arranged to pass him/her over by private adoption (legal then, not any more) to a good home – the obstetrician helped – in England. Having accomplished that, 'Theresa' went home, never to be heard of again – at least by me.

My coming into the world was in an anonymous East End London hospital, where perhaps 'Theresa' had discreet friends in the neighbourhood. Or perhaps she just stuck a pin into the map to find somewhere no one would think to look.

My birth mother, brave woman, did not take the easy way. I hope she went on to have a good life. If she reads this book, she can contact me. My message in a bottle.*

As I say, I was lucky. And the luck kept running strong. I was adopted, at birth, by a couple who really wanted a baby. Both my parents, hereafter my mother and father, were highly qualified professionals. Egg-headed, as they say. Many notches above sales assistants in shoe shops. Or anything I'd ever be.

Both had PhDs – my father three of them.† Both lived and worked in a world of learning. Myself, I've read fewer books than my father has written.‡ I'd need a space suit to make a trip to Planet Learning. I don't miss it. I was programmed, genetically, for different things.

I came to consciousness of the world around me in a large South London family house, in a community of similar families who'd ended up in Herne Hill (lovely name) because it was the last place in outer London where, in the

* I ought, in honesty, to add that I had a series of midlife nervous breakdowns (read on) and a near-suicidal drug-soaked month in hell when the full implication of 'adoption' – being 'given away' – came back to haunt me. A common crisis for adoptees, I'm told. I had, I confess, spasms of hatred for 'Theresa'. It's all pleasantly numb now. But how can you love a shadow?

† One earned, two honorary.

‡ I must mention two. *Reflections of a Rock Lobster: A Story About Growing Up Gay* by Aaron Fricke, and *Out of the Shadows: Understanding Sexual Addiction* by Patrick Carnes. Both life-changers.

early 1970s, you could get a half-decent house for under ten grand. It had once been a 'hill of herons' – woody lanes and fields with herds of cows to supply inner London with its daily milk. Now it was a yuppie ghetto.

I could now buy that house, at its 1973 price, with my credit card. When I was at my highest earning I could have bought half the street. Holmdene Avenue, it was called. ('Sheltered valley', my father once told me. In fact it was a terrace developed in 1910, when the railway opened up the area to jerry-building developers.) I loved the house, which was all nooks, crannies, dark cupboards, coal-holes and long steep staircases. And dry rot, it was later discovered. That somehow figured. It seemed, to little me, as big as a palace, and mysterious as Oz. I took a look at it the other day (now I live down Half Moon Lane in nowadays des-res Brixton). It's just another blah terraced house. No magic. And they cost a cool million too. No yuppie need apply. Bugger off to Scratch End.

I was named after my father's father, 'Jack Sutherland'. He (John Sutherland) never knew his father, any more than I knew mine. Jack Sutherland the first had died, in the RAF, fighting Germany, in 1941. John's relationship with his mother was complicated. You can read about it in his memoir, *The Boy Who Loved Books* (and, no, I didn't finish it: I didn't even read the book he dedicated to me – something about Victorian publishers. But I was grateful for the gesture).*

On my mother's side, I inherited one of the very best

* *John.* The book you can't remember the name of is *Victorian Fiction: Writers, Publishers, Readers* (Macmillan, 1994, repr. 2002). Not your cup of tea, I grant.

things in my life: a grandfather and grandmother for whom I was the first grandchild, and by whom I was pampered like the little prince I always knew I was. They were Scottish and still spoke that way. And Presbyterian. It was my gran who made me pray at night, later on to my own peculiar gods (Buddhist, more or less). She'd been a Norland Nanny (to stars like the Redgrave acting family, oddly) and would like to have grandmothered the world. I soaked up all she had to give. What's best in me, if anything, I owe to them.

It should have been a dream Brady Bunch childhood. It wasn't. There were three reasons. The first is that I'm smart: everyone tells me that. But I'm smart enough to know I'm not book-learning clever and never will be. My parents later on shelled out six hundred bucks to subject me to a Wechsler intelligence test. The results confirmed what I already knew. I have a poor short-term memory – my brain's like a garbage grinder with dyslexia. But I have strong reasoning powers and higher-order skills when it comes to lateral thinking. It's like a benign ADHD, I've been told. But it did not equip me to do well at school – other than that I was genius at manipulating people. I've always, whatever I've done, been liked. Liking myself has been harder.

The second thing that fucked up my childhood made itself known when, at infant school (!), my parents were summoned for a grim conversation with the principal, Ms Bossyboots. I'd been found vigorously researching the joys of fellatio (still one of the few Latin words, along with some STD names, I've picked up) in the school lavs.* 'Perhaps,'

* She actually got it slightly wrong. I won't go into details.

the principal said to my entirely flummoxed mother and father, 'you let this kind of thing go on in your home?'

It was a permissive era, the late 1970s. The last hurrah for hippydom. But not that permissive in Holmdene Avenue. The only thing they sucked was the occasional joint. Fact was, I knew, in myself, what I was myself. It would take a long time to come to terms with it. And a lot of pain and confusion. Accepting yourself is difficult. Changing yourself impossible.

The third thing which made for a less-than-happy home in Holmdene Avenue was the fact that my father drank. An understatement. He was the most dangerous kind of alcoholic. He could 'cope'. Blur, violence and domestic hell came at night. During the day, most days, he could operate in the university where he worked and was well thought of. Less so by his 'loved ones'.

Having an alcoholic around is like living in a house which is on fire – but the fire never burns itself out. Every so often I would be scooped up for a night-time escape. My mother kept an ever-ready packed bag, and when I look back in mind to those days, I see her smoking cigarette after cigarette and crying to herself. Promises to reform – and sometimes a few weeks' peace – brought 'the family' back together again. In my own alcoholic/drugged periods, later in life, I too would be very cunning at keeping support networks, and safety nets, in place. Who knows, perhaps those horror times in Holmdene Avenue were a learning experience for later madnesses of my own. Like father, like son, etc. Looking back, I remember hiding under the duvet, and whispering to myself a Stevie Wonder song, 'Girl Blue' ('Little girl you're sad'), from *Music of My Mind*. 'Boy Blue Me'.

There were intermissions. Blissful holidays in Cape Cod where I learned to swim in a motel pool and love 'real' hamburgers, bubble gum (Hubba Bubba, by choice), popcorn and Captain Kangaroo.

But mainly it was waiting, anxiously, for 'him' to come home – Toblerone bar and a book for bedtime – and the unasked question: 'Is "he" going to be drunk, or sober?' The record changed when he came through the door. I learned to smell, at a yard's distance, whether there was alcohol on his breath. That might well mean a bad night. No bedtime story. At its worst (and worst happened) drag-out fights downstairs, shouting, the sound of breaking dishes and, if it got violent, tomato ketchup or whatever was splatted on the walls next morning, and warnings to be careful where I walked: broken glass. Everything broken, really. The bad nights in Holmdene Avenue, as time passed, became bad weekends and then whole bad weeks.

I was not a success in school but I made my way lurking around the edge of the place. Adopted myself, I've always found it easier to adopt other people around me as a kind of floating family. Tribes of Jack. There was always, though, something antisocial about these unofficial families. Not criminal, just mischievous and 'naughty'.

My parents had a weekend home in the country, where – once the local Suffolk village kids accepted the 'London hippy' with the long blond hair – I had a little-folks gang life. There were midnight rambles, over the barbed wire, to the great churchyard at Ickworth. We would scare ourselves shitless round the graves, calling up the ghosts of the corpses beneath. Pure exorcist. On more than one occasion the local constabulary were called to find us. High crime in that sleepy corner of the world.

I later taught myself to drive in Hawstead, aged eleven, while my parents were out of the house. I remember my father's mild wonder on seeing the car parked somewhere he couldn't quite remember putting it. Then just reminding himself that he was an absent-minded professor with a drink problem and getting back to his books. Even then, aged eleven, I was probably a better driver than him.

Driving, and a kind of GPS implanted in my head, would be one of the key skills of my later career in the US. Avoiding 'moving violations' and, on one occasion (in my customised Corvette), carjackers was not, alas, one of my key skills. But I discovered there were always lawyers who could get you off the speeding, illegal-turn and light-jump charges. (Most people don't know that California cops have to give evidence in misdemeanour auto-offence charges on their days off: they don't turn up.) It cost $1,200 a pop from Traffic Defenders (I recommend them), but it kept my wheels on the road. Without that I would have withered away, selling oranges at intersections with a cardboard sign round my neck: CARLESS – PLEASE HELP.

I always chose high-end cars – Jaguars, for preference (and patriotism).* And I learned how to drive them, expertly, little feet dangling over the pedals of a Fiat Panda, in muddy Suffolk lanes. Happy days.

But before all that, the drinking in Holmdene Avenue got

* My personalised number plates, in the high-life years: UK PAPI. British daddy.

worse. End of the road (morgue, closed ward, skid row, car crash, job loss) menaced for my father.

Then, out of the blue, John got an offer from an elite Californian university. Loads of money. But his drinking was at crisis stage. Blackouts, violence, even an arrest or two. (He tried to smash up a Scientology 'church' on Tottenham Court Road, offended by the fact that they dared offer him an 'intelligence test'.) It was the crunch. Moment of truth. Go off, clean up, or don't come back, was the ultimatum.

He was sent to the other side of the world. No great hopes. It was 1983. I was nine.

2: SCHOOLDAYS: SUNSHINE, DRINK, DRUGS, MURDER AND VIDEOS

A miracle. John cleaned up. He's written about it in one of his many, many books – the 'drunkalog' called *Last Drink to LA*.* Now I think about it, that's one of the few books I've read to the end, because quite a lot of it's about me. Some of it wrong.

He hasn't drunk a drop of alcohol ever since. Nor, thank God, has he become an AA bore with all those stale 'truths' ('Let Go, Let God!', 'One Day at a Time', etc.). Alcohol just left his life for good. Good in every sense.†

We still didn't know, after the first year at his new employer was up and a tenured job on offer, whether he could be trusted. But my mum (soon to be my 'mom') and I took the risk. She gave up a good job with one of the best publishers in London and landed a job just as good, no trouble, in our new home – South Pasadena. I took to SoCal like a fish to water. We were a six-figure (and we're not talking low hundreds) rich family.

A word or two about SouthPas. Following the 1964 Civil Rights Act, Americans got very steamed about 'ghettoisation'.

* *John*. Second edition, 2015. Classic.

† *John*. At time of writing, thirty-one years, three months and a few days. Though after all these years I'm too bored, or old, to count.

Inner-city schools were all black and immigrant underclass, and catastrophically underachieving. The solution: bussing. Shipping kids out from deprived areas, and shipping kids in from upmarket areas.

It looked good in Washington. It didn't go down well on the ground. Poor black kids, one-language Hispanics, and rich white kids all shared one thing: they damn well didn't want to be sitting next to each other in classrooms. The greater Los Angeles area split into eighty-plus cities. Cut up into fragments by the bussing choice, they had the right to make the choice – bus/no bus – at local level. SouthPas was 100 per cent for ghettoisation. So long as it was rich, white, professional ghettos. Next-door Pasadena, which had a large underclass, bussed. The SouthPas solution to the post-1964 urban dilemma wasn't white flight – it was white self-defence. Racist as hell, of course.

So I found myself in a city which was vanilla-genteel. You probably haven't been to SouthPas. But you may have seen Michael J. Fox in *Teen Wolf* (that's set in SouthPas), or Robert Altman's *The Player* (SouthPas's historic Rialto Theatre is where the murder happens). Or the freeway where Dustin Hoffman's car runs out of gas in *The Graduate*.

SouthPas was, in the 1980s, 'heartland' America. Soda fountains, Trader Joe's for stocking the fridge organically, and a youth curfew after nine for its well-behaved youth. The cop station was fronted by 'Officer Friendly'. (I came to know him well. He wasn't always friendly.) The good life in SouthPas was, of course, pasted on: thin as tissue wrap. But if you didn't think about it, you could believe in it. We Believed.

We had a big 'Spanish' house (patio, Mexican tiles, redwood panelling, succulent 'desert' plants in the gardens). It was located in Floral Park Terrace, so called for its avenue of flowering jacaranda trees and kerbside borders of birds of paradise – the state flower, if you're interested.

Technicolor suburbia. The day we moved in, neighbours brought us chocolates and flowers. Welcome, Sutherlands. You're our kind of people. White, professional, upwardly mobile. We were principally welcome, of course, for what we weren't. No blockbusting in SouthPas.

Our street was a few hundred yards from the oldest freeway in the US, the Arroyo Seco Parkway (now the State Route 110). When the Santa Anas blew hot and dry over the San Gabriel Mountains you could hear the murmur of the 24-hour, 60-m.p.h. traffic jam. 'Just like the ocean,' the realtors would say, hopefully. For me it was the soundtrack of Southern California. I loved it.

I had my own annex to the house – which I painted all black. Black walls, black bed, black satin sheets. I shared it with my dog, Bear, a sweet-and-sour mix of Rottweiler and Labrador. I had privacy, my own phone, TV and sound system, but no toilet. The succulents had a hard time round my annex.

I was a lucky kid cushioned in privilege in Reagan's bright-new-morning America. Was I happy? Fuck, no. I wasn't smart in a school whose pride was all tied up in 'achievement' – academic, sporting and dating the hottest pupils on campus. I was a closet-gay D student with a hatred of ball games (I couldn't catch or hit the damn things). 'Everyone a Winner!' was the big sign inside the door. I was a loser in a world of winners. And, by the age of fourteen, I was an adolescent junkie. No other word for it.

I found myself an alternative dropout community to feel at home in. A 'family'. Not Crips/Bloods gangsterism, but a group of unhappy, maladjusted SouthPas fellow losers with big grudges against the world. Our 'colours' were black. We played Led Zeppelin ear-blasting loud. Not protest, just noise.

Our main drug supplier, and stylist, was another member of the family, whom I'll call Paul – my best friend – along with his girlfriend, Jennifer.* Very cool, Paul got the stuff from his even cooler older brother. The mother was a lesbian. It was a tolerant family. The leader of the family was lowlife Dave Atkins (no need to rename him for reasons that will appear). Dave was dark, film-star good-looking, and streetwise. He was clearly destined for something big and certainly criminal in life. Pizza-faced, dumb, even lower-life Vinnie Hebrock was his gofer. His punk. They were obsessively interested in girls and thoughtlessly homophobic. So, for appearance's sake, was I. I got suspended from junior high school for verbal abuse ('Die, you buttfucker!'). My pathetic, and cruel, smokescreen.

But, like men in prison (which is where Dave and Vinnie are now), the others were not, as I discovered, unwilling to try the guy, when the mood took them. It did, suspiciously often.

* Paul and Jennifer were among the first friends I had who were sympathetic to my being gay. I still keep in touch with Jennifer on Facebook. We talk about the old days. It's like shouting to a friend across the Grand Canyon – so much time and life has passed, taking us different places. Paul, I last heard, was working on ski slopes somewhere.

They loved porn videos, for the reasons all adolescents do. I got myself a copy of *Deep Throat*. They would sit around jerking off, looking at Linda Lovelace taking it in all orifices. I would jerk off alongside – looking at them jerk off, not the screen. Nothing there for me.

For appearance's sake I dated some girls at the school. Women, I've observed over the years, quite often go with gays. They feel safer – less eye-raping or clawing at their bodies. I even had sex with a couple of them – enough to give me locker-room bragging rights and impress the guys. But no satisfaction beyond that. But I've always loved the company of women. Still do.

My breakfasts, by choice, were Chicken McNuggets and S&S sauce from the SouthPas McDonald's drive-through. My father would drive me to school and we'd have man-to-man conversation. He could see more than he liked to admit to himself, and he told me, with that phony 'wisdom' dads put on for their kids, that most boys go through 'sexually transitional' periods – he had himself. I clung to the belief that my conflicted sexual feelings were a 'phase'.

LSD was the drug of choice in the later stages of my junkified school career. It supposedly left no trace in the blood, unlike marijuana, which would hang around for weeks. Wise parents (mine were too trusting) tested their kids once a month. I was free to smoke, sniff and pop what I wanted, so long as I didn't look visibly high. I've always had a strong tolerance for drugs. Dentists can shoot their whole pharmacy into my gums, I've found, and I still feel the pain. Vodka, meanwhile, was the drink of choice. It left no smell on the breath. I started drinking it in the seventh grade (around age twelve) and routinely kept it in a water bottle in my school locker.

On long, warm evenings I would tell my parents I was off to the nearby Arroyo stables with my friend Janie Morgan. A rich kid (with a powerful father), she owned a couple of horses. Mares – Queen and Baby. My parents would give me the $20 stable fee, and sometimes I would indeed spend it on a ride on Queen. I've always loved dogs and horses. Mainly the female of the species. Other times it would be weed and then chili-cheese fries at Hi-Life on Fair Oaks Avenue, washed down with a throw-it-all-in, sixty-two-ounce cup of a soda drink we called 'Suicide'.

If my parents smelled something on my breath I'd get all shamefaced and say I'd smoked a cigarette and how sorry I was. I always carried a pack of non-filter Joe Camels for cover.*

Sorry I was not.

Every weekend, one way or another, we'd get fucked up. I loved it – not for the kick, mainly, but for the forgetfulness of what I was, and what, inside, I now hated being.

IF YOU GO DOWN TO THE WOODS TODAY

If I could add it all up, I guess that of all the sex I've had in my life, 90 per cent has been anonymous – where neither I nor the other guy knew, or wanted to know, each other's

* They don't sell them any more, I heard. Probably 'collectable' mint packs go on eBay for $50.

names. Business, not personal, as they say in *The Godfather*.*

My first 'grown-up' encounter was when I was fourteen or so – well, not grown-up and very much jailbait. At this time, Janie, my closest girl friend – innocent bedmate, even – was my 'girlfriend'. Friend, nothing more, and having her around was cover for what I really was. For years afterwards she was always ready to be my beard when required. We ran an LA Marathon together.

I loved riding – Western-style, low stirrups, broad saddle. In America, going back to frontier days, it's working-class. Janie and I used to ride the trails for hours in Griffith Park. You may know the place, though you've never been there. It's where Hollywood used to shoot all the B-Westerns. It's home to the planetarium which is big in *Rebel Without a Cause*, and it's where the Terminator lands in the first of those films.

There was this wooded part of the park where you'd see men, just men, walking by themselves, going nowhere, looking round. For what? Sex in the wild, of course. We were kids – Janie two years older than me (which meant car-licenced). We were both curious and decided to investigate, on foot, the lonely-guy trails. A 'recon mission', we called it. What's that line in *Bambi* (a film I hate, by the way†)? 'Man is in the forest!' Why were these men in the forest? We'd find out.

* I had a good few heterosexual encounters around this time. Disaster.

† Because of the shooting of the mother. Why do that to children? But I'd forgive Uncle Walt anything for the Pirates of the Caribbean ride at Disneyland. I once went round it nine times on the trot.

The recon done, we made a second trip. Of course it was sexual curiosity on my part. I could guess, vaguely, why those guys would hang out in the woods. They weren't birdwatchers. There was a churning feeling in the pit of my stomach whenever I thought of those trails and fantasised where, deep in the shadows, they led. Janie went along with it. For our mission she pulled her hair back into a ponytail, put on one of my hoodies, and looked boy-drag enough for any chicken hawk. It raised the excitement level.

We drove over to the park for an hour or two at twilight. It doesn't last long in Southern California; night really falls. When we got there, Janie stayed within sight of the car. Nothing in the woods for her. I was petrified but by now excited enough to be reckless. No turning back now.

I went, all by myself, through the trailhead into the woods and bushes. Light was now fading fast. I was soon hit on by a guy – in his early twenties, I'd guess, perhaps older. White and clearly with a taste for young meat: it was a lucky night for him. I could almost see him slavering in what was left of the daylight. He knew the park well. After a few exchanges of the 'Hi, howyadoin'?' kind, checking me out, he beckoned me along a side trail which soon petered into wilderness. It was now dark.

What followed couldn't have lasted more than seven minutes. But it felt like a day-long trek through the San Gabriels to me. And frightening. Griffith Park was a place where you could get raped and killed and end up coyote food for days before anyone found what was left of you. We're talking 1988 – no cell phones, no pagers. Rangers rarely got out of their vehicles unless they had to. Why get their nice uniforms scuffed?

It happened – my sexual initiation, that is – in the bole of a big eucalyptus. I can smell that oil to this day, with faint echoes of the excitement of that night. He kissed me, touched my groin, gently took my pants down. Rape wasn't going to happen. He knelt and went down on me, after slobbering all over me and feeling my nipples. I was now terrified but let him do what he wanted. Then he asked me to go down on him. No way. I didn't do that, I said, pretending I knew all about sex in the park. The truth is, I just wanted to run. I jerked him off. As far as I could bring myself to go. He climaxed, looking me in the eyes, grunted a bit.

When we'd finished, he upped and left. Sprinting. Not even a goodbye or a look over his shoulder. He didn't want to be caught with a fourteen-year-old, pants round his ankles. The vice division of the LAPD was doing occasional plain-clothes sting-sweeps through the park – not to stamp it out, but to keep it from frightening the joggers. My guy had just committed a criminal act for which, if he had a record (he must have done), he could get life plus twenty-five. That puts wings on your heels.

I made my way back to the parking lot and Janie. I told her to drive fast. When we were out of the park I had her pull over where I could puke in a lay-by. Projectile velocity. I felt guilt, shame and fear. But, somewhere inside me, I knew I'd be back one way or another.

I would have that nauseous reaction after any kind of sex – particularly oral – for two years after that. My body saying no. And I never, thereafter, ever went with older guys. Still don't. I read a lot, nowadays, about young victims of Jimmy Savile whose lives are forever ruined or blighted by what he did. Mine wasn't. If anything, it was opened up. Why? Because I *chose* to go down that trail in Griffith Park. It was *my* decision. My leap in the dark. What I found at the end of the trail, under the eucalyptus, was, at the time, painful and horrible and nauseating. And I wish, to this day, that I hadn't done it. But it wasn't 'abuse'. It was me. I would work on that 'me' in the years to come.

PLAYGROUND PUSHER

Life goes on, even if you hate yourself. My parents could see, at last, through their haze of love, that I was 'troubled', and put me under the best child psychologist ($150 p.h.) in town. I liked Dr Eckel, and fooled her. We spent most of the sessions drinking herbal tea and playing Uno. She never even discovered, or wanted to know, that I was gay. Or that, young as I was (barely a teenager), I had a dangerous drug habit.

Drugs, even in Southern California, which is tsunami-awash with them, cost money. There were only so many pizzas my parents could credit me eating – more so as I was verging on clinically anorexic. Bone-thin. Part vanity – I liked the skinny look – part stress which was building up inside me all the time. To raise cash, me and Paul hit on the idea of mail-ordering weapons to be delivered to his house. His parents were separated and his mother and brother wouldn't give a toss what UPS brought Paul thanks to a fake ID. I'm talking knives and Rambo shit advertised in survivalist magazines. Ninja-themed stuff sold best of all.

Those throwing stars, winged daggers, and stupid chained truncheons that only Bruce Lee could twirl without spraining his wrists.

There was a brisk market for it in the school. But someone, caught with their feeble lethal weapon, ratted me out and that profitable line of business ended. I was warned. My dead-loss friends and I then worked out we could make useful, and safer, money selling drugs, mainly marijuana, to unconnected school kids. Paul's brother always had enough spare for the family's use and for selling on. We cut the stuff with herbs (sometimes from my mother's kitchen. I once saw her looking oddly at the jars – 'We've used *that* much oregano and basil?'). The suckers at school had no clue. They were excited by the 'idea'. *Drugs!*

One afternoon during lunch break, I saw the principal crossing the yard towards me at high speed, another teacher behind him. I was carrying a baggie with five or six wraps. It wasn't often the principal left his office, even less often that he sprinted on 'his' campus. I'd been ratted out again and was now about to be busted. I was marched off to be strip-searched in the gym. On the way I managed to crumple the incriminating wraps and toss them into a trash can. The principal, no fool he, fished them out from the garbage and held them aloft, like a sports trophy. It didn't sweeten his temper. The strip-search found more weed hidden in places which might have put my clientele off, had they known.

I ratted out Dave and Vinnie myself. Everyone cops pleas in that kind of situation. None of that Mafia omertà. This time, though, the police were called – good old Officer

Friendly. The three of us were arrested, handcuffed and marched through the school grounds, gawped at all the way. Perpetrators. I felt – no other word for it – 'cool'. Respected. Pathetic.

'Intention to Distribute' is serious, even if you are under sixteen. At the station – my father had been summoned from the Huntington Library, where he was wearing his eyes out, as usual, on manuscripts – they tested the herbs and found there was so much of my mother's oregano in the weed that it didn't even qualify as marijuana. Perhaps it ended up in a cop's pomodoro sauce that evening.

We were released, with more warnings. Much good that did. Occasionally my parents would find large bills in a pair of jeans on the way to the wash. I always came up with some persuasive cover story. Parents, I discovered, always wanted to think well of you. They fool themselves – love will do that. I fooled myself royally in later life.

I know enough about AA/NA/SA (sex addiction) 'sharing' to know addicts exaggerate. What I'm telling you now is God's honest truth. It's not James Frey lying shit.

It was in the ninth grade (age fourteen to fifteen) that things reached car-crash level. My life was becoming a blur. The crash itself began one weekend when, in the men's toilets at Pasadena Ice Skating Center, Dave and Vinnie passed me some cocaine. I took a couple of lines. I'd seen enough movies to know how to do it: plastic card – forged ID in my case, not yet a credit card – flat shiny surface, $20 bill, rub of the gums afterwards. Big let-down. Coke, it turned out, did nothing for me (it never has) except burn the fuck out of my nasal membranes. I'm coke-resistant.

I didn't dabble with it again until much later – never worked. But that weekend it set off a small explosion, a kind of recklessness.

A couple of days later, at school, I took my first tab of LSD, with my friend Lila, a regular marijuana buddy.* It was her first time as well. This was morning break. As usual I'd steadied my nerves with a shot of vodka from the locker before the first period. We both prepared ourselves with a quick puff on a joint. Lila took a half tab. Me? I've never believed in half measures.

The LSD exploded my brain into pulsing fragments. You can never tell how strong that stuff will be. Today was nuclear. At first I liked the effect. Halfway through the next period I slipped another full tab.

I wasn't tripping by noon – I was in outer space heading for the rim of the universe. But somehow holding it together. The trip got wilder. In the lunch break a couple of seniors, who'd noticed me lurching and could guess why, took me down to the school football field. 'Try a "cool",' they said, passing me what looked like a store-bought cigarette. Narco sadists. This was fun for them. I thought by 'cool' they meant menthol cigarettes – Kools. I puffed, hoping it would clear my scrambled brain. It was, of course, a stick of PCP, angel dust. You dip a regular cigarette in the juice and let it dry. Then smoke it. Then it all gets slippery.

Vodka, marijuana, LSD, PCP. *Fast Times at SouthPas High*. Halfway through the afternoon history class I was

* I'm still in touch with her, on Facebook. She's gone on to make something good of her life.

hallucinating wildly. I thought the ceiling was on fire and started screaming, lunging for the alarms.

The school put me in a quiet, dark place, the nurse's room, and tried calling my parents to say I 'wasn't well', please come and take him home. Indeed I wasn't well – but they didn't, at this stage, know the whole story. I'd had one or two genuine fainting fits (anorexia again). This, the school presumed, was another. I dodged yet another bullet.

They couldn't get through to anyone and decided, when the bell rang, to let me loose on South Pasadena. Lila took me, staggering, to Hi-Life. I took another hit of marijuana, which slowed me down. But it made me ravenously hungry – I'd eaten nothing all day. A senior (those guys were all SS Nazis at heart) 'kindly' offered me what was left of his cheese fries. I gobbled them down before Lila could snatch them away from me. The bastard had emptied an ashtray from his VW bug into it. Tasted good to me. I finally got home and managed to blag my way through the evening, claiming tiredness. All that studying. Night-night.

SouthPas High participated in this programme called SPARE: South Pasadena Response Effort. I hope they still do. In its way the school cared about its kids – even the ones like me, who didn't deserve care. They couldn't, after a while, *not* know that I was frequently wasted on school grounds. That, of course, made them legally liable and morally responsible. The faculty were, most of them, good people. For known juvenile users/abusers they recruited counsellors from nearby twelve-step groups, to nursemaid troubled kids like me, one-on-one, back to the straight and narrow.

The school didn't tell my parents what was now in my file – at least, not the worst of it. Which was extremely decent of them. (Decent, too, that the school hadn't by now simply excluded me for good.) I was lucky in the choice of counsellor they got on my case. Michael Leary. He was in his thirties and a former crack addict. He'd gone all the way and paid a high cost for his addiction. He had that tired-of-life look on his face that end-of-line addicts have. I catch it in my own mirror sometimes.

We would smoke cigarettes together and he would talk sense. He didn't talk down to me. But he didn't talk me out of using marijuana, which, like many, I didn't really regard as a drug. Still don't, really. I went with him, in his beat-up pickup, to the Friday MA (Marijuana Anonymous) participation meeting on Rosemead Boulevard. I listened. In a way, I even enjoyed the meetings, and the bull sessions afterwards over coffee and many refills (second cup's free in California).

But I still got high, sucking the bong with Dave, Vinnie, Paul and Jennifer most other evenings. Sometimes we'd shroom. Mushrooms were unpredictable but the high was never that high. It was all moderate compared to that nightmare drug-cocktail day at school. I even ditched the morning vodka. My grades crept up to around C. I'd made myself a little halfway house. Michael didn't approve, but he cut me some slack in the hope that I'd eventually clean up completely. Baby steps, and all that. I was 'maintaining' – the word they use.

My hypocrisy was noted at the meeting. Hard things were said. But I couldn't stop using marijuana. Compared to PCP or LSD, it just didn't feel like *really* using. In the words of one of my favourite songs, the stuff kept me comfortably numb. And stopped me thinking. About what? My crappy sexual orientation, mainly. I did not *want* to be gay. And if I couldn't fix being gay, I didn't want to be conscious of the fact. Straight or, failing that, zonked out: that was what I wanted. Amnesia. Anaesthesia.

Most twelve-step groups don't like you using them as a support mechanism for continued usage, even if it's controlled. 'Recovery' is what they are into, not 'maintenance'. Leave that to the methadone/Subutex clinics.* The Friday Rosemead group was no exception. On my third week, one of the external counsellors, a cool, badass black dude in his mid-thirties, got really snotty and challenged me to stay clean for seven days, or fuck off.

I can do that, cool black-ass dude, I thought. And, God help me, I did it. And it was disastrous. With a clear head I saw what was driving me to fuck up my head. I saw only one way out. 'Kill the poof.' Release the homicidal inner homophobe. The death cure.

There had been a teen suicide – it was reaching plague levels in SoCal at that time – in the house down the street. The kid – I never knew him – played loud, heavy-metal, ear-splitting rock for two days non-stop. Neighbours

* Heroin substitutes, if you don't know. Madness, in my opinion, to give one habit-forming drug to replace another habit-forming drug (especially methadone, which gives you a high). Like giving a whisky-drinking alcoholic a daily bottle of gin.

complained, but the parents were away. The music played on and on, followed by a loud bang. Gunshot and silence. I programmed my farewell from the world differently – no rock anthems. I left a note promising to be waiting for my loved ones, after what I thought would be happier lives for them with me out of the way.

As it happened, I didn't make it to the hereafter – not permanently, at least, only long enough to leave a rope burn, throttle bruise. There was a loud choking noise in my ears, then unconsciousness. Strangulation, if you've never tried it, is incredibly fast. That's why so many guys die of sexual auto-asphyxiation: they mistime it. One hears of a lot of guys who've got it wrong and gone to meet their maker with big erections and foolish looks on their faces. Myself, I've never been attracted.

I was found, dangling from the upper beam on my bunk bed, on my knees, in a praying position, elbows on pillows (why leave the world uncomfortable?). The farewell note had sounded the alarm. I'd left it in a prominent enough place: on my plate at supper time. Had I factored last-minute rescue into my plan? Was it a cunning 'cry for help'? I'll never be sure. Probably it was more in the nature of a gamble. Another three minutes and it would all have been over before supper cooled.

Mine was what psychiatrists call a 'structured attempt' – not impulsive or accidental. It had a narrative. A backstory. What that meant, clinically, was 'Take it very seriously.' Seriously meant incarceration and heavy therapy.

At that time in the United States there were close-confinement institutes for adolescents and children. They worked like rehab/detox centres, but with the difference that they had prison-style max-confinement and one-on-one supervision by nurse-attendants who could get very physical. Forget Brat Camp; these were juvenile penitentiaries. Hard time. Exclusively for the well heeled. Cost? Five grand a month. Multiply it by three for today's value.

My parents shipped me into one such well-intentioned lock-up, nestled off the I-10 freeway at Ingleside (not to be confused with the rappers' hangout, Inglewood, where a young white junkie like me would be lucky to last ten minutes). It was nicknamed 'Ingletraz' by the inmates ('patients' doesn't fit). The name was well chosen, if you know the Clint Eastwood movie *Escape from Alcatraz*. Escape over the wire and wall was not worth it. I tried and ended up with ten minutes' freedom, a sprained wrist, and a spell in the institution 'cage' – close-confinement unit. CCU. They loved acronyms.

There was a school in the basement at Ingletraz, run by a teacher nicknamed Boss, who looked like Morgan Freeman in *Deep Impact* but acted like kick-ass Louis Gossett Jr in *An Officer and Gentleman*. You could earn 'privileges', like 'air time' in the yard (where they let you smoke just one cigarette), or coffee (the only stimulant allowed), or a three-minute phone call. Otherwise it was hard time, and early wake-up, for the young folks, with never-ending twelve-step groups, family counselling, one-on-one psychiatric treatment.

Ingletraz and 'Boss' were the saving of me. A particularly

good shrink (clearly gay himself) made me come out to my parents. It was difficult. I couldn't look at them; we were in a big, empty former dorm. I put my head under the table, out of sight, when I came out with the awful fact. The shrink had insisted it must come from me. They took it well. My father even seemed nonchalant – an act, probably. They knew, of course, but had chosen not to be conscious of what they had long known.* I graduated from Ingletraz clean, sober and gay (at least to myself, my parents, and a circle of close friends). Southern California, I realised, wasn't Kansas. Gay was just another colour in the great human rainbow.

There began fifteen years of sobriety and a move towards self-acceptance. Gay, faggot, whatever. I was me. Things looked up immediately. On the morning of my sixteenth birthday I got my driving licence (100 per cent in theory and practice – who says I can't pass exams?). Free! Free at last! That same week I got my first ticket. (Why, I wondered, were all those power-line poles with yellow smiley-face signs flashing at me?) I had the third car in the three-person family: initially a heap-of-shit Subaru ('cheap to buy, built to last that way'), with ninety thousand on the clock, which I punished mercilessly, going for the six figures in record time. I racked up so many speeding violations with that car that only one firm in the whole of greater Los Angeles – Survival (I love the name) – would insure me. They gave you the paper. Your chances of a payout, if you had an accident, were remote. But you could wave the paper hopefully.

* *John*. You're right. It was, oddly, as big a weight off our shoulders as yours.

Things came round in other ways. My parents taught me to work for what I wanted. I worked long hours at a bijou coffee house in a mall off Mission Street, run by a couple of gays, doing customised drinks ('Latte, soy, go easy on the foam', etc.). I worked in a hardware store, helped out in a convalescent hospital for seniors and, when all else failed, shovelled horse shit down at the Arroyo stables for less than minimum. I did voluntary stints at the local Planned Parenthood, and qualified as a teen counsellor. I've always loved work. I lose myself in it.

Things looked up when, aged seventeen, to celebrate my two years C&S, my parents bought me a car more suited to my style: a Chrysler Laser XE, the first vehicle I chose myself, legally owned and registered in my name. I paid, easy payments, for half of it. The car itself was all me. It was low on the road, whitewall tyres, and black as sin. It was, I suspect, modelled on the KITT car from the TV series *Knight Rider*. I loved that programme. The KITT car was 'intelligent' – super-computerised. The Laser was stupid, but also computerised – at least, as far as the American auto industry had gone down that route in 1989. 'Your door is open,' a deep voice would warn, as if you didn't know. Or, 'Warning: your gasoline is running low' (I often heard that). The dashboard display was digitised, green on black, just like the first-generation desk computers. It was a clumsy, awkward, piece of Detroit junk – but it signalled the way of the future. Smart cars. I felt, when I was driving it, I was already in the twenty-first century.

The good things kept rolling in. I was entered into a good school, private, hugely expensive. Southwestern Academy was a demilitarised military school, but it still had some of the disciplines. I got to be student president and head proctor; everyone loved me. In a sense, I had become me. My sexuality was an open secret, but everyone was cool with it. I was too. Dyslexia meant one-on-one tutoring by the principal, Kenneth Veronda, and a teacher whose name I'll mention in gratitude, Lee Mothershed.

Happy is a bit boring. So I'll keep this short to save your yawns. My own as well.

When I was eighteen and recently graduated, John got an offer from UCL back in the UK. Big in terms of prestige, a third of the pay and three times the work, but he and my mother wanted to go back. Caltech gave him a split appointment, so they had a foot in both places. Eight months there, four months here. They sold Floral Park Terrace and made a fortune.

ABANDONED: NO PAIN THIS TIME

I stayed on as a 'resident alien' – green-carded.* How could I not? California was in my blood. My parents bought me a farewell BMW and put a year's down payment on a nice apartment in Pasadena for me. Guilt money – I played the abandoned child ('Don't leave me, Daddy!') scenario expertly. But I genuinely missed them.† Southwestern, having

* *John*. You once told me the green card was the only worthwhile present I'd ever given you. That hurt rather.

† *John*. To be honest, love you as we did, we weren't entirely broken up to have you 5,000 miles out of our lives. You were 'of age'. And very expensive when you were around.

educated me as well as I would ever want myself educated, kept me on as a salaried 'administrative assistant', assisting, mainly, with applications and interviews. I'd decided against the kind of college which would have accepted me. It was more fun selling the school to likely customers – which, it turned out, I was pretty good at.*

I was held out as an advertisement, not to the parents (the office staff made the hard-head deals), but to the kids. I had long, clean, blond hair. My ponytail was long gone. I looked wholesome, tall, free-range and sporty – I was, until I crocked a knee, a half-decent long-distance runner – and polite. As for clothes, I was into fine silk shirts which hung flowingly on my lean body, and black leather jackets. Looking back I can see it, from where I am today, as a style mix between South Beach Miami drug dealer and *The Matrix* – the worst look I've ever gone with. But I was young. I could have worn a bin bag and looked good.

It was a job, and I was, in my little way, a success story. But I was marking time. For what? I wanted more than just being the cheese on somebody else's mousetrap. More than just being clean, sober, hard-working and a credit to the twelve-step rehab programme ('It works!'). But what did I want?

Oddly, my big break was due to, of all people, Dave Atkins – with whom, and whose crew, I'd broken after cleaning up at Ingletraz (switching, at the same time, my loyalties from Led Zep to moony Peter Gabriel, who'd helped me through my drug withdrawal. More of which later).

* *John*. It saved us a couple of hundred thousand, I might add.

A couple of years earlier, Dave, Vinnie and another side-kick (I'll call him 'Clay') had found themselves in Dave's girlfriend's house, in SouthPas, over a long weekend. Two other girls were around. The parents were out of town at a convention. The kids all got high. There was loud music – perhaps sex, I don't know. No neighbours – it was an 'estate' house in its own grounds. The parents had left their gun cabinet either unlocked or easily broken into. There was an argument. Dave and Vinnie left then came back, armed and dangerous. It was never clear which of them took the lead. Whichever it was took his 12-gauge and blew the heads right off those three poor girls, who'd done nothing more than open the door to them.

No 'motive' was ever established. Just madness of the moment. That's no defence, even in California. Clay was sleeping and woke upon hearing the first shot, followed by the immortal words from Vinnie, looking down his twin barrels, 'We *smoked* them all, man. You with us or against us?' Clay decided that, on the whole, he'd rather not be smoked.

Dave and Vinnie took all the valuables they could find, packed their weapons, and took off for Las Vegas in the best remaining family car. They dropped quivering Clay off at his house. He lied to them, saying he was leaving town for New Mexico. Instead he phoned the cops and reported the crime.

There were reports in the SouthPas police gang register with my name as a KA (known associate) of the pathetic Atkins outfit. But I was, at that time, in Ingletraz. It might have been tricky if I hadn't been. Just an unreported phone call from them could have brought arrest for being an accomplice. Paul, who was at home, had a really hard time. His house was turned over.

As it turned out, the murderers never made it to the Strip. They were apprehended, outside godforsaken Barstow, speeding down the freeway. The last 'free' the dumb couple would ever know for the rest of their lives. Clay wisely decided he wasn't 'with' Vinnie and Dave after all, now that being smoked wasn't in prospect. He turned state's evidence and, quite rightly, got off.

The authorities were not forgiving of the other two. They kept Dave and Vinnie in remand until they could bring full adult sentences against them. Dave got life, without possibility of parole. Vinnie got fifty-one years to life. Same thing. Vinnie and Dave will die in hard-time prison. By now they'll be well past the youthful years in which, quite likely, they were cell punks, passed around like prime meat. Perhaps they're now big guys in the yard themselves. I sometimes think of them when I watch *Oz*, or that series everyone's talking about, *Orange is the New Black*. Stupid bastards. Would I have been with them that awful weekend, but for Ingletraz? Chances are I would have been. Would I, however high, have pulled a trigger on those girls? Never. Or so I tell myself.

As it stands, where I do come into the story is through a writer, Leon Bing, who had made a name for herself with a book called *Do or Die*, the story of a South Central Crips/Bloods hoodlum called Monster. It was a bestseller and she had decided to follow it up with a book about the Atkins/Hebrock murders, called *Smoked*. One night after work, I heard her on a local radio talk show, promoting her book, and I phoned in to say I had some details which might be of interest to her.

Smoked is a great book. And what it's about is why adolescents in cookie-cutter communities like South Pasadena explode, regularly, into 'inexplicable' teen violence. Why would SouthPas, of all places on God's earth, go Columbine? Why, come to that, did Columbine go Columbine?*

While we were writing this book, someone sent me a link to the most recent SouthPas teen 'atrocity'. South Pasadena High School again. The *LA Times* headlined it 'South Pasadena – Columbine'. A sixteen- and seventeen-year-old were arrested in September 2014 for planning a mass slaughter of fellow high school pupils and staff. Their declared aim was 'to kill as many people as possible'. They got into quite a lot of detail about it on Skype. They sincerely meant to do it. The 2014 academic year opened with a lot of nervous parents and heavy police presence on the campus. It'll happen again, believe me.

You can blame *The Basketball Diaries*, rap music, reefer madness, phases of the moon or whatever. But that doesn't explain the deep-down anger at – what? Teen spree-killings are a middle-class thing. And they seem to be done by kids who have a lot to live for. Why did Dave and Vinnie kill *all* those girls ('We smoked them *all*, man')? They weren't Saturday-night-special-wielding ghetto kids trying to gather tattoo teardrops round their eyes. Why not shoot just one and claim accidental discharge, or whatever that legless guy

* I don't buy that Michael Moore film, by the way. He's forgotten what it's like to be an angry teenager, if he ever was one.

Oscar Pistorius claimed. (Shot the girl, didn't mean to do it. She got in the way of my cop-killer bullets, poor thing.) Dave and Vinnie would still have gone down, but not for ever.

Leon didn't have the answers. But she could ask the questions in ways that made you want to turn pages. She and I met up and she pumped me for corrections and additional material for the second edition of *Smoked*, which was selling well. Leon was (is) a smart, glamorous, fascinatingly ditzy woman – pure West Coast. We hit it off. I'll go further: I loved the woman. It so happened she was writing a book about juvenile re-education camps like Ingletraz. Were they rip-offs for guilty parents or tough love that worked? I've got good reasons for believing in them. Ingletraz saved me. She wasn't, I think, as much in favour of forcible juvenile rehab as me but I was very useful to her.

3: VIDEO WORLD

Leon had contacts. One of the most recent was with Errol Morris, the prizewinning crime-documentary maker famous for *The Thin Blue Line*. Morris was in the process of adapting *Smoked* for Propaganda Films. Leon was closely involved and she got me an internship. Propaganda was, in the early 1990s, one of the most dynamic independent production companies in Hollywood. Their bestselling line was, at that time, music videos (MTV had by now taken over the world). And that's where my career in the entertainment business started. 'Intern' overstates it. I was at the very bottom of the prestige ladder, sweeping floors, flushing unflushed toilets, fetching what anyone (i.e. everyone) higher up the studio chain chose to want. I loved my MTV, to quote Dire Straits – even with a bog brush in my hand.

Propaganda were, at the time, doing $10m-plus videos – Janet Jackson's 'Scream', Madonna's 'Bedtime Stories'. You should, if you can, get a look at a video production set in full flow. It looks like a kindergarten on speed and steroids – teenagers, male, female, all ethnicities, moving across the floor like greased lightning, twenty-five hours a day, to get the shoot wrapped up in three to four days. (Artists – 'talent' – won't hang around; the concept's already been worked out by the star director and exists as a worksheet;

post-production editing will be done in a $500-p.h. studio.)

Leon got my foot through the door at Propaganda, but it was, for several months, as an unpaid intern – what, on UK video sets, they call a 'runner'. In fact, I was an even lower life form: a 'pre-intern'. Foetal. I had to prove myself to move up. My break came with a two-day recording session at a Burbank sound-stage studio for Des'ree's 'You Gotta Be'. Propaganda were doing the recording. The product was for Sony UK.

The track and video would go on to be mega-hits for Des'ree. The biggest she would have in her career. Deservedly. It's beautifully performed and it hit a black-feminist nerve. A 'stand up and fight' thing like Franklin's 'Respect'. Just listen: 'You gotta be bad, you gotta be bold, you gotta be wiser.' African Americans of both sexes also took it up as an anthem. It's played on MLK Day.

Paul Boyd was directing. Because I clearly didn't have a fucking clue how to do anything useful on the set, I was assigned by the producer (nice guy, forget his name) to 'look after' the star. I was, although I didn't quite realise it, a forty-eight-hour PA. I learned a lot, in those few hours, about how to do the job. It was not easy.

This, 1994, was before health and safety regs had kicked in. To get the thing wrapped in two days meant long, long, shoots – eighteen or nineteen hours, sometimes. Celebrity performers hate videos – really hate them. Why? Because they have to take orders from people whose names they can't remember and a couple of days later they'd have no reason to remember. They have no control. They're just cogs in the machine. They get real diva-ish in reaction. Cranky. I had a head start with Des'ree. Both of us came from South ('Sarf') London. I dragged the accent out of my Herne Hill memory bank.

I treated the lady like a goddess. When she came off set, for a break, I'm there, holding a cool bottle of pure water, with a straw. She's a vegan. Famous for it. I found a place nearby (in Burbank!) that made the fresh wheatgrass juice that she drank. It looks like the stuff you pull out of the bottom of the lawnmower when it jams, and tastes worse. I even found a vegan Indian restaurant nearby (I repeat, in Burbank! – where you could starve looking for a Big Mac). The dressing room, when she comes, exhausted, off the sound stage, is full of things she can refresh herself with. And the flowers I've discovered she likes. In short, I made her comfortable and the experience less about the pain of what she had to do. She did an eighteen-hour day, I did a twenty-hour day.

I got such good feedback via Des'ree that I was made a 'must-hire'. I was, thereafter, paid. Not only that, directors and producers found me useful and called for me by name.

I made, at the same time, one of my longest and most useful relationships – personal and professional – with the ace video producer Line Postmyr. She, like Leon Bing, opened doors for me. I became a kind of father figure to her son, Luka, whom I love. I'd by now left Pasadena behind. Line, Luka and I moved in together in a ranch-style small estate halfway up Topanga Canyon. I had the annexed studio apartment. In the paddock outside, Luka could be amused by two hyperactive Shetland ponies, borrowed from Daryl Hannah. They would wander into the dining area sometimes. Luka's actually living with me for a few months as I'm writing now – the same age as I was then: nineteen. No Shetlands in the kitchen. I bollock him for spooning baked beans out of the can and leaving the damn things beside his bed for days.*

I loved the hustle-bustle and sheer damn *life* of it all at Propaganda. In no time, I was what was called, loosely, 'talent liaison'. I had a title. Gofer double-plus. 'The Diva needs a freshly-laundered hand towel – get it, Jack! Now!' Hey presto, it's there. I'd found, at last, something I was very good at. That and driving. Propaganda were soon trusting me to drive their forty-foot customised Winnebagos, hired out from firms in the valley, tricked out with dressing rooms and restrooms, to serve as trailers on set or at concerts. I would sometimes cruise around in them after work, picking up dates in East LA. What else were they? Beds on wheels. But it was foolishly risky.

More risky, as it happened, than I or Propaganda knew. I did not have a legal driving licence. It was, incredibly, an unfixed speeding offence that had done it, returning from a day trip to Las Vegas with a visiting English friend. I was eighteen, and showing off my KITT car (OK, Laser). It couldn't fly but, I boasted to Joel, it could do a ton-plus. Indeed it could – 118 m.p.h., to be precise. A radar gun proved it and the highway patrolman holding it made a precise note of the fact. I managed to sweet-talk him into changing the 118 into 99. Anything over 100 m.p.h. is, in California, reckless driving: a felony. That means criminal charges, handcuffs,

* *John*. Welcome to the pissed-off fathers' club.

impounded car, loss of licence, thousands of dollars in extra insurance costs for the rest of your driving life – if, indeed, you have one. The patrolman did me the favour, I think, not out of the goodness of his heart but because he couldn't be bothered with the reams of paperwork. Cop laziness: the speeding driver's best friend.

I vaguely remembered getting the ticket and the domestic bollocking (another one?) in Floral Park, but apparently no one had settled the fine. The traffic courts in California are so clogged that the system had never caught up with me. I was a 'scofflaw'. It eventually did catch up with me and I had a lawyer fix it for me. I was, as I say, lucky at that period of my life.

My people skills and quick-delivery talent were noted. Artists – Kylie, Isaac Hayes, Mötley Crüe, Steven Seagal – 'took to me'. And I took to them, with occasional exceptions. Seagal, doing a Japanese rum commercial, was, oddly, the trickiest. He turned up hours late, with full entourage and enough bodyguards to storm the building. He walked into the middle of the set, on the phone – firing some poor guy, it sounded like. He then, overriding the director, instructed the camera crew in how to angle his shots. His good side, or something. There was to be no smoking allowed 'within a hundred feet of Mr Seagal's trailer'. I was a chain-smoker at the time. The biggest diva ever. But I like his good-bad movies and his famous 'Fuck you and die!'

All this was nothing long-lasting; it was just for the moment. But that's enough in that world. It's all flash photography and flash relationships. In the entertainment world you need three kinds of luck: knowing the right people, being in the right place, and being there at the right time. Any craps table in Las Vegas gives better odds. I was on a winning streak.

Not that you didn't also need skills that not everyone has. The star wanted a cup of green tea, three minutes' infusion? It was at their side in three minutes and ten seconds. Where was the limousine? I'd arranged to have it purring at the kerb. 'Thank you, Jack, you're a treasure.' Five minutes later: 'What was that kid's name, the helpful one with the shy smile? Oh, no reason.'

ON THE SET

Propaganda saw I was doing the job for them. I went up from 'minimum' to 'premium' pay for my lowly rank. They offered me a job as vault manager. Benefits, solid salary ('Take it!' screamed my parents). But I wanted to stay on the front line. In contact with the living talent, not down in the vault with the dead talent on tape. And I didn't want to be driving a VW Rabbit with two hundred thousand on the clock and a sinister clunk in the transmission aged forty.

I loved that phase of my life. If I ever had a taste of what heaven would be like it was driving surface streets towards Burbank at six in the morning, in a Nissan 300ZX sports car, the sprinklers wetting the lawns, the rising sun behind me, the day ahead of me.* Music blaring on maximum:

* There's a story behind the sweet vehicle. I got it on long loan from the car shop, saying that it was for my dad (you, John), who was going through a midlife crisis and wanted a sports car. The $45K sticker price? No problem. A belated thanks.

KISS-FM or Power 106. And that most lovely of lighting effects, 'starglow'.

My route took me past Forest Lawn, and I would remember one of Janie Morgan's boyfriends, Jeff Langley. A 'special medic' with the fire department, he was nicknamed 'the cowboy firefighter' for his love of horses (hence the bond with Janie). In his spare time he taught sport to the blind. The nicest and bravest of guys, Jeff was killed when he fell off a helicopter skid on an Air Operations rescue of a hiker injured in Topanga Canyon. This was 1993 – round about now, as I'm describing driving to work. The mayor and firefighters gave him a hero's send-off. I was there. He was twenty-eight years old.

When they picked up Jeff's body they found a poem in his pocket:

> To leave the world a bit better,
> Whether by a healthy child, a garden patch,
> Or a redeemed social condition;
> To know even one life has breathed easier
> Because you have lived.
> This is to have succeeded.

Jeff succeeded. Most of us don't. There's a simplicity about Western heroes, even to this day, that I love.

What was the video I most enjoyed working on in those years? No question: 'Sending My Love' by Zhané (pronounced 'Jah-nay' – Renée Neufville and Jean Norris), in February 1994. I was just twenty. They can't have been a whole lot older – just out of college. Preachers' daughters, I think. They wrote their own songs – kind of gentle soul with jazz inflections and a strong influence of Youssou N'Dour. It was Neufville who wrote 'Sending My Love'.

The music was already on tape. It was the filmic MTV accompaniment that was needed. A short shoot, and not much money, was allowed. I drove the singers several hours through the San Gabriel Mountain passes, all of us crammed in a Lincoln Town Car. They weren't big enough for the convoy uber-famous groups could demand. They were the nicest company. We stayed at a budget hotel on the down-side of the range. Modest all the way.

Antoine Fuqua's video is a masterpiece. Check it out wherever you can get Freeview (you can't, irritatingly, buy it). Fuqua, like the duo, is African American. Both the girls were conscious of their heritage and put it into their art. It was shot in the Mojave Desert. Fuqua brought subtle ethnic nuances, close-ups of the couple in Nefertiti profile, hints of Grace Jones – but without her aggression. Nubian static nobility was the effect aimed at. Both singers were daubed in gold cosmetics. The video opens with a gold weathervane spinning in the desert wind. A golden eagle stares, unblinking and cruel. A (gold-tinged) sandstorm is brewing. Two men, caught in long shot, run, in flowing native dress, across the dunes towards the singers. (Neufville had penned the song for her faraway boyfriend.)

Fuqua found his ideal spot – a dry lakebed. One of the effects he had in mind was swirling sand in the background. It didn't make for comfort for the singers – sand, body paint and Mojave heat are a horrible mix. The first idea was to mount up a powerful, generator-driven fan dropping bags of dust (sand is too heavy) into the air current. I was in charge of throwing the dirt, keeping the whole thing outside the range of the wide-angle lens. It didn't work. It looked like what it was. Flying dirt. Not at all the romantic, shimmery effect the director had in his head.

This, recall, was the early nineties, before the introduction of crippling health and safety regulations – the kind of control which has, for example, forced Southern California porn stars to visibly wear condoms. I'm in favour of anything that discourages mad risk-taking – how many people did porn star and junkie John Holmes, who hired his ten-inch cock out for sex sessions to bored, rich people, infect with HIV? But I'm not alone in thinking the H&S regulations have sadly cramped video style.

Antoine Fuqua came up with an ingenious idea (some might say dangerous as well): for me to do spinning donuts* on the lakebed floor, in the Lincoln Town Car. Literally kicking up a storm into the fan. I'd hired the car from Galpin Ford Studio Rentals, who rent everything to the entertainment industry, from ten-ton trucks to go-karts. They make good money from it but they most surely didn't want their classier vehicles used like stock cars or Humvees going into battle against Saddam Hussein in Iraq. You're talking vehicles that cost $100K and are not engineered for any damn desert.

But it was fun and 'creative'. Everyone there felt the excitement. I did the donuts as asked, with Antoine shouting

* You crank the steering wheel in one direction and hit the gas. The vehicle skids round and round, like a spinning top. Best done in deserts, not on the freeway.

on the car radio, 'Nearer! Nearer!' I'm meanwhile shitting myself. I was doing things that might well have invalidated our insurance. If I bolloxed things and a too-near skid went wrong it could have caused an accident that would have been hard to explain to the local sheriff. ('You were doing what? Donuts? Why don't you go to Winchell's, like we cops do?') Meanwhile, the singers – looking cool and poised – were inwardly hot, pissed off, and getting very uncomfortable. They didn't come here for any sandblasting workover.

My donuts were still whipping up too feeble a desert storm for what Antoine had envisioned. So we called in the 'dually' two-crew Ford truck that had brought in the heavy equipment. I did tighter and tighter spins in this behemoth, spurting up dirt for the fans to blow.

It finally worked for Antoine.

As I say, the H&S regulations have since made what I was doing legally undoable. Particularly by an eighteen-year-old short-hire kid (who, it later emerged, had no legal driving licence).

There had been too many accidents on sets where directors got too imaginative. But, as I say, it worked. And I am proud to say I did my bit. Zhané did other things before they shut up shop and went their own ways in 1997. Their mega-hit was 'Hey Mr DJ'. But for me, their best thing is 'Sending My Love'. I did the dirt, you know.

This kind of work, ground-level that it was, got me close to other big names doing creative things. Directors like Paul Boyd, Mark Romanek, Gore Verbinski, Michael Bay, Danny Boyle. Via the last I came into close contact with the iconic Iggy Pop, who looks, when he takes off his leather jacket, as if he's still wearing an even thicker leather jacket. When he waves his arms he looks like a Jurassic Park pterodactyl. He waves his arms a lot. Croaks a bit, too. But, I have to tell you, very polite to whatsisnames like me on the set.

For the Iggy Pop video 'Lust for Life', Danny Boyle brought in some of the guys from *Trainspotting*. I haven't read the novel, but I've seen the film. Iggy's a god in the video. I can understand why – he's fuck-it-all with a bare chest.

When I was trailing along behind them all, I felt part of the big scene, feeling, you might say, a bit fuck-it-all myself. In fact I was the smallest knob on the great MTV machine. Half an amp, in Spinal Tap reckoning. Iggy was eleven, at least. But I was young. It was enough to be inside the fence that kept those millions of fans out.

4: MONSTROUS

I was now rising twenty. And, photographs confirm, a very good-looking young man. With nice English manners, when I chose to turn them on. And getting very competent at fixing things, almost before you noticed they were unfixed. I felt I was on my way up at Propaganda – I had a future there.

In mid-1994, REM had come to Propaganda to do the promotional track for their upcoming *Monster* album, 'What's the Frequency, Kenneth?' What do the lyrics mean? Don't ask.* The video was directed by Peter Care and is harshly strobed. Should have an epilepsy warning. One of the things which people commented on was Michael's cropped skull. (It wasn't shaved, as some wrongly said, but close-clipped.) Why did he go with that look? His secret.

The four-day set-up was done by my friend Line. There was a lot of artist liaison and pre-production stuff to get worked out. It was a big deal, even for Propaganda. REM were routinely described as the biggest rock group in the word. For the 'Frequency' shoot the band were taken in a luxury motorhome to a huge abandoned warehouse in Burbank.

* *John*. I wrote an article on what the lyrics mean. It attracted a slightly snide comment in the *TLS*. *Jack*. What's the *TLS*? *John*. You'll find out when they have a go at *Stars, Cars and Crystal Meth*.

I did the dressing-room prep, fresh flowers, magazines, drinks, fruit – the vegetarian food Michael Stipe was known to prefer. I was the band nanny for four days and, as was now usual, I did it well. It was noticed. As the shoot was winding up, Jeff(erson) Holt, one of the band's senior team, came across and made conversation. To be honest, I thought he was gay. I was cool, charming, and slightly distant – the polite put-off. Later I realised he was feeling me out rather differently from what I had assumed.

Among other things, Jeff mentioned that they were about to set up a mega world tour, and Michael didn't have a PA. He'd vaguely asked if I was interested. I was very flattered, but not interested – I was already booked solid, and, ambitiously, heading to be top PA in Los Angeles.

By now I was an ever-present studio face on set, making myself useful. Michael Stipe clearly liked the face and valued the services I discreetly provided him and the others. We exchanged a few words. He's a man of very few words. I saw him looking at me, thoughtfully. The subject of Michael's tour PA kept coming up and I was by now taking more interest. Before committing I had a man-to-man with Michael himself.

'You should know this,' I told him – rather hoping it would put him off – 'I'm a recovering addict, five years clean. I cannot be around drink or drugs.'

'Those days are behind REM,' Michael replied.

'OK,' I said. 'If you trust me, good. If not, I'll stick with Propaganda. Oh, and by the way, I'm openly gay.'

Michael chuckled at this. 'That's fine,' he said.

Like I said, a man of few words.*

I was still in two minds. He invited me to hang out a bit with the band. He and I drove to the Chateau Marmont in a stretch limo, then on to a restaurant on La Brea, where I was introduced to his friends Stephen Dorff and Samantha Mathis.† We ended up in her house for wine and quiet conversation. All very un-rock-and-roll. If it was intended to impress me, I was impressed. Friends I asked said I'd be a fool not to jump at the offer, if and when a formal offer was made.

It looked as if it would be. To ensure we were right for each other, Michael proposed a trial run. I was flown to New York, to his favourite Four Seasons Hotel for five days. He was doing *Letterman*, I recall. I was loving the rush. And, I think it's safe to say, we got on well enough together. Jeff came back with some figures. I'll think about it, I said. My head saying yes. But I needed a little while to get over my nervousness.

A few days later, in my apartment (one of his gofers must have got my number from Propaganda), I got an unexpected phone call from Michael. He was, he said, being driven through the Texas Panhandle. His people had done a full background on me. Would I like to be his personal assistant on the upcoming *Monster* tour, he quietly asked. Yes or no. He mentioned figures. Not only that – he would double what the tour management paid, from his own take. The offer was firm. His word.

* He would come out publicly himself a few months later. It made headlines worldwide.

† Stephen Dorff made a movie set in the Marmont, *Somewhere*. It came out in 2010, a period of my life when the hotel was no longer somewhere for me. Sadly.

Would I like to? Yes, I think I would, I replied, just as quietly as he'd asked. He put the phone down and I let it all out with a scream so loud that all the birds flew off the trees on Mar Vista Avenue and thought twice about ever coming back.*

Here I was, nineteen and pulling in, I was amazed to calculate, $150K a year, all told. And I surely liked telling it to myself. For current purchasing power, double that figure. What's a yuppie? Twice his age in annual thousands of dollars. What did that make me? Eight yuppies rolled into one. Yippee. And still routinely being carded and barred from entry in Los Angeles clubs where alcohol was served.

It was as if that big finger you see in the British lottery advertisements had decided, for its own mysterious reasons, to point at me. I was prepped up for the eleven-month world tour, signing ten-page document after twenty-page document. The dollar figures on some of them left me breathless. Chump change for 'the greatest rock band in the world', of course. *Brewster's Millions* for me. (You remember, the movie where Eddie Murphy has so much money he can't find a way of spending it in one year.)

I got rid of my Pasadena apartment, put what little furniture and effects I wanted to keep in store, and sold the Datsun 240Z I was now driving. Once I'd got my head round what the REM machine was offering, I knew, in my heart, I'd never have a car that low-end again. Nor, for the next twenty years, did I. Nowadays, when I look at my

* *John.* Oddly enough I was in Jack's apartment during this conversation. That's indeed how it went.

Oyster card, the cold London wind whipping my arse, I feel very strange, and envious of that lucky nineteen-year-old.

Wells Fargo (I chose them because I liked the name and that crazy wagon-and-horses icon) treated me with new respect after I had a conversation with a VP about deposit arrangements. Words like 'premium' came into play. American Express, it transpired, had not the slightest objection to my carrying their platinum plastic. I was someone – Michael Stipe's main man. I made sure a lot of people knew that.

THE MAN

Michael Stipe had – probably still has – two main requirements of his PA. One was to keep people he didn't know from getting physically close to him. The other was for the PA to be physically close, in his necessary duties, while staying as far away from his private life as the rest of the human race. I had no difficulty respecting that, then and now. His line on 'substances' was absolute. His idea of a drug, at this stage of his career, was St John's wort – and perhaps not even that to excess. I was as-a-whistle clean all the time I worked for him and for quite a few years after.

REM in 1995 were the hottest rock band in the world, though with them, Peter Buck said, the word 'rock' should always have inverted commas round it. The *Monster* album had gone triple-platinum before the tour took off for Australasia in January 1995. I would be closer to Michael Stipe, 24/7, than any other human being for a year and sixty-nine gruelling performances.

I didn't presume to know what was going on inside his head over those eleven months. But he was still, as he put on public record, grieving over the deaths of River Phoenix (to whom the *Monster* album is dedicated) and Kurt Cobain. River had died fifteen months earlier; Kurt had killed himself just nine months before the tour. Dark shadows.

I knew nothing of what he felt beyond what he let out to the world – although you could feel a kind of grief in some of the tracks. On the twentieth anniversary of the *Monster* album release Michael recalled, 'There was so much sadness around us at that time.' There were also lots of rumours circulating about Cobain and Michael. I never found any reason to believe them. They had been personally close and deeply into each other's music. *Automatic for the People* was found on the record player in the room where Cobain died. There were also lots of rumours about that death: the 'Who killed Kurt Cobain?' sites are still going strong. Paranoia never sleeps.

I never got any sense that Michael suspected foul play. What I may have sensed, which others did, was that he felt, as people do after a friend's suicide, that perhaps he might have done more. I'm not a REM-ologist (there are lots of those going strong on the web too) but I hear that track on the album, 'Let Me In', as regret that he didn't push the door harder. But pushing wasn't him. Michael opened up a bit more in his April 2014 eulogy to Kurt, when Nirvana were inducted (why so late?) into the Rock and Roll Hall of Fame.

What I did observe, over 1995, was that he was incredibly loving to Cobain's widow, Courtney Love, at a time when she desperately needed it. She was in terrible shape, still destroyed by Cobain's death, tormented by allegations that she was, one way or another, responsible. She began performing with her group, Hole, just two months after. On her first show, she came on in tears, stretching her arms out, as in crucifixion. One critic said what followed would have been over the top for a lunatic asylum.

Hole were playing in Japan when we were there for three days at the beginning of February. At the first REM concert in the country, Michael dedicated 'Crush with Eyeliner' to Courtney. They (Hole) were doing club gigs; we (forgive the royal 'we') were filling vast stadiums. We went clubbing to hear her one night. Drew Barrymore, then dating Hole's drummer, Eric Erlandson, was with us. (Barrymore famously later fell out with Courtney, her one-time best friend, and did a cruel skit on *Saturday Night Live*. You can check it out on YouTube, if you're interested in how a broken friendship can go gangrenous.)

The name of Courtney's band was provocatively vaginal – and so, full-on, were her performances. Still in extreme distress, she was sometimes smashed on stage and, one read, prone to picking fights with members of the audience. (The Japanese, I have to say, were very polite on the night we saw Hole. No fights.) It was a hard time for her. I think Michael helped. Courtney was his escort at the big MTV Video Music Awards night later in the year. I arranged the transport and drove in the front of the vehicle for what REM historians rank as the highest high spot of the band's career. Courtney, at the next year's event, had a spat, now viral on YouTube, with Madonna. Clash of the Titanesses.

I followed in the rear along the red carpet that MTV night. If you can find the event on the web, you may catch a glimpse of me. Or not – I wasn't very visible. Dolce &

Gabbana, when we were in Milan, had given the band a free pick of their range. They surprised me, several months later, with a posted goody package containing a rich, old-school, burgundy velvet tux, cummerbund and pants. Price tag thousands, with that designer label, and pimp daddy all the way. But I wore it that night. (Fuck, why not do my little bit for product placement before it goes to the thrift store?) The outfit was so crimson I merged into the MTV red carpet, like Robert Patrick in *Terminator 2*.

Before the tour got going, while shooting the 'Bang and Blame' video in New York, Michael squashed speculation by coming out publicly in an interview with MTV's straight-talking Tabitha Soren on set. I was in the room, silently cheering. She asked the question direct, he gave the answer direct, adding: 'I've always felt that sexuality is a really slippery thing. In this day and age, it tends to get categorised and labelled, and I think labels are for food. Canned food.' What he said, and how he said it, was a huge thing for gays like me.

That closet door, of course, had never been firmly shut to the fan world. As Michael said, a performer who liked to appear on stage in skirts, as he had in his younger, wilder days, was either a fag or a Scotsman. And he sure as hell wasn't Rod Stewart.*

He liked my company as well as my services. Or, at least, I like to think he did. We did a CNN documentary together

* *John*. Michael, who's recently formed a civil union with his partner, told the *Guardian* in 2014: 'As I understand it queerness is the obvious acceptance that the world of sexuality, identity and love isn't just black and white, or simple – it is every shade and gradation of the rainbow.' Wise words.

in which he impersonated Brando in *Apocalypse Now*. Then he borrowed my black leather jacket and did Travolta. If I'd been wearing a kilt he might have done his Rod Stewart.

He could be fun that way. Not a side of him the fans often saw. I introduced him to the joys of midnight rollerblading – beats nightswimming – buying him top-of-the-range boots, screwing the brakes on. The money men would have killed me if they'd found out what I was doing with their 'property'. A broken Stipe ankle would have cost them tens of millions.

MONSTER CATASTROPHES

As it turned out, a broken ankle would have been a minor injury, and a tiny cost, compared to what actually happened. *Monster* turned into the most afflicted tour in rock history. Was there, MTV News asked, 'some weird medical curse' – a voodoo spell, a shot albatross, or something? It was eerie. The band were in their mid-thirties: prime of life. True, they hadn't toured in six years, and might have been somewhat out of training. But the disasters were biblical. I wouldn't have been surprised if it had rained frogs.

As Peter Buck recalled, even if things go smoothly, world tours are pure hell for stars:

> It's not sightseeing and eating nice food and all that. It's this chaotic whirlwind you happen to be at the center of – like taking a portable hurricane with you wherever you go. There's all this stuff going on around you that doesn't

make sense. You don't really know where you are. You're always kind of tired, always hungry, and you always have two more things to do than you have time for.

'Things' did not go smoothly. By a million miles, they didn't.

The disasters began, mildly, with Peter Buck himself being hit by flu virus, early in the tour. All the band (me as well) would go down with it over the year. It was no joke for Buck, one of the hubs around which the band's music revolved. But that was small change compared to what happened on 1 March, at the Patinoire de Malley in Lausanne, Switzerland.

During concerts, I had, by now, two assigned PA roles. Primary was assisting Michael, if needed. Often I wasn't. He liked an aura of solitude around himself at these moments. The three other band members happily shared a behind-stage dressing cabin and had a lightly tasked PA between them. Michael had his own space. And me. It was specified ahead of time that he had to have a star-bulbed mirror. He, unlike the others, made up for performance, applying lip gloss and eyeliner for the standout look he wanted under the stage lights. Sometimes he would want a shoulder massage from me, or, more likely, from the rock and roll masseuse (best in the business) the tour had hired – Dr Zadanoff.* Usually, though, he wanted to be alone.

* I loved Dr Zash, as I called her. A striking-looking woman with magic hands, she could do everything from chiropractic, through acupuncture, to aromatherapy and incense, and induced meditation recuperative trance state. If there was no one more important ahead of me, I would be lying on her table twice a day ('Off to see your wife again, Jack?' the crew would joke). Without her I'm not sure the band could have got through *Monster*. I couldn't have.

The time he took, pre-show, was in direct relation, I noticed, to how tight his nerves might be strung. He needed to be alone in those meditative minutes, or longer, before going out.

Once I was sure he didn't need me, my second role was to patrol the crowd, with some security back-up, confiscating any professional recording devices and cameras. Owners were told they could keep them, in return for surrendering their ticket and being frogmarched to the exit. Or they could hand in their stuff and collect it after the show. It was a symbolic thing. REM are one of the most bootlegged bands in rock history. Peter Buck, I read somewhere, has a magnificent collection, acquired at great cost, which he'll doubtless deposit, one day, in the Library of Congress.*

After the sweep I'd go to the side of the stage to keep an eagle eye on things. Twat that I was, I felt important at this stage of the evening. As it happened, that early spring night in Switzerland, I was rather important – or, at least, more useful than most nights.

It was the end of the concert, the fans behaving with Swiss decorum. (Wildest, oddly, on the tour were the English audiences.) The end-of-concert routine was this: Bill Berry leaving his drums to pick up Kurt Cobain's Jag-Stang guitar for his party piece, usually 'Let Me In' for the encore stint.† Courtney had given the instrument to the band. It was a sacred object for REM.

* *John*. Some PhD student is going to do a dissertation on Peter Buck's bootlegged tapes one day, I hope. I'd love to supervise it.

† I've seen and heard various accounts of what happened next. Mine I think is true as I remember it. It was hard to forget when you were ten feet away.

As he moved to the front of the stage, Bill staggered and put his hands (guitar swinging) to his head. I assumed he'd banged his head on the mike over his drums. None of the band would have claimed to be Jagger-calibre movers, even in their mid-thirties. I'm meanwhile on high alert. Eyes swivelling. The end of the show was the danger time for stage invasion. What the hell, the fans thought, they can't kick us out now, let's go for it. Manhandling was sometimes needed.

Another kind of manhandling would be necessary in Lausanne that March night. Bill collapsed, front of stage. The band momentarily froze. At which point I and a couple of music technicians came on, and lifted Bill bodily. He's not a big guy. Around 170 pounds, then. Meatloaf would have been something else. We would have needed a block and tackle.

There was faint, uncertain, applause – the fans thought it was somehow part of the show. Odd, but what the hell. Quite likely, some thought 'overdose' – like Eric Clapton having to perform lying flat on his back during his high-intake years. But none of the band, and certainly not Berry, was into drugs. Whatsoever.

After a short pause the band continued to play, and they finished the show without Bill, but their thoughts were well off-stage. Someone, I recall, stepped in – probably one of the session musicians – for the final encore songs. Meanwhile we got a stretcher and carried Bill to his dressing room. The fans were by now royally perplexed. 'I Feel Fine', another showstopper, was not entirely appropriate. Bill didn't feel fine by a long way. But he was now conscious, if woozy, and in obvious pain. The local contract physician, in attendance for just this kind of emergency, diagnosed severe migraine. Medication was administered and Bill calmed down – in less pain, apparently. He was discreetly motored back to the hotel, on his stretcher, on the tour bus.

Lausanne is a charming old town. No war has touched it for three hundred years. But it hasn't yet quite got out of the 1700s. There wasn't a lift big enough to take a stretcher or gurney to the suites on the upper floors, where the band were staying. We had to bundle poor Bill up the stairs manually.

It got worse. Bill still had severe head pains next morning A second doctor was called in. He took one look, and Bill (those stairs again) was in a klaxon-blaring ambulance to the nearest ER. 'Severe migraine' proved an understatement. Two aneurysms. One haemorrhaging. He was bleeding to death in the head.

God moves in mysterious ways, they say, and God is clearly an REM fan. What saved Bill Berry's life was the coincidence that the world's leading neurosurgeon was based in Lausanne. He operated, in a state-of-the-art operating theatre. The whole top of Bill's head was removed: pure Hannibal Lecter. As Buck later recalled, 'We were in Taipei just the week before. Can you imagine what would have happened if we had been in Taipei when the aneurysm happened?'

Only too easy to imagine. But that surgeon and Swiss hospitals were the only bright spots. We were now stuck for several weeks in this Swiss town. A total mind-fuck, psyched and hyped up as everyone was for a world tour. We'd by now, three months into the tour, grown used to a different country every few days and ten-minute naps to catch up before waking with a dozy 'Where are we today?' Now it was cowbells in the morning till who knew when. Hear one Alpine horn, you've heard them all. Lunch and dinner in the same restaurant every Groundhog Day.

Michael eventually suggested I go on furlough, and I took off for London to be with friends and family. It was a whole six weeks before Bill Berry could get back behind his drums. The band stayed with him. Then, out of sheer loyalty, he re-joined the band. He could/should, I thought, surely have gone back to the US for long-term recuperation. (I suspect that was what his doctors recommended.) But the show went on, though after Lausanne, Michael would occasionally greet the audiences with, 'Welcome to the aneurysm tour.' It got laughs.

Mike Mills was the second to be cut down. Appendicitis 'adhesion'. He'd collapsed during the studio recording, a year earlier, of 'What's the Frequency'. Simple appendectomy at that stage. In and out with the scalpel, and a healthy multi-instrumentalist again. But a complication, 'adhesion' (bits of his insides sticking together, like Scotch Tape on your thumbs, I assumed), struck him down in July during the tour.

Mike did a couple of shows with what must have felt like ferrets fighting for exit from his abdomen. There were yet more cancellations of booked-out events. The showrunners were going crazy, as were the money men at Warner Brothers. REM were raining rain checks on the world.

The kibosh (nice English word, whatever it means) was Michael getting an inguinal hernia which required surgery in August. The pain had become critical in Prague, where the band were playing a sold-out concert in the city's Sports Hall. He was in the hospital an hour before the show. But Michael – against medical advice, probably – did that show, the last before the band flew back to Atlanta, for a break before the American segment of the tour.

It was for him a point of honour to do that Prague event. It had been postponed, in March, for Bill's surgery. Then postponed again for Mike's surgery in July. Michael felt they owed their Czech fans. I personally (for what little it matters) don't think he should have gone on stage that night. If MTV awarded purple hearts, Michael Stipe should have got one.

Michael's surgery in Atlanta was successful. I'd gone with him, on a private plane, my bed by his side. I can say, without breaching confidentiality, that he bears pain stoically. No performances had been scheduled for the planned rest month, August. He had time to recover – but his slick moves in front of the stand-up mike and reading lectern he used on stage were a trifle less slick for a while.

One of my more important tasks on concert days was to staple to the lectern Michael liked to use the lyrics of the songs he intended to sing, in the strict order he planned to sing them. He surely knew the lyrics by heart (although quite often there were handwritten changes) – but the point he was making, not everyone got it, is that 'words', not rhythms or guitar riffs, are at the heart of REM creation. Like Dylan and Patti Smith, he's a poet.

But he's also a great showman. At the end of the number he would throw the lyrics into the crowd, like Madonna and her intimate apparel. By the end of the year I had a collection of them – some with those handwritten corrections. EBay gold dust, not that I would have sold them. They got lost, with a lot else of value to me, in the later upheavals of my life.

By the time the leaves were falling off the trees, I'd picked up quite a respectable Latin vocab. Inguinal, aneurysm, adhesion. If it went on like this I'd know as many ten-dollar words as my dad. It had its grimly humorous side. The band should have brought their own infirmary, MTV joked, and come on to the accompaniment of ambulance horns.

A MOMENT OF CLARITY

One night, a while before the tour started, I'd picked up a street date. Not a prostitute. Just a guy hanging out, looking for a casual encounter. The street in question was Santa Monica Boulevard. If you wanted gay, or transgender (like prattish Eddie Murphy), that was where you went. If you wanted straight (like prattish Hugh Grant) it was five hundred yards north, to parallel Sunset Boulevard, the 5,000s and up.

On Santa Monica, whatever you pick up will have a cock. Do what you will with it – if you can pay the price (sometimes, as I would soon find out, that price could be a little while arriving and it wasn't always money). My friend that night – perhaps longer – was very handsome, Latin and lithe. My type. I'll call him Hugo. I was in my rented Mustang convertible GT, cruising down the boulevard like a sultan in his harem. Round about Astro Burger (favourite hangout of stars, they tell you), if you know the boulevard.

Mexican in origin, Hugo had come north to LA with dreams of becoming a ballet dancer. A gay with that particular dream might not find Mexico the happiest place to pursue it. We liked each other. It went past one-off to a kind of loose hooked-up thing. Not quite a relationship. One thing that struck me as curious was that Hugo always wanted it condomless. This was the 1990s. They even put rubbers on kids' popsicles, so frightened was everyone by the so-called 'gay plague'. Retrovirals were still things guys in white coats were playing with in test tubes. Safety first. Particularly for recipients. But not, apparently, for Hugo. We drifted apart after a few weeks. It was fun, but there was no lastingness to it. We were both free spirits and too young to settle down. No hard feelings.

By the time the tour got going I'd hooked up with another Latino, Eric, to whom I was more solidly attached. With one notable, and exquisitely humiliating, lapse (see below), I was faithful to Eric for the next eleven months – a record for me at that time of my life. He came out to join me on the tour when we touched down in the US. Eric was young and skinny but, unlike other partners of my preferred ethnicity, he was my age, not younger. He was also better educated than me and well off. When he travelled to join up with me it was on his own dime. And I could introduce him round. That relationship with Eric helped glue me together over that year. Hugo, however, would make a traumatic re-entry into my life.

NA and all the other twelve-step groups have a term for it: 'moment of clarity'. Suddenly the fog clears, and you see what it's all about. It's precious and it doesn't last long – sometimes no more than an hour or so. It can be terrifying. But it's the fork in the road. Go one way and it's salvation – perhaps. Go the other and it's the morgue, the closed ward or prison. No perhaps about it.

Looking back it's hard nowadays to recall how high I was riding that year, without assistance, amazingly, from any substance other than youth. It was as if I was carried up by a swirl of golden bubbles. Gold's the right word. A tour by a mega-famous rock band like REM generates more money than many small countries. There's so much that it loses value. You're no more conscious of it than of the air you breathe. It's there. More of it than you could possibly find a use for.

I was physically close, for a year, to the one person who was the radioactive core of the *Monster* enterprise – Michael Stipe. His factotum. I didn't generate it but I shared that sense of omnipotence that vast amounts of money give. If Michael needed shaving cream (for his chin, not his scalp – which was clipped), I'd order a limousine to go to Rite Aid. Damn, I'd even do it myself if I felt like a pecan-vanilla cone from Häagen-Dazs.

We stayed in the best suites in the best establishments, like the Chateau Marmont, where you'd find specially printed notepaper with your name on it (even me). Keanu Reeves, apparently, liked the Marmont, a few yards in distance from Sunset, but in a different galaxy. He'd sit by the pool, with his laptop and his melancholy for company. Michael liked the discretion it offered. But in New York it was the breezier, open-to-all (paps behind every bush) Four

Seasons, on 57th. And it was here, at the NY Four Seasons, where this 'moment of clarity' I'm talking about took place. Hugo came back. He'd made his move to New York, hoping to make it as a dancer. He tracked me easily enough and phoned. I agreed to see him again – just as a friend. I wasn't going to cheat on Eric.

I, little Lord Snooty, refused to meet Hugo in the lobby. But he could stay the night, I said, when he came up. There was a rollaway bed in my suite. I showed him where it was and told him to watch TV. Then went off by myself to soak, luxuriously, in the deep bath, bubbles to the neck. Room service had brought in my usual evening meal. It was on a tray alongside me in the bath. Vegetable soup, medium-rare hamburger, apple pie à la mode, washed down with ginger ale. The bathroom TV was quietly muttering. I was softly crooning whatever song was in my head that day. I heard a click. The door? I shouted, 'Hugo!' – no answer.

Hugo had got the message. He'd gone. Not so much as a 'Fuck you, Jack.' I confess, to my shame, that my first thought was, 'Thank God that trash has left.' My second thought was, 'My God, I'm a bastard.' Things started falling into place. I saw, with awful clarity, the fool's paradise I'd created for myself. I'm not a rock star. That's not my private plane – I belong in the unpressurised hold with the luggage. I'm a dumb dyslexic kid from South London who got luckier than he deserved. And cruel. I was a shit.

I burst into tears. I threw on some clothes and ran outside. I walked the Manhattan streets for an hour, looking for him, wanting, somehow, to make amends. Hopeless. It was a life-changing moment. I never saw Hugo again – but I would hear from him. That would be another life-changing moment.

MY ONE LAPSE AND THOUSANDS OF INTIMATE GROIN NEIGHBOURS

What follows is crude and crass. I'll stick a vulgarity alert on it. Skip to the next section if you're easily offended.

As I said, I was faithful to Eric over the tour. But there was one gross lapse. It happened in Japan. Michael and some friends were relaxing in a restaurant, after a show. My body had collapsed on me. I was whacked. I'd been sleepless for days, getting by on twenty-minute naps. Michael saw me nodding and ordered me back to the hotel to get some rest. It was the only time I left my post on the tour. But in the state I was in, I was no good to him or myself. It was kind of him.

I thought a walk through the Tokyo streets would refresh me. In five minutes it was a *Takeshi's Castle* maze. I was lost. The hotel was near – I knew that. But where was it? A couple of taxis couldn't understand me and drove off. Or perhaps they didn't want a shambling foreign devil speaking gibberish in their cab.

A Japanese guy in his early twenties, by the look of him, approached me. I guessed he was gay but he was chubby and definitely, most definitely, not my type. He saw me doing the headless chicken and asked, in broken English, but English, thank God, if I was lost. I told him the name of the hotel and he said he'd take me there. Just direct me, I said. No, he said, he was going to take me.

When we got to the hotel he asked if he could come up to my room. I didn't want him to – too many REM people up there. (Hello Bill this is my new friend don't know his name wish he'd go.) And I was still resolved to be faithful. And, frankly, I didn't like the look of him.

I made an excuse – security problems. His solution? A nearby park where we could 'talk'. We would both need subtitles for that, but talk wasn't what Oddjob had in mind. But outside I thought it would be easier to get rid of him. We went to the park. I surely didn't want to stay in the lobby, starring on that evening's CCTV as the security staff did their nightly screen review.

When we were out of sight (he had clearly cottaged in the place many times), he damn near tore my jeans off, me squealing like a Victorian virgin, 'Oh no, sir, no!', him like a sex-maddened sumo wrestler. Finally I let him get on with it so I could finally go back to the hotel – fifty yards away. It was freezing cold. He dropped his own jeans to reveal a horrific sight. A pubic forest. Most Asian guys don't trim – it's a big joke among gays. In this case it was complicated by his tiny penis being a babe in the wood – invisible. Not that it was needed. The strangest thing: he just wanted to sit on my naked lap, no penetration. There was some limp, get-it-over-with hotdogging (penis between thighs) on my part. After two minutes I felt sick and pushed him off. That was it. I pulled my trousers back up and legged it back to the hotel, a shower, and eight hours' sleep.

It wasn't infidelity. 'I did not have sexual relations with that fat Japanese man', as the president would have said. I could have forgotten it but for one thing. When the tour got to Taipei a few days later, I noticed in the bath what I thought was a spot in my pubic area (neatly trimmed). I picked around and, horrors, the spot grew legs and started crawling, interestedly, around my hand. I was infested. Invaded. I felt I should get a leper's clapper: 'Unclean! Unclean!' It would not have helped me at this particular point in my career to ask around if anyone knew anything about venereal lice – 'crabs'. I was, by now, itching madly.

I confided my plight to Louise, the nanny looking after Peter Buck's twins, Zoe and Zelda. She was a bubbling, English Mary Poppins. We got on well. Louise arranged for the hotel to have a doctor come to my room. He looked me over and later had three kinds of pills sent to me. They did fuck-all. By now I was panicking. There now seemed to be thousands of them. I was a walking crab farm.

A little research helped. If you need to know (I hope you don't), you have first to clip and shave off all your body hair – the human-egg look. That doesn't kill them but it stops them spreading. We were now in Italy. Louise and I went to a druggist. Neither of us spoke the language. She explained, giggling, with a charade, pointing at me, what the problem was. I was mortified. The two pharmacists were crippled with laughter. They gave me three bottles of shampoo that worked like crab napalm.

So there you are. If you get crabs from a Jap in a park, my advice is to go to Italy, find a drugstore, and go through the motions of scratching your groin. Problem solved.

*A TOUCH OF THE REAPER'S SCYTHE**

The episode with Hugo in New York had been life-changing. The changes kept coming. A few weeks later, when we were in the Bay Area, I found a voicemail on my Motorola Flip. No callback number. Just a short message, in a cool, casual voice.

'Hi Jack. Remember me? You may want to call by your doctor. I've just found out from mine I'm HIV-positive. Bye.'

The world turned black.

I fell apart. And suddenly it was Michael Stipe, God bless him, who was looking after me. And here I was, bringing incurable disease into his private world. It was a period when no one was quite sure how else you could catch the virus.

It was also a distraction – something he sure as hell wasn't paying me for. The day I told Michael about my likely infection was big for him. He'd had a meeting with Patti Smith – a singer he hugely admired. (They'd sing on stage together, a few nights later.) And here was I. Sorrier for myself than in the whole of my sorry life. Staining it. Crying inconsolably. (Can you catch it from tears?)

Michael embraced me. It was role reversal. He talked to me like a brother, not a boss. He instructed me to fly to LA, where the best, and quickest, 24-hour diagnostic clinics currently were. Result? Negative. I broke down on the phone. Michael was my first call.

* These titles are John's. I asked him what the word 'skithe' was. He said he'd tell me if I could spell it correctly. We moved on.

I'll always love him for what he did.

And Hugo – was he merely putting the frighteners on me? Did he have someone as compassionate as Michael? Did he hold out till the drugs came in, if he really was positive? If he was positive was he still barebacking? I'll never know, and I don't look too closely, nowadays, for good times on Santa Monica Boulevard.

THE KINDNESS OF MICHAEL STIPE (1)

Michael Stipe was not just boss-kind to me but also sweetheart-kind to my family. When *Monster* did Milton Keynes (Christ, I hope I only go there once in my life), on a burning-hot evening in late July, he put my mother and granny in VIP seats on the side of the stage, and personally gave them earplugs. Mike Mills's mother was also there. They were a family band. For an hour or two, I too was 'family'.

Before the show got going, my grandmother, making conversation (and, to be honest, queening it a bit), asked Mrs Mills what *her* boy did? Oh, he plays the guitar, she said, pointing vaguely to the stage. (Blur, I recall, were warming things up for the local Milton Keynesians.) 'But I hope one day,' Mike's mother sighed, 'he'll get a *proper* job.' Granny nodded, sympathetically. Same with her Jack.

I swear that story's true.

My granny, for whom Andy Stewart's *White Heather Club* TV performances at Hogmanay were a tad too wild, idolised Michael when, on her birthday and at Christmas, he sent cards with a lot of OTT praise for me. They were given a permanent place of honour on the sideboard. Alongside my picture.

THE KINDNESS OF MICHAEL STIPE (2)

I was getting off Michael's tour bus (the band had different vehicles) in Chicago and someone in the crowd (there was always a crowd) called my name. Nothing strange about that. I was listed in the tour book. Fans – the kind who shook, drooled and went into convulsions during performances – studied that book like devout priests. Not fans – fanatics. REM fans, of all ages and sexes, offered me, with a meaningful look, 'everything', if I could only get them a backstage pass. Not many – but enough to give you the creeps. Quite a few asked me (me!) for my autograph and snapped me.

This was different, though. There was something pathetic about the wail. You could hear pain in it. It came from a middle-aged white woman, with a mixed-race teenager hanging back. About fifteen, I'd guess. Her mother it was who shouted out my name, 'Jack Sutherland!' She told me – gabbling, worried I was going to run off and do my job – that the girl had been abused by her father, over and over. She was crying.

The poor girl had made suicide attempts and was eventually hospitalised. The only thing which had saved her, the mother said, was the REM track, and video, 'Everybody Hurts'. She played it again and again. You'll know the video and Michael's lyrics. Universal pain, and 'You are not alone', as the eye sweeps jammed cars on a freeway. Subtitles.

I would have listened to the woman whatever. But what she was saying struck a chord. I teared up. Peter Gabriel, particularly the track 'Don't Give Up' he did with Kate Bush, had helped me through my suicide episode five years before. I'd say it 'helped save' me, if that didn't sound embarrassing. It seemed to be a song written for me, personally, in my gay pain.

They'd got tickets. It wasn't just an evening's entertainment. It was a religious act of thanks. She told me, hoping against hope I would thank Michael and the band. She gave me a letter, and some flowers. That was all. 'Thank you, Mr Stipe, for saving my daughter's life for me. Bless you.' A very big 'all'.

I told him about it before the show – interrupting what was usually a time when he required to be alone. He went thoughtful. Then asked for the girl's name, and that night, in the concert, he stopped the applause – creating a moment's silence – to dedicate his performance in the encore of 'Everybody Hurts' to the girl, who he named. Jennifer. He went on to add that her friend Jack wanted to see her after the show, pointing at me on the side of the stage. Meant nothing to the audience – except two people. And it meant everything to them.

They came up afterwards. Tearful, silent, overawed. I took them backstage to Michael, who showed them around. He introduced them to other band members and chatted with them, by themselves, in his personal tour bus (and this, recall, is a guy who's just done an exhausting two-hour concert). He asked them polite questions – with that Southern courtesy they have (very un-Chicago). I'm fairly certain (I'd left to do my after-show things) that he took their address and wrote them a letter.

These weren't fans: they were hurt human beings. Victims of a very horrible crime. His song had helped them and he, personally, could help a bit more. And he did. He didn't claim to put their world right. No one could. But he could help. On MTV they still play that song, 'Everybody Hurts', more than any other by REM. I never hear it even now without a pang, thinking about that night in Chicago.

THE KINDNESS OF MICHAEL STIPE (3)

I met (in a manner of speaking) any number of celebrities and stars on the tour. Everyone, it seemed, wanted to pay court to Michael – he was, there's no other word, revered in his business. Tori Amos, Johnny Depp, Bono, Red Hot Chili Peppers, The Cranberries, Oasis, Radiohead, Blur, Sarah Jessica Parker, Samantha Mathis, Stephen Dorff, Brad Pitt (just after the release of his movie *Seven*, which I shivered through and loved). I could fill a page with VIP names for whom Michael was a Most Important Of All Person. All of them were polite if they were obliged to notice me.

Nor did they matter to me beyond a name check, a spasm of awe at the name and, usually, the private thought how normal they all looked off-stage and off-screen. There was, however, one exception. I got more kindness from Michael than I can recall. Only once did it go wrong. He'd regularly ask me if he could introduce me, personally, to anyone I particularly wanted to meet. Peter Gabriel was coming to one of our shows. I can't now remember which.

I'd explained to Michael how Gabriel's albums (among other things, the soundtrack album he'd done for *The Last Temptation of Christ*) had saved my life when I was in the pits of suicidal despair. We were in Michael's dressing room, a few friends saying hello after the concert. I was doing my usual packing up, but staring, all the while, at Gabriel, as if I was hypnotised. Meaning well, Michael took me by the elbow, walked me over, introduced me with the words: 'This is Jack Sutherland, my assistant, Peter, and your greatest fan.' He didn't say 'number-one fan', like Kathy Bates in the movie *Misery*. But it had the same chilling effect. The last thing, it was crystal-clear to me, that Gabriel wanted behind stage was 'fans'. He got enough of the buggers front of stage.

I was too overawed to do anything but stand there, jaw sagging. I could have saved the situation. ('Where, precisely, do you stand on the Resurrection, Peter?') But I wasn't fast enough. Dumb and dumbstruck.

He politely shook my hand, nodded, and slipped away to carry on his conversation with Michael.

The three people I've most dearly wanted to meet in life, the Dalai Lama, RuPaul, and Peter Gabriel – I only managed one. Ru. The other two, nada. If they read this – a second chance, Your Holiness and Peter? No, I didn't think so.

THE KINDNESS OF MICHAEL STIPE (4)

It was 28 January 1995, Auckland, NZ. Winter's summer there. It was rainforest-hot and damp. REM were playing an outdoor concert to eighty thousand fans. The biggest thing that happened in the country since the Japanese didn't invade in 1943. The fans were caked in red mud. People were passing out, and being 'surfed' down over the packed crowd. Some had fainted and couldn't find room to fall over, so jammed in were they.

During the last break, before the finale's eight songs (crowd-rousers like 'What's the Frequency', 'Sidewinder', 'Losing My Religion', etc.), Michael called me on stage and thanked me for doing my job so well. Then he told eighty thousand New Zealanders, 'Let's give Jack a song.' They broke into 'Happy Birthday'. One of the roadies threw a cake in my face: I stood there dripping icing. The sound guy made a tape of the whole thing.

If I've ever felt on top of the world, it was standing on that stage, down under, with enough noise to frighten every duck-billed platypus in the country. Master of the Universe. For two minutes. If Andy Warhol's right, I'm still owed thirteen.

MOMENTS OF CREATION

So what did I get from the *Monster* tour? I made a shitload of money, far more than a teenager should have, and saw the world. Which every teenager should do. I grew up a bit.

Not enough. I slept and had some occasional sex (with Eric) in interesting places – but for once in my life sex wasn't a primary thing. And, when I got back home, I found out Eric had been cheating. Just one of the occupational hazards of being young and gay.

The lasting thing I took away from the tour was being around to see how great art happens. PAs, who are close-up and (if they're doing their job) invisible, sometimes have that privilege. I'll give an example.

It was 13 February. We were flying to San Sebastian, Spain, from Singapore. The world tour was at its most 'world'. First-class cabin. Michael, rocking slightly in his set, wrapped up in thought, quietly crooning, suddenly turned and barked, 'Get me some paper and a pen.' I burrowed, obediently, in my carry-on bag.

I'll inventory the contents of that high-end Mandarina Duck (a birthday present from Michael). I carried it with me at all times, like POTUS carries that briefcase with the big red button which will end the world as we know it. In my Mandarina were contact lens solution, the rolling paper and tobacco Michael preferred for his occasional cigarettes, Drum. American Spirit, if he wanted ready-made. Witch hazel. Mobile phone. Less mobile than most because Michael was suspicious (so am I) and had one the size of a brick with elaborate radiation barriers. (Wise man, in my view. I had to use a standard Motorola flip.) Usual first-aid stuff. Washbag stuff in case the plane was diverted. (Can't remember the toothpaste brand, but he would certainly have specified it.)

The bag weighed a ton. And, of course, it had writing

materials – supplied, on this occasion, in seconds. A few minutes later Michael is jabbing at the paper. People around are looking at him a tad nervously. Pop stars, planes – you know the headline stories. Where is the nearest exit door again, steward?

In fact he was he was composing a song, 'Departure'. Catching that moment, between take-off and landing on long distance, when you're nowhere and in no one time zone (we were actually 'losing' a day). The band's rapport was so close that they would, on landing, build the music round his lyrics. It was what Michael called a 'throw-up song' – spur-of-the-moment inspiration.

You may know the opening line: 'Just arrived Singapore, San Sebastian, Spain, 26-hour trip.' (It sounds a lot better than that looks.)

A few hours later I saw him debut the song, my back still twanging from that twenty-six-hour trip, at the Velódromo de Anoeta, San Sebastian. It's a beautiful composition – and I saw it being born, just like a proud father in the maternity ward. That's what remains. My personal *Monster* legacy.

RANDOM THOUGHTS

I've swapped job gossip with career PAs who've had to pick up drugs, hold them, ration them out, and wipe celebrity noses as they emerge from restrooms, powdery-white round the nostrils. Others who've had to arrange (even inspect) 'escorts', and inject B-complex into some of the more respected buttocks in show business.

Celebrities tend to have retained doctors in every city they go to. Up where they are the pressure is unbelievable. Pills are staples of celebrity life. The PA will often hold them. And then wonder whether they should dispense so many. Look at the post-mortem report on Elvis. So many pills inside him his corpse rattled like maracas. The doctors prescribed them, and who administered them? The PA, I'd guess.

Pusher, peddler, pimp, human pillbox. They don't put that in the job description.

And then there's the humble domestic stuff. Washing underwear with special soaps in bathroom basins (room service, even five-star, isn't fast enough for one-nighters), when all you're desperate for is a few hours' sleep before you get up (early). My know-all dad tells me the Romans had no word for 'no'. Neither do celebrities. You don't really know them and you certainly don't ever 'no' them.

They're frightened to death of hearing that little word when they ask for something wholly outrageous. It's a test for them. 'No' would mean (1) they haven't yet quite made it to the very top of the slippery pole, or (2) they're on the way down. When Beyoncé,* or whoever, demands that, before she/he arrives, the dressing room be repainted in puce (no, hold that, lilac), and orchids flown in from the Tibetan foothills, she/he doesn't probably give a shit about the décor. They want proof they are all-powerful. Still masters/mistresses of the universe. And, looking around, who has held on to the top celebrity position? Jagger, Streisand, Clapton, Neil Young and very few

* I read somewhere that she demands the toilet paper in her private restroom be red. Good for her. I feel sorry for her PA, though.

others. Not many people get old up there. When the world stops obeying their outrageous commands, and their toilet paper turns white, like everyone else's, celebrities know their day is over. They fear that day more than death itself.

So the last thing a PA can say to his/her celebrity is 'no'. People still ask me, hoping for dirt, about what I really 'did' as a PA. I tell them I never had to do any of the above kind of stuff with any of the names mentioned in this book. That's the legally unenforced truth. I've been lucky, and I chose well, except for a couple of occasions, with other clients who aren't mentioned here (or in my CV at the back), when I had to go beyond Michael's 'Lemon tea, please, Jack.' (He'd sometimes, for a laugh, ask for it on stage.) OK. You really want to know something close-up and personal about Michael Stipe? Apply to be his PA, and find out for yourself. I think I can say he likes fresh tabouli in his dressing room without betraying any confidences.

The only problem for me in the PA business, and what eventually turned me away from it, was handling emotional slippage. The relationship changes so fast. When you start, the boss wants you to keep your distance. You're the helpful stranger. Respectful of the boundaries. Then, if you do your job well, boundaries melt. First it's Jeeves the gentleman's gentleman and then, before you know it, it's Mrs Doubtfire. Except, it gradually dawns on you, you're not that Robin Williams tranny granny who can put lives right. You're just hired help.

It rankles, once it hits home – usually after a month or so. And the bitch is, you can't have personal relationships that last more than hours. The talent can bring wives, husbands, girl- and boyfriends or family on tour. Children, even. And do. The PA can't. You're close enough to celebrity, and its lifestyle, to smell it. But most of the time you're an over-paid, two-legged alarm clock, tea-maker, trouser-presser, door-opener, UPS guy, cigarette-fetcher. And occasional trouble-shooter – the moments that make you feel more important than you are.

They're tired. You're tireder. In the nature of the job, you get less sleep than your boss – phone, switched to 'listen' on max volume, close to your ear. Always at the ready. First up, last to bed. First to the door, at the end of the entourage. It's wearing. But you, unlike the boss, can never be grouchy. And never forget a bag.

There are PAs who've stayed with their artists for long periods. Elvis Costello, I'm told, has had a long-serving PA. Chris Martin, I'm told, likewise. Good for them. But most PAs I've known have moved on as I did when or even before their short-term contracts were up. And, to be honest, it's just as well they do if they want a life out-side PA-dom. Friendship with a star is something else. And it only works, long-time, if money doesn't come into the equation. Jump on to me and RuPaul if you want to see what I mean.

The best, if entirely OTT, depiction of the downside of a PA life that I know is Kevin Spacey's film, *Swimming with Sharks*. It's about a PA, bullied and publicly humiliated by a shit Hollywood boss. PA kidnaps said boss, ties him to a chair, and gets to work on him, Hannibal Lecter-style. I've been lucky enough never to have had to console myself with those fantasies. Spacey, by the way, is an actor I love. He's one in my very select 'I'd work for him for nothing' category. He's crafted his own image of cool which is irresistible to a gay man like myself – whether Spacey himself is or is not doesn't matter.

5: *CLUBS, PARTIES, EYE LINERS, OCEAN LINERS AND PORN (VERY LITE)*

CLUB SCENE, PARTY SCENE

I was never a to-the-death fan of REM. My favourite track is one they did later, on *Up*, 'Day Sleeper'. They were a college band for fans who dug poetry. That wasn't me. I still loved Peter Gabriel's psychedelic spectaculars. A hangover, perhaps, from the LSD I no longer took.

After *Monster*, I could, quite likely, have got permanent staff appointment in their hometown, Athens, Georgia. That's where they'd come together and made their Four Musketeers pact – all for one, one for all (an even split of money). It's a college town. And Deep South. They, particularly Michael, liked it because there they weren't stars – they were just guys who lived there and had done well for themselves. They fitted. I didn't think I would. And, of course, out of the big cities, and below the Mason–Dixon line, you couldn't be too flamboyantly gay. I wanted hustle-bustle. In two words: Los Angeles.

It was no secret that the band were in fracture mode. They had been close to breaking up before the tour, when there had been published accounts in the papers of 'fuck you' rows. True or not, I don't know. I never witnessed any arguments like that. What I saw was a band in a family relationship. It's true they seemed to be careful to reduce friction by travelling in different buses and having different dressing rooms.

The strains of the tour itself wouldn't have improved things, if there were indeed growing differences. But whatever else, the near-death experiences reminded these four supremely gifted guys that there were more important things in life (life itself, for example) than making even more money than would get you on the Forbes rich list. I wasn't the only one whose neck had been touched by the reaper's scythe.

LA, the Nowhere City, was now my home. My favourite night resort was Arena Cafe, the largest gay, and gay-Hispanic, club in the world. I have always been drawn to golden-skinned, smooth, slim Hispanics as lovers, friends and people. They still owned California, I thought: the gringos had merely borrowed it for a century or two to bring it into the twentieth century. During my time in the city, Hispanics became the demographic majority. I adopted the look – cholo-shaved head, goatee died jet, cold eyes, toothpick at the corner of the mouth, baggy 4XL clothes that hung, and could have fitted three of me. It was all pasted on, of course. Ming the Merciless crossed with Ali G and a dab of Antonio Banderas. But it made a point I wanted to make. *Junto contigo*.

I drove an open Corvette at this point, the colour metallic purple. I got a lot of Barney the Dinosaur teasing for that, but I liked flamboyant – in the world's face. I spent thousands on customising and had a stereo loud enough to shatter glass. (I got a ticket for that noise and had to protest my way out of a stint in traffic school. The fine I didn't mind. I could have papered my bathroom with tickets.)

I was forever being stopped by the police on suspicion of being a little Latino gangster. Here I was, twenty years old, in a car no honest officer could dream of owning without a painful visit from Internal Affairs. They would sometimes open the questioning in Spanish. Hostile street Spanish.

Just to say again, I was drug- and alcohol-clean at this point – and would be for the best part of fifteen years, 1989 to 2004. Good years. But I'd forgotten where I'd come from and I had drifted out of the twelve-step world that had saved me. Fool that I was. It would be a few years, though, before I discovered that fact.

I was by now increasingly involved in the gay Latin scene. The GLS social life was split into two sections. One was the house party scene, the other the club scene. The reason for the split was the fierce liquor-consumption laws. Only twenty-one and older could drink legally. The police squad didn't go for the drinkers themselves – they targeted the bar or store owner. Latinos come of age early and are desperate for full 'manhood'. The biggest gay Latin club, Circus & Arena (more of which later), would have Under-21 Fridays, with the club organised as ground-floor for juniors – food only – and twenty-one and over, with a bar, on the floor above: entrance strictly by ID card only. Fake cards are almost always recognised by trained security, and in any case they don't have to let you through if they're the slightest bit suspicious, which they are by nature. Gay Latinos of the kind I was friendly with did not want to go clubbing with a BLT in one hand and a Diet Coke in the other.

The house parties took place at weekends and were organised by party crews. The crews had names like Happy Happy

Joy Joy (one I used a lot and whose crew chief, BJ, I came to know well*). The crew would take over a back garden (paying the owner handsomely) and set up sound systems. The location of the party, and the crew organising it, would be advertised by same-day fliers. At the party they'd charge entrance and sell alcohol to all and sundry, no questions asked. But alcohol wasn't the big item: nitrous balloons, inflated from tanks, were the intoxicant of choice. Cost: a dollar a balloon.

Kids would suck down the contents and be sky-high for a few minutes. Then another dollar and another suck. Nitrous had the advantage that it made you 'happy', not drunk or violent. You were literally 'incapable'. And it fired the party spirit. And, of course, it was legal. I personally never touched it. There were rumours of brain damage – as with glue. But I liked the wild effect it had on partygoers.† And it was very profitable: two hundred kids, ten balloons each, beer at double the store cost, dusk till dawn. Do the maths.

The house parties I patronised in South Central ran the risk of being broken up two ways. The first, which was the less risky, was a police noise patrol. That would probably mean a fairly peaceful dispersal and a warning to the householder; nothing illegal about juveniles drinking in a home environment. The cops, generally, did not cruise that dangerous part of town at night. They were too busy guarding Beverly Hills mansions.

* Too well, as it happened. See below.

† Nitrous is no longer big in LA, I'm told, but I'm amused – from my current viewpoint in Old Compton Street – to see it's recently taken off big time on the London gay scene. A legal high.

The other risk was the arrival of local gang members offended by their barrio being invaded by a horde of maricones, dressed like wannabe real cholos. If they were really angry, they'd fire a few shots in the air. All the maricones would run, screaming like little girls, for their cars. I saw that more than once. The gangs would probably threaten the crew chief, scoop up the night's takings and issue fierce warnings about respecting their turf. If the outsiders were pussies without gang back-up, there were occasional fist fights. I threw the occasional punch, though generally I left it to others. As always, I was sober and careful. Partying young Latino gays are generally peaceful. They just wanna have fun, as the song says.

I had organisational skills from my Propaganda days, and I was recruited into the 8-Ball Crew by my friend Byron. He was a best friend – in recognition of this I had his name tattooed across my chest.* He had mine on his. Byron set up the locations. I did the organisation and logistics. I picked up some easy money, and had weekend fun myself at the house parties. But I wanted more (money, that is). I formed my own crew – The Reckless Bunch. I later renamed it Tallwhiteboy Productions. There weren't too many white boys at these house parties. I was now a fully-fledged party monster.†

I didn't need a crew – I could get the assists I needed throwing around a handful of twenties on the night. Or I'd partner with some other crew – there were no hard feelings.

* It's now covered by a black strip. See below.

† Like Macaulay Culkin, 'party kid' organiser, in the movie *Party Monster* – which hadn't yet come out.

We all liked each other. There were plenty of young Latin gays to go round for the house party scene to boom. A good party would yield me, by the time dawn broke, a couple of grand. My angle, which proved very successful, was to offer cabaret entertainment. My entertainer was Miss Martin, a 300-pound Divine-inspired 'chola' drag queen, with a hilarious Spanglish falsetto patter, a great wardrobe, and terrific diva-mimic skills. He/she would have made it to the top were it not for a fatal love of crystal meth, which was just beginning to appear on the party scene. I would set up a stage, get some spotlights. (I knew the equipment renters from Propaganda days.) If it was going to be a big night, I'd lay down a dance floor. Tallwhiteboy Productions was a leader in the field after six months or so.

I was pulling in good money and having fun myself. But I didn't stick with it. It took me too near the fringe of violence – just one person shot, or stabbed, or beaten to death in or around a party, and the consequences could be awful. Over the years I've known at least fifteen people close to me who've been killed. There are a score of homicides every weekend in LA – mainly in the area the police call Ghettoside. We're not talking Phil Spectors; mainly black on black, or Latino on Latino.*

There was one near-miss event, particularly, which was career-changing, if not life-changing. I was living at the time in a nice apartment in Atwater Village. It was a quiet residential street but cab drivers who knew the area would warn

* Armenians, in Glendale, and Asians, in Alhambra, are not homicidal. *John*. There's a book on the subject just been published, *Ghettoside*, by Jill Leovy. Very relevant to what you're saying here.

passengers not to walk to the far end of it. Gang territory. If they're suspicious (cholos never go round less than four to a car), there's the one question, 'Where are you from?' Turf defence. They don't fuck about; they see a shaved head and a face they don't recognise and they close in. Wrong, or unsatisfactory, answer and they move fast: 'whoever draws first will walk away' is their code.

Brushes with gangs happened to me often enough. When they asked where I was from I'd go into my Jeeves routine – exaggerated English accent, make it clear I 'respected' them. It worked. They had no quarrel with the Queen of England. But they were in a state of perpetual inter-Latino war. The 18th Street gang, for example, were Mexican and in constant turf confrontation with MS-13 (Mara Salvatrucha), who were Salvadorean and called Mexicans 'serote' – 'shit'.

This night I parked my car by the apartment and I saw a low-rider cruising up from the end of the street. It was moving slowly, no music. The lights were doused – a danger sign. They didn't want the licence plate picked up. In some places, sometimes, it could mean a drive-by shooting (as common here as in areas like Compton or Watts). I was with my friend Miguel (Mexican-Puerto Rican). They'd seen two shaved heads and were investigating. Or perhaps they were just bored and wanted some action. Quite recently, round about here, there'd been a sixteen-year-old Latin boy killed on his skateboard. Didn't give a satisfactory answer, presumably. Or got smart. I told Miguel to stand behind me and not move. Run to the house and you'd risk a bullet in the back.

We stood in the driveway, empty hands dangling. Let me

talk, I said. If they were Salvadorean it might not be good to be recognisably Mexican, as Miguel was. Their ears could pick up an identifying accent. I did my cut-glass English stuff, but – it was late at night and I was tired – not humbly enough. And I made the mistake of stepping forward towards the guy (there were three more behind him) asking questions. A gun came out, a foot from my face.

He was, I'd guess, eighteen, a short five-eight in height, slim. I was six-two, 210 pounds and muscled. I could have snapped him in two. But he had that $50 hand gun – 9mm, I could see. I'd be dead, one shot in the face, before I knew it. And they'd shoot, run, and I'd be another unsolved crime on that night's police file. I managed, without showing fear (by Christ, I was feeling it) to talk him down. Required respect was shown them. I was let off with a caution.

There were a couple of other experiences like that. I decided, mid-twenties approaching, that party-monstering was too dangerous for me and moved on, looking for lines of work where you were less likely to have a gun put to your face. But when I got really short over the next couple of years, I'd put on a party to fill my pocket.

The mega-big, Latin-gay-friendly Arena Cafe and its sister Circus club were where I liked to spend my leisure hours, which, nowadays, I had more of. They were the creation of a remarkable man, whom I came to know and admire, just this side of worship. Gene La Pietra is a quietly spoken, courteous Angeleno – even though, like most of the Los Angeles power elite, he didn't start in the city. Gene has, through his clubs, given the Hollywood community more good times than Disney – he is, for example, the moving spirit behind the City of Hollywood New Year's street party (one of the funnest public events in the Los Angeles calendar, particularly for the city's gays). But La Pietra himself is never seen partying. I went very occasionally to his mansion on Los Feliz. It would be quiet company. So quiet you could hear the ice in the glasses tinkle.

Gene came to Hollywood from the East Coast in the late seventies. He was no celebrity and no big shot. According to his published profile he was:

> in search of his fortune and a place where his homosexuality would be accepted. As he tells it, the early years in Hollywood were a struggle, a mix of odd jobs, roach-infested hotel rooms and occasional nights asking strangers for change. An especially low point came in 1972, when La Pietra was arrested for selling pornographic movies at a store he co-owned, BookCity News. Because La Pietra was under 25, the conviction for using the mail to send obscene materials was expunged from his record.

Gene went on to manage a couple of 'low-level' bars in Hollywood. They can get very low. He found that clubs in this part of town – even if they were gay-friendly (we're talking mid-seventies) – 'turned away patrons who were not white'. Golden-skinned Hispanics qualified as 'not white'. Olive-skinned Americans of Italian descent might be so misidentified. In 1975 he raised some cash and opened Circus Discus in the scuzzier end of Santa Monica Boulevard, where big parking lots could be installed. He called it 'Circus' because all and sundry were welcome. Even 'non-whites'. 'Discus' because it was circular and disco. It was hugely successful. In 1990 he went on to set up Arena Cafe on the same vast plot, a converted warehouse with a 3K-plus legal customer capacity. All his outlets were linked by an archipelago* of linked parking lots. The clubs – three of them, eventually – made him super-rich and not a gay in Hollywood grudged him a cent of that money. He was giving, not taking, from the community.

Gene could have devoted himself to his clubs and to getting even richer. He didn't. He became a social activist, raising funds and forming pressure groups for everything from cleaning the West Hollywood streets to AIDS crisis response. He forged close ties with the LAPD, advocating diversity quotas. Cops needn't be the gays' enemy. He contributed to politicians, muscling up his causes in Sacramento. He had a vision.

One minority was a minority no more – gays and lesbians. After West Hollywood was incorporated in 1984, they flocked there. To live. But the place was a mess – an eyesore. Tourists to the holy sites, Gene complained, took one look and ran back to the safety of the valleys:

> They get off the bus, they look around and they say, 'My God, what have you done to this beautiful place?' They see a few stars [on the Hollywood Walk of Fame] and then they get back on the bus and go somewhere else to spend their money.

* Thanks, Dad. Ever parked there? I thought not.

Gene wanted to go all the way – secession for Hollywood from Los Angeles. He spent millions on the campaign to become mayor of an independent Hollywood – realising, probably, it was hopeless. Los Angeles needed the tax revenue Hollywood generated: it was LA's money box. But it fitted in with Gene's larger mission – to make all of Hollywood more like chintzy West Hollywood. If you know Los Angeles, you'll know what that yawning difference was.

There was no shortage of gay activism in Hollywood. But Gene was a prime mover and the big hitter. He spent most. And because of it La Pietra's a hero to the world's largest concentration of gay and lesbian citizens. There's quite a few single straight women as well who choose to live in 90069 (lots of jokes about the zip code), free from gropers, gawpers, and stalkers as neighbours. The city is now what realtors call 'desirable' (as if you could fuck a house). It can afford to be. It's rich. For the same reason that Hamelin must have got rich after the rat-catcher moved on.* No kids, no schools, no crippling education taxes. West Hollywood has the lowest crime rate in LA County nowadays. You could walk down Santa Monica from Fairfax to Doheny at midnight, with hundred-dollar bills fluttering in your hands, and not get mugged. The grassy lawns you pass look like they've been trimmed with nose clippers. The police cars have the gay rainbow embossed on their sides. Where else in the world would you find that – Brixton?

Gene liked me for the same reasons I had come to like myself. I was young, trans-ethnic, Hispanic-loving, clean and

* *John*. Glad the poem I read you one bedtime stuck in your mind.

sober, smart, good-looking (though I say it myself), English-polite when I chose to turn it on and confidently gay. It was a real possibility, at one point, that I might have worked for him, in some club managerial role. I suggested it to him several times. The night side of me was attracted. It could have really gone somewhere. But he thought I might be, as he said, 'overqualified' – by which he meant qualified for other things.

Arena was managed in my time, expertly, by Gene's partner, who had begun at floor level and rose on ability, not because he was passing the cornflakes to his boss every morning. Who knows, I too might have risen if I'd gone to work for Gene. But when I thought about it, my abilities aren't suited to club management. I'm too restless by nature. I've always needed jobs where ADHD is a career asset – running clubs, year in year out, isn't one of them.

There were other reasons. I admired what Gene did for Hollywood. And I respected what he and his clubs had done for the LGBT and Hispanic communities. But, truth to tell, I never bought 100 per cent into the West Hollywood Boys' Town concept. For me there was a 'real world' in which gay was in the mix but without making a big deal about it. I was embarrassed by all the 'pride' days and demonstrations. No need to proclaim it – just *be* it, for fuck's sake, and get on with the rest of life.

I didn't (still don't) like, as a look, those West Hollywood gay white boys with their sporty Cherokee jeeps, muscle-Mary bodies and designer T-shirts. Or walking the sidewalks with their dinky little tricked-out dogs, stopping at every boutique window to squeal delightedly. What drew me to the Hispanic communities was their admirable love of family, respect for elders, their concept of honour. Their 'manhood'. Loyal Gay Hispanics, most of them I was close to, chose to live with their multi-generation families in places like East LA. They weren't 'self-orphaned', as most of those gay whites in West Hollywood had chosen to be. Rootless – with only gayness gluing them together as a community. I've never chosen to live there permanently. I don't think at this stage (I was growing up) I was a self-hating gay, or trying to escape from myself. I just have problems with some styles of gay.

Style apart, I admired then – and still do today – Gene La Pietra. Unreservedly. LA should, one day, do him the honour of a named LAX terminal, like they did with Tom Bradley, the first black mayor.

PAINT JOB

What was I going to do? I tried out for Winona Ryder, who needed a PA. A bizarre experience. I was interviewed by one of her trusties – who knows, she might have been watching on CCTV. I felt like a suspect in *Law and Order*. I flunked. Perhaps deliberately. Truth was, I didn't much want to go back to PA slaving.

I was picking up, for as long as I wanted, all the work I wanted on videos, bumping from job to job. But it was subsistence, given my enlarged lifestyle and car expenses. (My insurance was horrendous.) The *Monster* money was melting away fast in the California sun. And I wasn't too fond of getting up at five in the morning after three hours' sleep any more, which is what video work meant. Comfort had corrupted me. I wanted a six-figure salary which would allow me to live a life. Perhaps even have that thing I had never so far had in that life, a 'relationship'.

As a first step I got myself a penthouse split-level loft near La Brea and Third. I shared it with my old friend Janie, the one who had always loved animals more than humans. I grew quite fond of her three-legged cat, Ellen. Less fond of the Chinese water dragon she installed in the master restroom, watching human personal ablutions with a cold eye. It scared the shit (literally) out of visitors who didn't know about it. I fitted the place out with dull-grey custom-made suede furniture. Dark tones throughout. Pneumatic bed. It had a high-rise Jacuzzi in the roof garden, where I could watch sunsets, icy tropical juice in hand while my body poached.

I didn't stay in that area too long.

For an interesting few months, I went into cosmetics. Not selling Kiehl over the counter in the Beverly Center (which is what one of my prettier boyfriends, Louis, did), but working in the place where cosmetics meets art. The relevant name? Joe Blasco. I met Mr Blasco through my best friend at the time, Noah Marino. A gay who liked risky sex with straight Latin guys, Noah had given me a necessary style makeover, mirroring his own look. It was Rocawear, the bigger the better – triple-X FUBU. I was now a cross between Latino and hip-hop wigger.

Noah and I were the only two white boys around our part of the Latin gay scene. He was found dead in a New York hotel apartment a couple of years later, with fifty stab wounds. A conviction followed – straight guy, of course. He claimed he'd come up for drugs (Noah dealt), and that Noah, a stranger till that point, had raped him, and the wounds, front, back and groin, were self-defence. What happened to Noah still shakes me up. But we knew it would happen. He took too many risks in life. A short life – he was just thirty.

At the time I joined him, Mr Blasco had two personal assistants: Noah was one. The name 'Blasco' probably means nothing to you. But check out the early masterpiece of his art on YouTube, the Naziploitation flick *Ilsa, She Wolf of the SS*.

Blasco did the make-up on Dyanne Thorne – sexy but marble-white – making the other Nazi scum ugly and puffy, sweaty, and the concentration-camp inmates haggard, scarred, grey.* Truth is, he used movies like *Ilsa* as a laboratory, always trying new techniques to refine old techniques. Blasco's genius was that his talent was directed head-on at the motion picture industry. His customers were the studios, not bored ladies wondering which Mac lipstick would make their husbands really interested. In the process, he was raising film make-up to a higher level of art. His skills meshed with lighting, special effects, moods, lens and filter variation. Make-up was not the right word – what he did was closer to prosthetics. At times, illusionism.

Make-up is usually about fiftieth on the credits of any movie ('Face paint by Who the Fuck Cares'). And by the time it scrolls down you're out of the theatre, throwing your empty popcorn carton in the bin. But it matters. Ask anyone who works on the studio floor. 'Make-up', in the hands

* *John.* There's a post on the YouTube film I like: 'Hollywood Jews will stop at nothing to denigrate the German people.'

of a master like Blasco, can do as much, on screen at least, as 'work' (surgery – which is often disastrous. Check it out on those 'Hollywood's Worst Cosmetic Surgery' programmes on the Entertainment Channel).

You'll surely notice how 'ordinary' Jennifer Aniston looks when a pap catches her at Ralphs, or wherever she picks up her groceries, but how she glows in front of the camera and on the screen? That voltage is at least 70 per cent cosmetic. A good part of what gives you the creeps in Cronenberg and Romero, and all the Leatherface rip-offs, should be credited, directly or indirectly, to Joe Blasco. As his Wikipedia entry says:

> Blasco is often credited as inventing the bladder technique presented in horror movies, as well as special effects, such as bulging blisters and rashes on the skin.

Despite working with the man I still don't know what the fuck the 'bladder technique' is. (Sounds like the kind of thing they mention as personal preferences on Grindr – 'Chemsex with bladder technique only, please.') But what I was hired for, after being introduced by Noah and given the once-over, was helping reshape an organisation that was growing out of its old movie-studio line of work. Blasco was expanding from theatrical work into store-retailed cosmetics (an industry that was going crazy in the 1990s, every B-list star starting her own line) and cosmetology, with his Blasco School of Makeup. He had another branch in Orlando, Florida.

He didn't want me for my non-skills with the brush and palette. What he wanted me for was as a blunter instrument

– hatchet man. I was to help slim down and shape the new organisation. I'm good at that. I don't mind firing those who have to be fired and then being around to be blamed. His organisation was (he would have been the first to agree) in a bit of a mess, and needed someone to feed back to him as to what next. Like other great artists, Joe's mind had been too long on higher things. He'd had to fire all his senior staff.

He took a chance on me, and I owed him big time. I got my MBA ('equivalent') from JB Cosmetics. I know I did a good job for Blasco Enterprises (though believe me, Orlando is boring as fuck. See one alligator, you've seen them all. And it has the most hazardous traffic lights I've ever known – Floridians regard them as a challenge to their manhood). His academy and 'lines' for the general market – introduced around this period – have thrived. Particularly the school. Last time I looked, to get a certificate of training from the Blasco Academy ('The Mercedes of Make-Up Schools') costs close on $40K for a top-line course. But I bet every premier make-up artist in Hollywood has Blasco products in his/her bag, and Blasco-devised techniques at his/her fingertips.

After I'd done what he took me on to do, I left Mr Blasco amicably enough. To be honest, I found it a bit not-my-style – that face-dabbing. And no one wants the guy who had the guy at the neighouring desk fired hanging around. It makes for a bad office atmosphere. I was unpopular. Particularly, I think, with Joe's boyfriend.

But I did what I was paid to do and it was a learning experience. I'll never see movie faces, or any faces, the same way again. And Mr Blasco (it never fully relaxed into 'Joe and Jack') was a nice guy who treated me nicely and paid me nicely. He was a genius at what he did, and what he'd done for the film industry.

And, my God, I smelled good over those months.

ON THE OCEAN WAVE

After Blasco I spent the best part of a year as production manager for a company whose main line was organising live cabaret and stage entertainment for cruise liners.

There's a backstory. I had a Latino boyfriend, BJ, whom I loved but towards whom I was not the best of boyfriends. We'd met through the 8-Ball party scene crew (he was a chief), and hit it off. I was very popular, nowadays, on the dating scene and aged in my early-to-mid twenties had no intentions of settling down. Or, come to that, slowing down. Open relationship. That was the deal. BJ finally couldn't take it and wrote me a devastating farewell letter.

Shattered and self-disgusted, I decided to leave LA and return to London for good – or at least a long time. When I was able to think clearly, I thought my personal life through, and decided that, after all, BJ was what I wanted. He'd said, forcefully, he wanted no more contact, it was over, but I reached out to him by email and phone using all my powers of persuasion. I couldn't see my life without him.

I convinced him to come to London. I had a small apartment in Russell Square (then the cottaging capital of the Western world*). He'd had a terrible life – typical, sadly,

* They've since cut down the shrubbery. Spoilsports.

of what happened to Latino gays. When she found out the awful fact, his mother kicked him out, aged sixteen. That door would be forever slammed against him. ¡Maricon! For two years he'd camped – short-term, till it got embarrassing – with a series of friends.

I arranged for visa, passport, and bought him his ticket. One way. He arrived just before Christmas. First really cold weather (snow, even) he'd ever experienced. I bought him warm clothes. We went to my parents' country house in Suffolk with some of my long-time English friends. It was blissful. For BJ it was winter wonderland. And, for a week or two, so it was for me.

I couldn't but notice, though, that he was oddly reserved, as if he was holding something back. Just overawed, I thought. It's a new world for him. Then a bouquet of flowers, and some expensive chocolates, arrived at the Russell Square apartment. What the hell? The message attached said 'love, love, love'. Just my 'friend', he explained. He had been hitch-hiking on my AOL email account. I broke his password and found a slew of what were clearly love, love, love letters. Friend be fucked. I wasn't his lifetime love – I was a Christmas holiday. My heart was broken.

I raged but I couldn't really blame him. Joey, the other guy (who I came to know well, ten years later), was solid. I was flaky. I'd hurt BJ too much. He hadn't filled in either me or Joey as to what was going on: he was out of his depth, poor kid. I was angry but I was more scared than angry. Was this going to be the story of my life? One-night stands, one-week 'relationships'? I delivered an ultimatum: him or me. Him it was. I bought the ticket which took BJ out of my life.*

I'd come back to London thinking I could do something in the city's booming entertainment industry. They have world-beating music videos, I thought. I'll waltz into it with the kind of CV I have. REM? Wow!!! You're on board, Jack. Big mistake. Not only did London not have any Latin boys, or Circus & Arena, which was a pain. It didn't need Jack Sutherland to make its world-beating videos. Not one little bit, it didn't. I couldn't even get a job as a runner, if I wanted to sink that low.

I phoned up Line Postmyr, my friend in need, with a desperate 'help me back' plea. Line had done business with Anita Mann. An interesting woman, Mann was an ex-Disney dancer, world-class choreographer, and now, in the 1990s, was organising live entertainment for cruise liners. The deal was done, by me and Anita, over the phone. She wasn't one to waste time. I flew back to LA. Back home, it felt like, after those cold, disappointing weeks in London.

I was hired as production manager to all and sundry in the entertainment crew. Lots of feathered costumes, sub-diva temperaments and changing-room spats. The liners themselves were little Las Vegases on the ocean wave (which, thanks to state-of-the-art stabilisers, were never felt by the paying passengers. Nothing was really felt). There were slot machines everywhere – you could empty your wallet and

* For the tragic end of the BJ story see the Rourke chapter. The relationship with Joey ended when, a few months after BJ went home, Joey's 'true love' got out of prison. BJ, it turned out, was a stopgap. He got very promiscuous and contracted HIV (when it was still a dark age for the disease).

empty your bowels at the same time. And at night, while overeating, entertainment from showgirls, name comedians on the way up, or down. There was probably less fucking in the cabins on these ships (apart from in the showbiz quarters) than anywhere outside Mother Theresa's bedroom. But lots of drinking. I liked the entertainers.

But on the sun decks it looked, to me, like a living morgue. Guys with zippers running down their bare chests, mementos of the heart-bypass operations that every rich, overweight, well-off American male seemed to have aged fifty. And again aged sixty. And so on till the old ticker stopped ticking. Alongside women with atrophied right biceps from pulling on the slots. Very nice, most of them, but bored shitless. By what? Life. They gorged meals that their worn-out palettes couldn't appreciate and their bellies didn't need. I exaggerate.

It was hell's circle of boredom. Motto: 'Not dead yet, but when it happens how will we know the difference?' I saw the world (not as much as with REM) and got a terrific tan. And it was a safe, reasonably senior, job for a man in his mid-twenties. And I could have gone on with it. I liked Ms Mann.

I wasn't ready to be old. I moved on. But before I shipped out, I took my grandmother and mother on a cruise through the Caribbean. Truth is, I think they found it boring.

HUSTLING WITH LARRY FLYNT (ALMOST)

I never actually met Larry – in his golden wheelchair – but I saw him often enough at the Four Seasons and saw his

Bentley (licence plate HUSTLER) cruising, like a sex-shark, down the Hollywood boulevards. And I got quite close to some gay guys who worked in his Sunset porn supermarket, Hustler Hollywood, up around San Vicente. It blatantly shop-windowed bizarre paraphernalia – everything from sexual-assault blow-up dolls ('NASA technology!'), through baseball-sized butt plugs, to the kind of torture gadgetry ('sexual toys'!) I recall giving me nightmares for a week as a nine-year-old after visits to the London Dungeon. The penile tokens they gave you for the restroom were cute. I've never been a sex-shop addict (I prefer real things to unreal) but Flynt's place didn't seem at all dirty. It's wide-open windows were a world away from the other mega-big sex shop on Santa Monica – a big, dark, ill-smelling hole fouling up the boulevard. Larry's genius was to make the perverse not just acceptable but as 'normal' as what the missionaries recommended.

I was sent to Hustler Hollywood, not long after it opened, in my 'pre-intern' days at REM, to collect a life-size blow-up doll that needed to be made up to look like Björk. It was a birthday joke for her. Her boyfriend Stéphane Sednaoui had directed the hit video for 'Big Time Sensuality'. I don't know if she laughed. Everyone else did. And she's a good sort, as the English say.

People pucker their noses when you mention his name but Flynt has a skyscraper with his name on it in a prime spot on La Cienega. LFP. Larry Flynt Publications. I never drive by without thinking of that building Marty McFly's evil stepdad has in *Back to the Future Part II*. What's it called?* While on the subject of films, you remember in *Volcano*, when the massed power of the LA Fire Department stops the lava reaching the sacred Beverly Center mall on La Cienega? The massed hoses of LA are also saving, for humanity, the Larry Flynt Publications building just down the road.

The beautiful Spanish word, Cienega, few realise as they cruise down the boulevard to the airport or beach, means 'swamp'. That seems about right.

My next career jump would take me into Larry's swamp – or might have done had I gone through with it. The porn industry is huge and, via web subscription, recession-proof. Guys, even after they've been wiped out, always have $4.95 left for the last cheap thrill. And I bet every barrack-room in the US military had, at that period, much-thumbed copies of *Hustler*, like every motel room in the country has a Gideon Bible. American manhood jerks off to Larry's product. You could fill Lake Tahoe with the ejaculate the man's inspired. You couldn't grow up, at least as I'd grown up, in the place and not have dipped your toe (and other parts) into the swampy stuff. A lot of it with the LFP brandmark on it. At this time, I myself was spending a fortune buying DVDs (good for one viewing only), often four at a time, fifty bucks or more. Nowadays it's all free on the internet.

I was a looky-loo. I didn't want to get into the muck, crime and human exploitation of that industry, which I sincerely don't like, but there was a variety of gay(ish) porn that

* *John*. 'Biff Tannen's Pleasure Paradise'. I read, in October 2014, that the building has just been sold for $89m. Presumably in the face of internet porn taking over the nation's gonads.

did interest me – careerwise. It grew out of my most visited site – Latinboys – and my experience with weekend parties. What I had in mind was not filth. In fact, by today's standards, it's quite innocent. You could call it 'can we talk?' porn (with apologies to the late Ms Rivers – whom I arranged the occasional limousine for, later in my career).

I opened a limited-liability shell company called Tallwhiteboy, recycling my weekend party title. The base 'CWT?' scenario I came up with went like this. There's a huge number of Hispanic adolescents who come into LA every week, hitching, by bus, walking. They're looking, poor souls, for new lives and whatever work they can get. They all need a few dollars to get started. You recruit the ones who can speak English (many can, if badly – it's part of the ethnic charm), check their age for the 18+ laws ('Latin Boys' usually look younger than they are), and get them to talk about why they've come to El Norte, what they want – to talk about themselves. Su vida, hermano. To open up, in a sense. Not just the zipper.

They're not necessarily gay – most, in fact, won't be, and those that are mostly won't admit it. But you ask them if they'd mind undressing and posing – modestly, if they're embarrassed. Like that lovable old queen Quentin Crisp. But younger and cuter. And, if they're willing, jack off. If not – de nada, hijo. Their refusal has a certain charm. Would they just mind if the camera took a peek (think the end of *Boogie Nights*)? The kids only go as far as they want to go. Timidity adds to the charm. No coercion. Most of them, if the questioning is gentle, are proud of their big dicks. A Hispanic thing.

The fee (paid up front) is generous by the standards of stoop work in the fields, or labour on the construction site. Mine, in the couple of trial shoots I did, was $100. For two hours' work. Their mothers would never see it. It wouldn't even offend the Catholic Legion of Decency on a broad-minded day.

I had a very close friend at this time, Hernando, strikingly good-looking, lithe as a panther and incurably mischievous, who did videos like this on odd occasions when he was hard up for a concert ticket. (Madonna, he liked to recall, was the first he'd jerked off on screen for, thinking all the time of Leonardo DiCaprio.) He gave me the idea.

The target market was lonely, white, shy gays with an eye for golden-skinned Hispanics. Plenty of them around LA. They wanted to feel close – but were frightened of getting physically close. They'd never 'do' anything. Just looky-loos. And there would be no problem getting them to part with the $4.95. No one would get hurt, or abused. I wouldn't market the product myself – too complicated and, frankly, too dangerous. I'd feed it through a porn wholesaler. Plenty of them around in LA, as well. I'd profit on percentage payback.

I borrowed $20K and got camera and sound equipment from Samy's on Fairfax. I knew enough technicians from my Propaganda days to help with a couple of trial shoots. It all looked good. It would have worked out. I know it would. But in the end it didn't. A number of reasons. One was self-preservation. A gay cop who hung out in Arena warned me that the porn-monitoring department at the LAPD would certainly open a file on me. Any kid who fooled me with fake ID could have got me charged with corrupting a juvenile. Then it would have been goodbye green card or worse. ('Hello Dave, hello Vinnie, how're ya doin'?')

There might have been licensing issues – with the health and safety regs coming in stronger every year. And, to be honest, the more I looked into it the more I didn't like the scummier parts of the business. Other well-paying things came my way over the next couple of years. But I kept the idea on a back burner. There was so very much money in it. Meeting a friend of my friend, RuPaul, Chi Chi LaRue, drag queen and commercial pornographer, revived my interest for a while. But it went wholly off-programme when my partner and frontman, Freddy B. (who was lined up to do the Spanish, English, Spanglish questions, do the graphics, and recruit the models from the LA bus depot), got jailed and deported.* With him gone I didn't have any cover. Not a closet I wanted to come out of.

I hocked the equipment. I'd already paid back the money I'd borrowed. It was an interesting 'never quite happened' in my life. And if you know any tall white guy who wants to buy an unused company name, let me know.

I'll never have that skyscraper in the LA swamp.

LOS ANGELES PARABLES

What did I believe in those days – as a rising-mid-twenties-year-old? What do I believe in now? Karma. How I found

* See below for more on Freddy, and his sad story.

my faith, and had it confirmed, is best explained with a story. Call it an LA parable.

At the Arena nightclub I met this guy, Jaime. Everyone liked Jaime. Why? Because he could get you anything you wanted, 50 per cent reduction. Anything, that is, from an electric toothbrush to an AK-47.

How did he do it? I asked, when I was close enough to him personally (just friends) for him to trust me. It was very simple. He'd drop by the Arroyo Seco Golf Course or the Rose Bowl parking lot on the night of a big event. He'd pick a dozen or so car locks. (You can do it with a bump key; if you don't know what that is, Google it.) Some of the drivers and passengers would have been sure to put their valuables in the trunk. Jaime could scoop up a handful of credit cards, driving licences, social security numbers. Then he'd consult his buyers' list and go off to the Glendale Galleria or wherever, and pick up what was required. The docs he'd throw into the nearest ravine.

I wanted some surround-sound speakers for my apartment. Why would I, earning what I did, give a fuck about saving $300? The sheer fun of it. So one night Jaime drove to Dodger Stadium for one of his serial trunk raids. Sure enough, he got what he needed and gave me the speakers I needed. No charge.

It was stupid, high-risk, and it hurt people who had done me no harm. And this is where the karma comes in. Seven days, precisely, after getting my speakers, I was carjacked in Elysian Park – one of my happier hunting grounds.

I was with a friend, David. Just a friend. When we stopped he remained by the car, smoking. Nervously. The park wasn't a good place to be standing by a new $80K vehicle. You might as well have put up a sign saying CARJACK ME, CHOLOS. I'd just finished paying thousands that morning tricking the Corvette out. It was metallic purple and glowed with pride of ownership.

I, meanwhile, was in the bushes being – well, picture me standing with a happy, faraway look on my face. Mid-happiness in the brush I heard the sound of smashing glass. I shoved Mr Anonymous off my private parts and ran to the car.*

Two guys were face to face with David. One of them punched him hard. Another, as I approached, fists up (fool that I was), put a shotgun to my head. I tried to disarm him. Christ, my car was at stake! My car! They'd already smashed in the driving-side window (looking for the keys). Three hundred dollars at least to put that right, the little calculator in my head clocked up.

They didn't shoot. One of them jumped over the driving-side door into the car (it was a T-top convertible, top down, no lock). They were still looking for the keys. Then everything went black. What saved my life was that the guy had pulled the gun back to smash my skull, and in the process smashed the other front window. The blow lost enough of its force to save me from death or permanent brain damage (I hope).

I was unconscious a minute or two and when I came round I couldn't see for blood. They were still whacking my head, shoulders and ribs, shouting – in Spanish – where are

* When I dictated this I used the words 'sucked off in the bushes' and 'kicked him off my cock' here. John, Nervous Nellie that he is, softened it.

the fucking keys? Donde *Bang* los jodidas llaves, *Bang* maricon *Bang*? I threw them the things, slippery with my blood.

They tore the Tag off my wrist (an REM memento) and the flashy rings I liked to wear at that time of my life. I had bruised knuckles (the smallest of my concerns) for weeks after. One of them jumped into their pickup, the other roared away in my lovely Vette. I would never see it again. It was either chopped that night or driven through the border to be sold in Tijuana.

I was in a bad way. But with an arm round David, I could just about stagger, blood streaming down my face. Elysian Park, once you get to the road, is just five minutes' walk from the Police Academy. From there, where I reported the crime (for insurance purposes, without going into detail about fellatio in the bushes), I was shipped to the emergency room at County Hospital, East LA, where they checked for internal bleeding. I remembered Bill Berry and Lausanne. Like him, I was lucky in the medical attention I got. County is the biggest hospital on the coast and has bright trainee doctors from all the LA medical schools, picking up their skills. My skull was fractured in two places, the MRIs recorded (at $3K a pop). But I'd live and walk out in hours. I wouldn't be running the LA Marathon that year.*

I was sure it was karma. Bad things you do will come back at you. Those scars on my skull remind me of that every time the barber asks how I got them. 'Expensively,' I reply. I wonder sometimes whether some of my later-life

* Did it once. Under four hours. Came back looking like tandoori chicken, one of my friends said; it was a hot day.

problems – anger management, for example – weren't caused by that head trauma.*

Confirmation of my karma beliefs came a couple of months after the carjacking, when I bought myself a SIG Sauer 9mm handgun. Fifteen-round clip, laser sight, hollow-point bullets (cop-killers). State-of-the-art weapon. I registered it legally. Self-defence. Fact was, I was wanting to big myself up. Gunman. Stupid gunman. I hadn't learned my lesson. I told Jaime I wanted some luxury bedding. He got it for me – usual discount.

I was now driving a sober-coloured Cadillac. Corvettes attracted too much attention from carjackers. Seven days (that same karma interval as before) after acquiring my bedding, at six o'clock in the evening, I was making the tight turn off the 101 onto Melrose, to drive the surface streets to Sunset and avoid the freeway jam. Nestled opposite the crosslights was an invisible cop car.

This was Ramparts territory – the most corrupt of the police divisions in the history of California, as later scandals, and a hundred overturned convictions, would reveal. That was in the future. Right now, I was used to being pulled over: young kid, expensive car, shaved cholo head, big baggy E. Smith football jersey. I also had a Hispanic friend I was fond of in the car with me.

The driver of the cop car flips a bitch (driving U-turn) and his loud speaker bellows: 'Driver! Pull over!' I know the drill.

* Newspapers recently have had stories about American football players having uncontrollable anger issues as a result of their head injuries. The NFL is all set to settle out of court, apparently. My fuse was a hell of a lot shorter after that night. I take medication for it nowadays.

I stop where it's safe, then, with no delay, put both hands, holding the keys, out of the driver's window, instructing my passenger to do the same. Then, 'Out of the car! On your knees!' Two cops, both Latino, one senior, one a rookie. I have committed no offence. What next? Ten minutes' plate and licence check and on your way, driver. They cuff us. SOP, standard operating procedure. But a bit tougher than usual, I noticed. My passenger (why can't I remember his name?) is by now trembling like a leaf. I'm cool. No big deal.

I put on my English-butler act. Not a cholo, officer, but Jeeves. 'Any weapons?' the senior cop asks. 'Yes, officer,' I reply, in my cut-glass accent. 'Legally held.' The SIG was, as the law required, in a gun case, between the front seats under the armrest. I give them the combination.

'Where's the clip?' senior cop asks. Law requires ammunition is stored separately, which indeed the clip is. Under the seat. I didn't see what came next – my back was to the car. But I heard something that chilled my blood. 'It looks,' says the older cop, laughing (the cruel bastard, how many times had he done this?), 'like we've got our first arrest of the night. You're busted.' He'd put the clip in the gun. What does that mean? Possession of a loaded firearm. Major felony, possible prison time, loss of green card. Now I'm shaking like a leaf as well. Justice, Ramparts-style, looms.*

Oddly the rookie cop, who I sense is gay, mutters to me,

* This couldn't have happened, or, at least, not as easily, if the police cruisers had, as they now do, cameras recording the stop. I'm all in favour of that – obviously enough – and of the next predicted step, cameras on the cops' persons recording it all when they make a stop or an arrest.

while his partner is radioing in to the station to tell them he's bringing in a couple of gangsters, 'Just fight it', adding, 'When we process you, just keep saying "alternative lifestyle". They don't want to get into any of that, it's too political.' Politics wasn't much on my mind at the time, but I got what he was saying. Camp, not cholo.

When we get to the precinct, still cuffed, the older cop shows the SIG to his fellow officers, who guffaw merrily. 'Sweet gun,' one of them says. Then he points it at me, and aims the laser sight at my forehead. Is he going to kill me for resisting arrest? They did that kind of thing at Ramparts. Fuhrman testified to it at the OJ trial. The walls, he said, were streaked with blood.

I'll never see the gun ($1,500, it cost me) again. Ramparts, I assume at the time, keeps a whole armoury of them – if they're not needed as court evidence, then as plants on jacked-up arrests like mine. My companion is let go. The expectation is he'll testify against me. I'm transported downtown to the Twin Towers, the largest remand prison in the Western world. Before I leave, the rookie (he *must* be gay) presses into my hand a piece of paper. On it is written 'alternative lifestyle'. I get the message. I'll never see him again, but I'll always remember him kindly.

Downtown I'm strip-searched ('Spread 'em'), relieved of my expensive jewellery and thrown into a holding cell. On the way, now in prison uniform, I pick up a blanket from a large plastic bin which looks like home to every scabies bug in the city. This was not 'luxury bedding'. Was God chuckling? By now I'm saying 'alternative lifestyle' like a mantra and I see what it means. I'm put in the gay 'tank', not the gangsters' 'tank', where, sure as hell, the veteranos would kill me as a wannabe fake. Which I was.

I finally get my phone call and, after a night and a day in this circle of hell, a friend brings my $1,000 bail. I hire an expensive lawyer and the case is, after costs which still make me wince with pain, dropped. 'Insufficient evidence'. What does that mean? The rookie cop refused to testify. Bless him.

I kept my eye on any news about Ramparts – and there was lots of buzz in Arena. Five years later I like to think the senior cop was prosecuted and jailed when that balloon went up. Damn him. Hard time, I hope.

All this happened, as I say, seven days after I idiotically asked Jaime to get me that luxury bedding and acquired that gun. Karma. I got the message and binned it when I got home. Do bad things, get worse things in return. In just one week. Karma has a very tight calendar.

THE STORY OF FREDDY

I was close at Arena with Freddy B., who'd been my accomplice in the porn venture. Freddy was a first-generation Guatemalan immigrant, brown-skinned, gay and green-carded. He did the early-evening DJ stint at the club. Freddy had nice looks, he wasn't a great voice man (in English, at least), but, more importantly, he was a genius spinner. He would, had things not gone wrong, have gone far.

He was the baby in his family. They lived in South Central. His big brother, Jose, ran a local sports bar and grill. It was a front. Jose was also financing the importation of large quantities of cocaine from south of the border. When he'd made enough from that he planned to go legit. They all say that.

Jose's drug business meant moving the product, and the money it generated, across state lines and national borders. He didn't know it but he had had attracted serious FBI interest. One of his couriers had snitched on him, probably, to plead a sentence down. Jose, as I say, didn't know that, but he knew the dangers of putting his own hands on drugs or dirty cash.

Jose had a problem. Beyond urgent. Money owed him had to be brought in from Salt Lake City. (Even the Mormons use.) He couldn't trust a low-paid mule. The sum, $60K, unmarked, was too tempting. Mule and bag would be over the border, speed of light, never to be seen again. He decided to ask his baby brother Freddy to do the fetching from SLC. It was an irresistible advantage that Freddy was entirely clean. No criminal record. He'd had nothing to do with his brother's dealing. He knew about it, of course.

Jose put a guilt and family-loyalty trip on his baby brother – if this money doesn't get delivered to the man I owe in LA, they'll kill me. I've never asked you to do anything like this before, have I? Anyway, it's not drugs I'm asking you to carry – just cash. Untraceable. Freddy refused. The pressure kept coming. He gave in.

He flew, domestic (no security problems, this is pre-2001), with a half-empty carry-on. Jose didn't know it, but he and his operation were being staked out. He was medium-size himself, but he was connected with some very big fish. Freddy was apprehended getting off his flight at SLC. He was clean.

But it terrified him. Frantic phone calls were made to LA – 'The Feds are onto us, Jose.' Jose talked him round. Bring the money or I'm a dead man. They've stopped you once, they won't bother again. It's just routine.

Wrong. On his return the Feds do pick him up again. Now he's carrying a vast amount of money he can't account for – except by telling the truth. And if he does that his brother goes down. The FBI is, at this stage, rolling up the case. Freddy is just one of thirty-eight arrests. He's given the option of testifying but refuses. His conscience is clean – he's no criminal, just a family guy doing his brother a favour. He didn't even know what was in the bag. The FBI stitch him into the operation. His lawyer (public defender) tells him it could mean life behind bars.

Freddy agrees to testify before a grand jury with the assurance he will get immunity, probation or a suspended sentence. All Jose's money and property has been seized ('asset forfeiture'). There's no prospect of any dream team getting the brothers off. Freddy's released on bail while the prosecution inches forward, closing down the network. For four years he doesn't know what's ahead of him. He's nervous. Witnesses in trials like this often 'disappear'. The trial itself is being held in SLC. The travelling is ruinous, eating up everything he gets from club work. His family is cold.

Finally, after having Freddy testify against his own flesh and blood, they fuck him. Three years in federal prison, no parole. And after a long, expensive trial they nail Jose to the cross. Life plus thirty-six. The living death sentence. He deserves it – Freddy doesn't.

When the date came for Freddy's surrender it was horrific for me. He was, along with Noah, one of my very closest friends. They shipped him to a godforsaken Texas prison camp for overflow detainees, where he slept on cold concrete, wrecking his kidneys. It was done – vindictively, one can suspect – to keep him far away from his family and friends. When he was coming up to the end of his third year they revoked his green card, which made him just another indocumentado, an illegal alien, banned for life from entering the US, where his home had been for twenty years.

I sent him what comforts were allowed and felt bad about not driving down. Having 'paid his debt to society', Freddy was deported, like so much human garbage, back to Guatemala. Not a happy place for a gay, with a criminal conviction, to spend the rest of his life. Deportation means they fly you back and just kick you off the plane. He keeps in touch, and sends plaintive emails inviting me there.*

DON'T CROSS THE BORDER WITH A MAXED-OUT CARD

I've known good cops but I've never had a warm spot for law enforcement, generally. When it comes to police, Mexico is bad, but in its way honestly bad. The corruption is naked. None of that lip service to protect and serve. Last time (and, by God, it will be) I went across into Mexico, I took three friends, all Hispanic but fully documented US citizens.

* I hope to go later this year, 2015.

I was driving a fast car with blacked-out windows. I looked, on the road, like a high-class pimp. Driving south of the border is sometimes iffy with insurance but I took my chances, as I had many times. I was, by this stage (2008), using again, my clean, drugless years behind me.

We spent the night in Tijuana, clubbing. Rather wildly, it must be said. You don't go to TJ for Earl Grey and cucumber sandwiches. We'd been smoking continuously. I had three tubs of medical marijuana, highest strength, in the car. On the way back to the hotel we were stopped by the cops in the middle of town. We were high and smelled it. My medical marijuana card was not much help. Nor was the too-flash car. Nor the fact that we were clearly gays. There were drawn guns and assault weapons pointing. And very cold eyes. We're fucked.

Particularly fucked since one of my friends panics at the prospect of a Spanish prison. He says, in Spanish, 'The gringo is rich. The white boy will pay whatever you want.' I thought of that Lone Ranger joke, 'What do you mean "we", paleface?'* They indeed wanted big time. They took all the cash out of our pockets and the marijuana from the car. (There would be a high time in the precinct tonight – it was LA medical, better than anything on the TJ streets.)

Eyewitnesses melted away. If it was drug-gang stuff (with a car like mine, it probably was), they didn't want to end up beheaded in a ravine or boiled alive in an oil drum. Neither, of course, did we. We'd seen the horror stories on TV. The

* *John*. They're facing the Indians and the Ranger says to Tonto, 'We'll have to shoot it out.' Tonto has an ethnic thought: 'What do you mean "we", paleface?'

cops didn't even bother to talk. They told my little Hispanic friends to stop jabbering or they'd throw their ID down the nearest drain and let them explain it to the migra on the way back. Me they took, at pistolpoint, to the ATM, and ordered me to withdraw my daily maximum. I got out $2k in five separate withdrawals before the card wilted under the strain. Then it was on your way, señor, and bienvenido a Mexico. The sarky bastard in charge actually saluted. Back at the hotel we consoled ourselves with a tub of weed the Feds had missed. A glum high.

It was brutal. But honest. The face behind the mask of authority everywhere. My advice? Never go there with a maxed-out card. The Feds don't take 'declined' politely. But, as I say, it's honest. The honesty of a fucked-up world where the police are as fucked-up as everyone else. I've never been back to TJ since.

6: CARS, LAMAS AND THE GREATEST DRAG QUEEN IN THE WORLD

I finally found my destiny for the next fifteen years. Cars and stars. Put them together and what do you have? The limousine. It's celebrity existence on wheels, and as much California's state icon as the golden bear. In Washington the vehicle of choice is the black Escalade. It says to the world 'power'. In New York the VOC is the yellow Checker cab with scuffed seats and a driver who was once a Lebanese professor of ancient anthropology. It says to the world 'melting pot'. In LA the VOC – what else? – is the Lincoln Town Car. Unstretched.

Famously, LA despises public transport. It's Disneyland's Autopia for adults. You can grow a beard waiting for a taxi. Imagine you've just de-planed at the Tom Bradley terminal at LAX. There's no bus or train connection. You stand on the sidewalk. Cars and hotel jitneys pull up to the white zone and cruise off, like little fish. Suddenly, a limousine with tinted windows and a black-suited driver who looks like he auditioned for *Reservoir Dogs* stops. Who's inside? Every head turns. Monseigneur in his carriage, the Lord Mayor's coach, Neil Armstrong in Apollo 11. It's all that rolled into one. It's LA on wheels.

In the years I was managing limousines, moving them around like pieces on a chequerboard, the star who I felt understood what they were was Faye Dunaway, who, a driver once told me, liked to have a dry-ice machine available in her limousine so that she emerged misty-ankled into the real world of little people outside – like one of the fanged beauties in Coppola's *Dracula*. Limousine lady. I admire her style.

To cut the story short, I decided to go into chauffeured transportation. The limo business.

Some legendary figures founded the industry when it took off, big time, in the 1970s. Most of them started as drivers, or car cleaners and detailers. On the ground floor. But they saw the future, grabbed it, shook it, and made millions. Some were still around, gods of the chauffeured-transportation business, when I started in the mid-nineties. The founder everyone in the industry knelt to was David Klein, who founded Dav-El* in the late sixties. Klein it was who switched the Cadillac (too swish) for the sober Lincoln Town Car.

Klein died in 1988, aged only forty-two. I never knew him. But I did know the man who took over from him, Scott Solombrino. Solombrino was another genius. He was the first to appreciate that credit cards and cell phones (he carries three, at all times) could revolutionise, and lubricate, his industry. None of that billing and filthy lucre. (Who knows what snotty, coke-sniffing nostril this twenty has been stuffed up?) Everything could be prepaid, on account, ahead of time. And everything synchronised perfectly. No wait. The cell phone was to the limo what air-to-ground radio communication is for planes.

Solombrino (who'd begun as a driver in a peaked cap)

* It's variously spelled Davel, Dav El, and Dav-El.

luxuriated the limo interior – installing sound, climate control, TV, drinks cabinet and office facilities.

Limos became the rage in the 1970s. And Dav-El was Hertz to every other firm's Avis. I would work for Solombrino, in a senior(ish) position, in a couple of years, but it wasn't my break-in job. My first position – behind desk and wheel – was at a smaller, dynamic firm, Budget on Sunset.* They don't exist any more, but they were located at the western end of the Plaza, as the ritzy half-mile around the 8,000s is called.

I got the job, indirectly, through Michael Stipe. That streak of luck was still running for me. REM, when they were staying at the Chateau Marmont, used BoS. I'd arranged the band's transport and had an in there with the owner/proprietor, Tony Phelps. They took me on first as a Jack of all trades called (laughably) 'special projects manager'. Special projects included handwashing vehicles and changing tyres. I soon earned respect and trust. Then I was office staff, then managerial.

BoS did high-end car hire (with celebrity show business clients – like REM) and were moving into chauffeured transportation. Their selling point was the superb fleet of cars they had on instant call. Either theirs or leased. At the top end, you could hire a Lamborghini.

BoS had humbler vehicles, a couple below even bottom-end. I would review the contracts and there was one repeat monthly renter who caught my eye. I saw him a couple of

* *John*. Opposite my world's favourite bookshop, Book Soup. If they want a signing session – we're on.

times; an angry-looking white guy with a woollen beanie (in California? Had he just had brain surgery?). He returned, months on end, to hire a heap-of-shit Toyota Corolla. All he could afford to drive, apparently. God knows why we had it crapping up the lot.

This customer no one was exactly jostling to serve was, the contract revealed, Marshall Bruce Mathers III, who'd just released an album no one was jostling up to buy, *Infinite*. He's recorded as selling a total of a hundred or so mainly from the back of his car (perhaps some of them from our Corolla).

You've guessed. Eminem, before anyone know who was Eminem was, and before he became world-famous with the success of his third album in 2000. He could nowadays buy a fleet of leased Mercedes (his favourite transport, his website tells me) to cruise up and down 8 Mile Road.

I'll always remember him fondly, clunking off the lot in that banger. I don't suppose he remembers it fondly.

Morgan Freeman strolled by one day to pick up a car. He's physically massive (as is his on-screen presence – the camera never seems to leave his face). The studio had only given him a 'full-size' car. Like the 'tall' Starbucks coffee, it doesn't mean what it says; it's an off-the-shelf, low-end vehicle. I felt so guilty and was (*Seven*! *Shawshank*!) such a fan, that I discreetly upgraded him. Fact was, he's so tall, he would have had to drive with his head out of the sunshine roof on a normal car, like a tank commander going into battle. On the basis of that one meeting I can say I didn't see a fragment of diva in Morgan.

The biggest kick for me during my three years at Budget on Sunset was that I had (remember I'm in my mid-to-high twenties) the pick of what was one of the juiciest fleets of luxury vehicles in the city. I would roll into East LA, where my Hispanic friends mostly lived, in a gleaming, fresh-out-of-the-car-wash Audi or Mercedes S-Class. And eye-catching: not quite Springsteen's pink Cadillac, but getting there. Sometimes, even, if my English roots were twitching, a Bentley: a surprisingly popular car for personal use in the US, among the star community.

On my birthday, my boss, Tony, gave me his flame-red Ferrari Maranello 550 for 24 hours. I only left the driving seat to piss – and that not too often. It was a $300K miracle of Italian engineering. If God has a freeway, that's what He's driving on it. I'd return it cleaned and detailed, aching for another twelve months to pass. There's no other word for what I felt at such moments (and they were regular at this stage of my life): orgasm.

BoS, as I say, wanted a slice of the Los Angeles chauffeured-transportation cake. They'd set up a separate outfit to do it, T&T Limousines (which stood for Tony/Transportation). I had a 10 per cent share and sales responsibility as general manager (I loved those titles). Most of all I liked hustling for clients. RuPaul, via the Outfest festival, was one (of which more in a minute). Our biggest first job for T&T (God, was I proud to have landed it) was the transport requirements of the Dalai Lama on his 1998 visit to LA. It came to me, as such things usually do, through 'contacts'. The buddy system. In this case it was Randy King, a rock and roll kind of guy and a sales agent who happened not merely to be a Buddhist, but also high up in the LA Buddhist community.

There are close on 150 Buddhist centres in Los Angeles

County. Relics of the 1960s hippy-Zen cult. There is even a colony of monks in Hacienda Heights, for whom the Dalai's visit must have been a taste of nirvana. And then he had his Hollywood supporters. Michael Stipe is on record as a fervent supporter of Tibetan freedom, and he gave concerts for the cause. Even more of an admirer was, and is, Richard Gere, a tireless Hollywood warrior for Tibetan freedom.* All in all, the five-day trip would involve a lot of in-car-time.

I'd like to wow you with a chapter on him and our conversations ('I have some queries about karma, your holiness . . .') but I can't. You had to submit, for security, the names of ten potential drivers with full background details, to the State Department. I sent in my name at the top of the list. This was one job I wasn't going to pass on. Not that I anticipated the tip to be stupendous. But there are (at rough count) 70,000 Buddhists in LA County – who knew, after this gig there might be 70,001. Buddhism has always attracted me, little that I know of it.

Anyway, to cut it short, Washington looked into my licence and determined that I was 'not a fit driver'. That page after page of 'moving violations' on my DMV sheet. Perhaps, too, the US Secret Service did not want the Dalai being whisked at 118 m.p.h. to Mr Gere's Bel-Air mansion. Un-tranquil. I was, shamefully, the only driver Washington kicked off the list.

* Gere's mansion, by the way, is no Buddhist cell. It outdoes even Phil Spector's 'chateau' in Alhambra (before he found his present, extremely non-Buddhist, cell). Check out Gere's Versailles on Google.

I knew RuPaul before I knew him – the way the public fools itself into feeling close-up to celebrities. (Read any check-out-lane mag that has 'Jen' or 'Brad' on the cover.*) They, of course, wouldn't know you from dog shit on the pavement. And care about you less, probably. I became 'acquainted' with RuPaul, of all places, at a 'gay night' in a pub in Great Bogwallow in the Marsh, or something, in Essex. Not Haight-Ashbury by two planets, at least. But even that village, as in *Little Britain* (I loved that programme), had its gay. More than one, it would seem.

I was there with my best English friend – from babyhood, almost – Sarah Upton. She was into extreme sports (and extremely straight sex) professionally (not the sex). The disco was blasting a song I'd never heard before (this was 1994), 'Supermodel'. They played it three times on the trot. I danced my arse off with Sarah. My booty, I have to say, is rarely shaken.

And (this is the truth) I felt, with a kind of orgasmic liberation, glad in that moment to be gay. No, not glad – relieved. Somehow that song, 'Supermodel' (I didn't, then, know it was Ru belting it out), made me feel normal. Not straight-normal, but gay-normal. A stone had been lifted

* I came close-up to the couple after an REM concert. Oddly Brad's skin looks bad, except when he's on screen. Blasco magic, I assume. Cameron Diaz and Ewan McGregor, who I met on the set of *A Life Less Ordinary* (crap film), have skin so good they could go straight past make-up to first take without stopping for the powder puff and paint. Megan Fox, too, who I saw on the set of *Passion Play* (underrated movie). Skin-close stars are different animals.

from somewhere inside me. And that was it: in a muddy Essex village.

There are only two full-blown celebrities I've been fan-crazy to meet. One was Peter Gabriel. For that floperoo, and Michael Stipe's kindness gone wrong, see above. The other was RuPaul, which led to the warmest friendship in my professional life.

Sammy Davis Jr was once asked on the golf course what his handicap was. 'I'm black,' he said, 'I've got one eye, and I'm Jewish. Ain't that enough?' RuPaul was six-five fully grown (close on seven foot in heels), couldn't play basketball, was black, and, as soon as he knew who he was, gay – born into a pre-emancipation sixties world where gays were regarded as lower than frogspawn. And drag-queen gays even lower than that. Ain't that enough?

Ru's written a lot, and candidly, about his/her* early struggles and miserable childhood. It's heartbreaking. He rose above it (six-five helps) to become the most famous, and tallest (and for my money most talented), drag artist of his time. Some would say all time.

When I was running T&T for Budget on Sunset, one of the big clients we landed was Outfest. If you don't know, it's a LGBT film festival. It's huge. One of Outfest's top icons was RuPaul. Ru's not just a pretty face and high heels. He's always had a mission, on his passage from supermodel to booty star, to do for LGBT culture what Warhol did for pop art.

* Ru apparently doesn't mind whether you call him/her him or her. I'll go mainly masculine in what follows. Visualise both. It began as fun before it became a career.

Anyway, he was in town in 1997 (it must have been), donating himself to the festival. T&T contracted for a car to take him from the house he was renting in the Hollywood Hills on a short trip to one of those old Art Deco movie theatres on Wilshire. RuPaul had done the voice-over for a movie the festival was showing that night. The afternoon visit was to set the star up for the evening red-carpet event. I've never gone weak-kneed around celebrities ('no man a hero', etc.*). But I remembered that night, in cold muddy Essex. For me, and several people I knew, Ru was the 1990s Abraham Lincoln of gay, a liberator. His Gettysburg Address? Sex does not 'divide', it 'joins'.

Long and short, I deputed myself to do the driving. Manager's privilege. I intended to take a Bentley. This client is trademark tall. English limos (like London black cabs) always had plenty head room. For top hats, someone told me. Not the greatest need in Hollywood. But with heels and wig, RuPaul has a couple of inches on Kobe Bryant.

Mechanical problems ('Those fucking British cars!' was the cry on the lot) ruled out the Bentley. I selected instead a white Merc S500. The colour gave me background 'standout', liveried as I was in my reservoir-dog black suiting. I made sure the interior was perfect. There was no partition glass – it was a sedan, not a limo.

Joelle, Ru's longstanding personal assistant and showrunner-in-chief for the Outfest thing, phoned in some uber-precise instructions. She's a sharp, no-nonsense lady. No cologne. Mr RuPaul is sensitive to odours. In fact, no air

* Peter Gabriel's an exception – see above.

fresheners of any kind. Just crystal-fresh air and a very clean car. Mr RuPaul does not like people using cell phones in his presence. Etc., etc. Divas, I thought. They're all the same. (He/she wasn't, I would discover.)

Ru, before locating more or less full-time from New York to SoCal in 1998, had rented a secluded house in the Hollywood Hills, just above the 101. Outfest takes place in the height of summer. It was a hot day, even for LA – nineties-plus. No problem getting to the street address. Getting to the house itself was something else. It was perched on a sharp canyon slope – the kind of house where you'd prefer not to watch *Horizon* programmes on earthquakes while you were staying there.

It had a driveway from hell. An eighty-degree incline, it felt like. Who the fuck thought that would be helpful? Clarkson could have built a whole programme round the access problems that driveway posed. If you didn't hit it right, at a steady, straight 5 m.p.h. (which felt too fast), all you got was screeching wheelspin and a deadly dust storm of burning rubber trailing behind you.

Somehow I couldn't see a tall diva in high heels making it down that slope. Catwalks, yes; north face of the Eiger, no. I made five attempts before finally drawing up to the portico porch, accompanied by a powerful stench of burning German rubber And driver sweat. This, remember, was a man who was strict enough about scent to instruct his manager to lay down the law about cologne. And I (no partition!) sure as hell wasn't smelling of cologne. Not cool. In any sense.

There was no terrace area outside the front door. Just a concrete apron barely the size of a coffee table. Joelle comes out. Speaking with her on the phone, I stupidly hadn't registered she's white. She's followed by a black guy, nondescript. Skinny. Luggage handler, I assume. Stars don't carry their own bags.

The first rule for limo chauffeurs is don't eyeball the client. But there I am, waiting for the great man. Or great woman? 'We'll get the doors,' Joelle had told me, crisply, when I made as if to move out. 'You stay behind the wheel.' Good thing, I think, as my underarm deodorant finally gives up the unequal struggle.

I'd angled the wing mirror to keep a sneaky eye on the house door, from which Ru, I anticipated, would emerge in all his/her glory. Engine purring. When's he/she coming?

Suddenly Joelle barks, 'Let's go, Driver. We're late.'

Shit, that guy in the back is him! Like most of the gay population of the world for whom he/she was god(dess) in high heels, I'd no idea what RuPaul looked like 'as a man' (whatever the fuck that means).

The whole way down to Wilshire the two of them, Joelle and the passenger, talk in the subdued voices celebrities and their guys use when they don't want people (e.g. chauffeurs) to pick up what they're saying. No word to me, though I'm driving not at all badly. I land on a spot bang in front of the theatre doors. The red carpet's there already, baking in the July sun. I wait there so Ru can make a fast exit when he's finished his business inside. Standing tall outside the car, arms folded, chin high – classic chauffeur posture. You've seen the pictures. Meanwhile I'm baking along with the carpet. Black suit. Hot day. Already fucked the job up, I'm thinking.

At some point Joelle comes out to inform me ('Driver') I'll be taking Ru home by myself. She, Joelle, has things to do. Important person. Unlike me. Ru eventually lopes out and jumps into the car, hardly waiting for me to open the door. It's a quick, effortless drive back down Wilshire, past Bonaventure, to the 101 Interchange and the Hollywood Hills, by Universal Studios. Rush-hour traffic hasn't yet built up.

Almost as soon as he's in the car, Ru comes alive.

'What's your name, Driver?'

In my cut-glass English accent (no cholo today), I tell him. He hits it back with his bantering English routine. Jeeves and Wooster.

We're suddenly loose.

The Merc, as I say, has no partition. And an engine as quiet as German Technik, and an $85,000 sticker price, can make them. As we approach the driveway from hell, my nerves begin to twang. ('You're going have to hike the last stretch, Mr RuPaul. Did you bring your crampons?') But he knows the problem and tells me to veer sharply to the right and jam my foot hard down on the accelerator – life-threatening as it will feel. (I realise he's a good driver himself – I learn why, later.) I make it to the house and its tiny concrete apron, first attempt. Mission accomplished.

I expect he'll jump out. He's just done an event. My duty's done. He's been friendly. I have that to feel good about. But no. He wants to talk. So I keep the engine on for air-con and we talk. And in a sense we've never stopped since that moment in a luxury car, on a hot day, in the Hollywood Hills, fifteen years ago.

Over the next two hours we exchanged life stories. They

have (given the obvious differences) similarities. I was a good few years clean and sober. He too (he's been public about it) had enough hard-won sobriety to feel he was over the hump. You can find his short autobiog on RuPaul.com and the full life story in his book, *Lettin It All Hang Out*.

I didn't know anything about him then – other than the image and the music. The same RuPaul the world knew and the gay world worshipped. Me with them. The following is what I learned, in those two hours, sitting in the car.*

He was born in San Diego. On a later road trip, he showed me exactly where. We're not talking mansions in the Hollywood Hills. We had a pleasant meal, I recall, with his siblings there. He's close to his family.

The name 'RuPaul' was given to him by his mother with the immortal words, 'There ain't another motherfucker alive with a name like that.' Very true. There ain't. Ru was loving-close to his mother, who sadly had died, after years of suffering, a little while before I met him. The hurt was still there. Aged four, he saw the Supremes on *The Ed Sullivan Show*. 'I fell in love with them,' he remembers, 'particularly, the skinny one in the middle.' He was already borrowing his sister Renetta's pink dresses. Aged six, kids were already taunting him as a 'cissy'. That went on for years. His parents were fighting a lot; his father drank. During the rows, the children would take shelter 'as if it was an air raid'.

His mother and father split when he was seven. 'I thought it was all my fault.' His mother fell to pieces. The family

* I've taken the following from Ru's published memoir – which I didn't know then – for the quotes.

went on welfare. People were by now routinely mistaking him for a girl. Aged eleven, 'I got shit-faced drunk for the first time and smoked my first joint.' The next year, he fell in love with a boy at school – but kept it secret. Sound familiar? It did to me.

He won dance competitions, dropped out of school and picked up work in the luxury-car industry, as a driver. 'I've always loved cars.' A week after his eighteenth birthday, 'I lost my virginity to a 36-year-old man named Richard. I had never even kissed a man before. I remember when he kissed me that first time I was so swept away, my knees buckled.'

He was still driving luxury cars for minimum pay. 'I never really made any money to speak of, a couple of hundred bucks here and there, and all the weed I could smoke.' He was preparing himself for something – he didn't know what. Aged twenty-one he realised what. 'RuPaul is Red Hot.' The rest is show business history.

The fit with my own life (even down to the car-love*) dovetailed in important places – particularly places where hurt had happened. Not that I was black, or had any star potential. Christ, he was probably even a better driver than me. I shared my own childhood and growing up with him – pretty much what I've told you in the early chapters here. We talked in that Mercedes, no exaggeration, for hours. Bantering from time

* His preferred vehicle: high-end minivan (for his height), custom rims (for the glitter). We tricked out the car after a 'ghetto-run', researching what the smarter African Americans were doing with their wheel style. Ru's words (in a rapper voice): 'I want some motherfuckin' rims for my ride.' We went to a guy I knew in the Valley for the badass rims he craved. It was strange. Minivans are 'mothers' cars'. Ru wanted a bit of 'pimp my car'. But not too much.

to time. It was a life-changing conversation. For me, at least. Evening fell. We swapped cell phone numbers and I drove off. ('Veer to the left! Veer to the left!' Thanks, Ru.)

There was some texting between us and a few days later I was invited to hang out for the afternoon at Ru's place in the hills. This, for me, was a whole new level. When I arrived (I'd chosen a BoS sporty Mustang, for the driveway problem), he suggested dipping into the pool and Jacuzzi. No sweat, this time, unlike the last. But it wasn't straight into our chosen waters – I hadn't brought trunks. Ru supplied a preposterous (for me) pair of bright orange Gucci Speedos.

I'm up for a laugh. So what. No one's around. And, if they were, I'm not *National Enquirer* material. Ru's wearing Speedos as well. I assume we're headed for a dip. He likes the pool. But before we get there, thinking I'm making polite small talk, I stupidly ask a couple of questions which, when I have my wits about me, I know you're supposed never to ask him/her. He's sick of (not) answering them. First was, looking at his body, 'How do you keep so thin?' Answer: 'The Supermodel Diet' (cigarettes and coffee). Second stupid question: 'How do you manage to walk so well in high heels?' He hates questions of that kind and always either dodges them, or gives misleading answers. As with other artists it's not his job to *explain* anything. It either explains itself or you'll never know. Asshole.

Payback. He doesn't answer directly. Before we get to the pool or tub he stops. Thinks. Then he asks me if I've ever walked in heels? No. Tells me that, since I look so cute (ho! ho!) in those Speedos, he'll teach me. He ruffles inside the house for an entry-level pair of heels – a mere four inches or so – and straps them on my feet. I have big feet, like him – fourteen American.

Because it's RuPaul, I can't say no. But I hate, hate, hate camp. As my look, that is. I always go heavy masculine, and preferably Hispanic. Already the Speedo is against my rule book. Of course, he's sized me up. I'm sitting on a pool lounger while the shoes go on. He heaves me up to my tottering feet. So here I am: white as a morning-doorstep milk bottle, alongside an olive-skinned supermodel.

Meet Mr Orange Speedo and Heels.

The lesson begins. The torture continues. How to do the catwalk. I'm like I need a Zimmer frame. Ru says, to graduate to apprentice drag-queen status, I have to do one full circuit of the pool.

'Sashay, shantay, white boy! Now you know what it means, eh?'

It's a rather large pool. I would have preferred the Jacuzzi. Or a fucking washbowl. But I did it. And I'm buggered if I'll ever do it again.

In the following years, Ru and I enjoyed a close friendship. I travelled on road trips with him. For fun, not money, I did bodyguard for him and chauffeured him more times than I can count, all over the country (not that there was much demand for drag in the backcountry). I took no pay. It was joy just being with him. Sometimes, on the road, we shared a bed. Just shared somewhere to sleep. Other times there were great sleepovers at his houses.

I always, ever since that catwalk round the pool in Speedo and heels, amused the hell out of Ru. If he was Supermodel, he was perplexed by my Superman complex. My need, for example, to ride to the rescue in situations that I wasn't involved in. I should carry my own telephone box around with me, he said. A good example happened on in LA, on Sunset – just where the boulevard meets Highland. I described it to Ru, hoping, as one does, for praise. 'What a good boy am I.'

A Corvette was speeding east, well over the 35 m.p.h. limit. Suddenly, from the cross street, against red, crossing two lanes (illegally), came a junky, piece-of-shit 'love van' (think Beach Boys). Impact. (It's uglier in the real world than in *Fast & Furious.*) Thousands of dollars' damage to the Vette; fifty-cent new dents on the van, joining all the other dings.

Out jumps Mr Corvette, gold chains swinging, like an animal. In his hand, his two-part club. He intended to use it for just that. To club to death the fucker who'd ruined his car. Unfortunately, as he swung it lethally at the grey-haired hippy, the club broke into two, and it was mano-a-mano, clubs at sunset.

Do I watch, like other Sunset passers-by on their way to In-N-Out Burger?* No. I pull my Nissan 240SX (nice sporty car) into the centre lane and rush up to disarm the aggressor and hold him in a rear-arm lock till the police show up. At the risk of being beaten to death by two crazies with clubs. A rare occurrence on Sunset Boulevard.

'Why the fuck did you do that?' asked Ru. 'Who the fuck are you? Superman? This isn't Gotham. It's Shit City. Do you want to save the whole goddam world?' Yes, I thought, I goddam do, remembering all those times as a

* If you're in LA, by the way, it's the cheapest, best meal in town.

kid when no one rode in to save me.

It all fizzled out in court. The Corvette owner didn't show. Probably didn't want the cops looking too closely at how he'd paid for his hundred-grand wheels.

Ru moved to LA in 1998, living around West Hollywood, where he'd bought a condo. I at that time had gone quaint and was living in Los Feliz ('the happy ones') in a midget cluster of houses themed on Disney's *Snow White and the Seven Dwarfs*. Pure Southern California. Charlie Chaplin once lived there. You may have seen the Disneyfied compound in David Lynch's movie *Mulholland Drive*. It's the setting the film opens with in that blurry 'is she dead?' scene. It obviously amused the fuck out of Lynch. Me too. My cottage still had the film-scene paint. Superior work.

The compound had starred in a number of movies. The owner, like many owners of interesting houses in LA, had a sharp agent, and it earned a hell of a lot more than my (very reasonable) rent. It suited me because it was cute and I liked the landlady.

I would meet Ru, many nights, in a quiet coffee shop on Los Feliz itself – great cakes. He was generally unrecognised (the staff were discreet). Just another good-looking black guy catching up from a hard day. From what I've seen of it, most people have no idea, if you're up there with the likes of RuPaul, how lonely seven-star hotel rooms can be. Or how empty a mansion is when you have to surround yourself with 'security', electronic and human.* Or how false most

* I love that movie, *The Bling Ring*, where the stars' mansions are like Egyptian pyramids and this smart teenage gang are like grave robbers helping themselves to what owners like Lindsay Lohan (who

of the people who want to be close to you are. Fame vampires, stalkers, fantasists. The occasional extremely dangerous weirdo. Ru has those.

As I observed it, most stars simply want, every now and then, to go to Bristol Farms and pick over the produce like all the other pass-you-by-without-a-second-look customers. (Ru, leaving his celebrity in the wardrobe with his wigs, does just that.) All I was to Ru, on those Los Feliz evenings, was a friend who wanted nothing other than kaffeeklatsch. I bought, he bought, just a few dollars and cents. Like a lot of artists who depend on quick wits on stage (my dad's friend Barry Humphries/Dame Edna, for example), Ru's a terrific conversationalist. He was very into addiction meetings at the time, and still a newcomer (all of which is in the public domain). The anonymity helped. I'd occasionally go along with him, although, alas, my regular attendance had lapsed. Trouble ahead, old-timers would tell me. I didn't listen.

It's hard to say without my nose turning a fetching brown, but I've been lucky, as a PA, in the people I've worked for and with. None kinder than Ru. None who paid less and gave more. When my back went crucifixion on me (details later), it was Ru who took me, moaning, to the ER. He visited me in hospital. That was kind.* What was more than kind was that he did this despite having a horror of hospitals. Read his autobiography. The long painful illnesses of his mother, being eaten from the inside, as he put it, gave him a lifelong fear of the places.

good-naturedly loaned her mansion) didn't even know they owned and never noticed they'd lost.

* He'd had the same operation himself at Cedars-Sinai.

My father, who made an emergency trip from England to see me on what, quite possibly, might have my deathbed (the hospital, since closed down, did its very best to kill me), was driven to visit me a couple of times by Ru, in his tricked-out (courtesy of Jack) minivan. My father said he looked like he was wearing whiteface, so fearful he looked. And yet he came. And when I was discharged (sicker than I'd been when I went in), it's not over the top to say he nursed me.

MY FIFTEEN MINUTES

It was Ru who gave me my fifteen minutes of Warholian fame, on Graham Norton's TV show. This is how it happened – with some necessary medical detail.

White men, particularly in America (I speak from wide experience), are usually 'cut'. A foreskin is unusual – except among Latinos (I speak from even wider experience). No one, of course, gets worked up about 'male genital mutilation' but men talk about it a lot among themselves – particularly as to whether erotic sensitivity is lost, along with the skin.

I told Ru about some of my childhood nonsense. Dare challenges on camping trips, where penises were involved. Bathroom escapades. Ru was perplexed at the idea of my having put random objects in my foreskin. I told him my prick had been nicknamed 'The Anteater' – from its ability to swallow anything in sight. He found it funny.

A spoof/poof movie came out of it. He told one of his contacts at the World of Wonder production company. The idea was to do a short video, called *Spunk'd*, spoofing Ashton

Kutcher's *Punk'd*. It was directed at the smart-ass gay community. They got a lookalike for the Ashton part – 'Gashton Cootcher'. Among the sections ('Hairless Hilton', etc.) was one called 'Foreskin Follies', which was where I came in. I had agreed on the understanding that I'd be ski-masked and my name would be kept out. I didn't think anyone would identify my cock. I should have said 'No!' but, what the hell, it was Ru.

Ru arranged to have the segment filmed in his basement. A cameraman turned up with a ton of gear. It turned out they wanted full-body, not groin-only. I wasn't entirely happy with full-on, but I went along. We had some discussion about 'objects'. One possibility was 'docking' (I know I'm losing straight readers by the score at this point). That is pulling the foreskin over some handy object, like so much clingfilm (the games gays play): Ru had a regular working-guy set of screwdrivers in his basement, handles the size of prize zucchinis; peeled bananas (American bananas, from Ecuador, are twice the size of the British West Indian variety); finally we settled on marbles (we're talking smallish marbles), stuffed into my foreskin bag until it could hold no more. Folly indeed. Someone was sent out to the nearest Toys R Us. (I don't think they told the salesgirl, 'Some crazy gay guy wants to stick them in his penis, dear.')

The camera began to roll, I put the ski mask on my face, and slowly inserted one, two, three marbles into the skinny bag and kept going until there were, believe it or not (even I was rattled), twenty-two. My poor foreskin was, by the end, down to my ankles.

Spunk'd went out, got its laughs, and was forgotten. No one, I was certain, would have known the face behind the foreskin. I was the Zorro of penis exhibitionists. I was wrong. Ru went on *The Graham Norton Effect*, with its audience of zillions. At one point Graham said: 'Enough of this small talk, Ru. Tell us about Jack and the twenty-two marbles.' And, God help me, Ru did indeed tell him. With an instruction to the curious millions as to how they could find the proof of what should be in the *Guinness Book of Crazy Sexual Records*. You can call up the whole interview on Google. 'Foreskin Follies', if your nerves are up to it, you can find on any number of restricted sites (where I'm listed as 'unknown male').

Over the next few weeks after the Norton interview, my phone and pager were on fire. I had the most famous damned foreskin in the world. What the hell, fame is fame. Who knows, some day I may decide to break my own world record and go for the whole twenty-five.

FAMILY LIFE

It sounds strange for a footloose gay to say, but at heart I'm a family man. I was lucky to have landed by fate in my own family – now thousands of miles away. But I've always been good at creating what looked like adoptive family relationships of my own. One example will make what I'm saying clearer – Fidel. I first met him when I was riding high at Budget on Sunset. Heading home in the early evening (the 'golden hour', photographers call it), it was my habit to cruise along Santa Monica, to see what action there might be bubbling up in Boys' Town. Usually just looking; sometimes a bit more.

This particular evening I was driving west up Sunset,

about to make the sharp left down San Vicente to Santa Monica. I was suited, booted and in one of the firm's three Jaguars, an XJ sedan. Sweet car, newly washed and gleaming, and inside a smart young Californian – feeling very good about himself. As I turned, half a dozen young Hispanics walked casually in front of the car, making me pull over. I wasn't nervous. This wasn't gang territory. I was gym-fit. And also, it became clear, identifiably gay, in an area of town where we were a majority. These youngsters start flirting with me; wiggling their hips, pouting. Not homophobic, flirtatious. I play cool, smile, say nothing and drive off. I hear an ear-splitting wolf whistle as I go.

I'm not exactly nervous, but cautious. On occasions like this – where there may be a 'roll the queer' set up (I'm carrying thousands of dollars on my wrist and fingers) – I do a kind of circling drive-by, round the block and back again.* On my second time round, the group's still there and my eye's caught by one of them. He's young (around eighteen), dressed in the approved Latin gangster style, and very much my type. Back again at the top of the San Vicente hill, I park, pull the windows down, and pretend I'm making a phone call.

When they see me again, they're confused. But they gather round the car. Head of the line is the one I've got my eye on – Fidel.

'You a cop?' he asks. He's got good reason for being careful himself: he's an undocumented Mexican.

'No,' I say. 'I'm just checking you guys out. How're you

* I'd got to be more careful after the death of Noah.

doing?' We chat, flirtily, for five minutes or so.

All of a sudden a younger, chubbier kid rocks up to the car and pushes his head between Fidel's head and mine. Fidel's younger brother Cesar, it turns out. 'Fuck off and leave my brother alone,' he says. 'He's only talking to you because you've got a nice ride.' As, indeed, I do. Cesar's not protecting Fidel's virtue. There's another kid in the group who has a claim on him.

Fidel's a rational kid and jostles back to the front and tells Cesar, who's now shouting shit on the sidewalk, to fuck off, for Christ's sake. Who's he going to go with? A rich, nice, sober, good-looking white guy – not too old, with a $100K Jag and a designer suit – or a raggedy Latin pal with not so much as ten dollars in his thrift-store jeans?

I don't push it. I give Fidel my business card, tell him to phone, and make my way down to Santa Monica and home. Inevitably he phones later and we start dating. I'm fond of him, and, in time, have real love for him. There's something paternal rather than passionate about our relationship. He's illiterate, no job, living at home with his mother and a crowd of siblings and half-siblings. His oldest brother (straight) is serving time in prison, father(s) long gone. Even in those circumstances, families are ironclad institutions among Hispanics.

After we'd met a few times, driving around, snacking in fast-food joints, having fun just talking, he convinced me to spend a night at his home, in an apartment complex in Montebello. We hadn't, up to this point, had all-out sex, just boyfriend stuff. There were two bedrooms for the kids – Fidel, I discovered, shared one with Cesar. Fidel didn't tell me that fact when he invited me over. Cesar still disliked me. The other thing was that once his mother got back from her bar manager's job, and picking up the younger kids (a lovely boy and girl) from school, I'd be shut in the bedroom. Neither of the brothers were out of the closet – nor, for that night, would I be.

It made for a rather awkward, but cosy, date. I snuck out in the early hours, while everyone was asleep. I saw more of Fidel over the months, and eventually years, but when we finally got round to sex it turned out we were incompatible. 'Two tops can't make a bottom', as the gays say. Neither of us was orally inclined and handjobs are for schoolkids. I loved him nonetheless, and we became, over the next three years, special friends.

Over that period I became close to the family and the mother who accepted, but never let it pass her lips, that her two younger sons were gay. It wasn't a problem with Fidel, who looked straight and, if anything, like a tough little guy. Cesar was babyish camp. The two of them were inseparable – Siamese twins, practically. I envied that: I'd grown up very alone. Fidel was jobless, living off his mother. Cesar had got piecework in a packing factory – minimum wage. The older brother was out of prison by now, and in Arizona living a straight life, in both senses. Cesar had eventually come round and was as devoted as Fidel to me.

I was a kind of godfather to the young kids. One of them, the daughter, was coming up for her *quinceañera* – fifteenth birthday party. Like christening and confirmation, it's a huge event for girls in the Mexican community. I was one of the compadres. They organise the hall, the cake, the new dresses and clothes for the family. I organised the transport. Rosa arrived, beautiful in white, in a matching white stretch limo. It cost me hundreds, and I never parted with money more gladly. I saw the family, and Fidel one-on-one, regularly over the years. Later tragedy would strike – more of which in another chapter.

7: LIMOUSINING ONWARDS AND UPWARDS

Those years at BoS were, no question about it, the funnest of my life. It had everything to do with being young, car-horny and lucky. It helped that gays were a powerful presence in the luxury-car industry. It had started up big time in LA in the wake of the Stonewall insurgency. And it was centred on Hollywood, where gays increasingly liked to work and play. A lot of hard-charging gays had, by the 1990s, risen to senior positions in the industry. I too would rise – although never *quite* to the top. But close enough to get a strong smell of what the air was like up there.

If you want to see my career history as a gay man in chauffeured transportation, it's in the CV at the back. (As I say, I'm always open to offers – my career in authorship, I've been tactfully informed, will not be a long one.) Very simply I moved – onwards and ever upwards – from Dav-El to CLS (Empire-CLS after the firm was reorganised), then Ridewell and finally Virgin Limousines. The full stories behind those company names I'll tell in a bit. But that, in short, was my twenty-five-year career arc.

T&T didn't go anywhere much, and I sacrificed my 10 per cent interest and moved on, by invitation, to Dav-El, where I was now fully suit-and-tie managerial. I was ambitious and to get my foot on the lowest rung I took a big pay cut – below $50K, no car package, no pick-of-the-fleet privileges, people I didn't always respect giving me orders. My first appointment was as 'assistant operations manager'. I hated that first word, but I knew in a firm as big and open as Dav-El, I'd make my way.

I busted my ass off for my first six months at Dav-El – working to get respect from everyone: chauffeurs, clients, top management. I glistened. I got particularly close to the general manager, Tim, the life partner of Jack Gonzales (later one of my closest business friends, and an inspiration to young LA gays), who ran the multimillion travel division at Sony. Triple-A client for Dav-El.

Tim moved over, by his own request, to the accountancy division, leaving the general manager, LA, position open. I put myself forward. It was an arrogant attempt to leap-frog over guys older than me, and a rung or two above. I wouldn't win any popularity contests and I knew at least three guys who'd walk away from me when I came up to the water cooler for a break. I was a twenty-something and had only been in the firm six months.

I'd never met Scott Solombrino, who managed the huge firm from its headquarters in Boston. I knew about him, of course. Short in stature, he was massive in his business presence. He exuded authority. He was one of the giants who had made chauffeured transportation what it now was. The LA Dav-El management were politely negative in response to my application. They realised how well I'd done but I was too young and too new. Get back in line and wait your turn, Jack. You've got lots of years ahead of you.

What the fuck, I thought. I'll play some employment

poker. It's a high-risk game, and you shouldn't do it too often, but I believed in myself. I filed a letter of resignation. I was grateful and sad to leave, but firm in my decision. I couldn't work where I felt undervalued. The LA management regretfully accepted my resignation. Plenty where I came from.

But by the end of the day (midday in Boston), I got a personal call from Solombrino. At Dav-El it was like the Queen of England phoning. 'What the fuck are you doing?' he asked. (Not quite what you'd expect from HM, I grant.) The promotion I wanted couldn't be done, he explained. I stood my ground. I can't live on this pay grade, I said. And it wasn't just money. My resignation was a done deal.

There was a stream of phone calls from his underlings as the evening wore on, which, sitting in Starbucks with an eight-ounce vanilla latte or two, I didn't answer. Finally, Solombrino came back to me himself. I took that call. They'd fly me, red-eye, to Boston next day for a face-to-face (remember, I'm just an 'assistant' halfway through the door. They could fill my job, twenty times over, by the end of the week). I declined; he insisted – it would be 'worth my while'. In fact he was a bit saltier than that: 'Don't be a fucking idiot.' I clicked my heels and accepted.

They pulled out the stops for me (me!). A chauffeured limousine picked me up at the crack of dawn to take me to Burbank (a sweet little airport, they use it for retro *Mad Men*-style films). First class, two stops, Mercedes waiting for me at Logan (wretched fucking airport). I was booked into a top hotel – suite, not room. It was midday. I showered, shaved and put on my pinstripe suit for what would be the most important interview of my life.

I was dropped off early at the palatial Dav-El HQ, and given a snap VIP tour. All this, of course, to make me feel important. As it happened, it did. Then a one-on-one with the man himself, Scott Solombrino, over lunch. It's hard to enjoy the beef wellington and Virgin Mary when you're being felt out. Then a meeting with the executive committee. As evening drew on, Solombrino came through with the offer. General manager was out of the question. At the moment. But I'd fly back as operations manager, with an enhanced salary and fat package. What about the current ops manager, I asked.

'We fired him,' said Solombrino. 'His office will be clear by the time you get back, tomorrow morning.'

My conscience was clear: I'd never bad-mouthed the guy I was replacing. But the power – fire the bum – was frightening.

On Solombrino's instruction (I assumed), a celebration had been set up for me, to make me feel big. I joined him for a Celtics game in the stadium's VIP restaurant, looking down on the game before taking up front-row seats. He was glad-handed all the way, by everyone from the cops outside to the ushers. He was like a star. And this was a businessman. I was surprised the players didn't bow before doing their stuff on the court. Later that night I was taken out by one of the reservation managers – young, Latino, gay – to one of Boston's gay clubs. A night's chauffeured transportation thrown in. They'd done a full background on me. I celebrated on Pepsi. A litre of vodka couldn't have got me merrier.

In my years in the limo business, I would bounce between two main sectors: operations and sales. Sales meant, primarily, schmoozing with hotels and institutions, building up a client base, smiling and glad-handing all the way. I loved that side of things. And I made really good friends in the process.

In operations, you'd be more like an airport ground controller, making sure, from the tower, that the fleet was functioning smoothly at full capacity. 'Dispatch', it's called. You'd be playing the phones pinball-wizard-style. There are a lot of pinballs to keep moving. On the nights of major concerts, each star band member needs bus-sized transport for their entourage, and a personal limousine for themselves and any escorts. We're talking motorcades. No waiting – you have to arrange for all the lights to be green, which means cops (all retired, sitting in front or driving) and escorts. If you have to jump the lights or do illegal U-turns, the cops handle it. I did that pretty much every time the Stones came to LA, on tour or to an event. Fuck up (as one of my chauffeurs did, with Christina Aguilera) and you lose a client for ever. The chauffeur too, perhaps – though it's usually not their fault.

For award shows, you have to buy a big portion of the parking lot, then mobilise a fleet of golf carts (no crumpling of dresses, if you please, Driver) to bring the celebs to the carpet. It's a tricky part of the evening. I remember, as a hands-on manager, going to the front line on the biggest night of the year, driving Kylie Minogue. (As nice in person as her image – she actually remembered me from Propaganda days, which was sweet.) You have to keep the paps at bay. It's not the stars' most elegant moment of the evening, being unloaded like nine-irons, legs splaying.

Once offloaded, the stars progress (no other word for it) like royalty along the red carpet. But they leave, after the show's over, like thieves in the night – all this has to be arranged to the minute – by the back fire exit, via a specially cleared lobby, and go back to their hotels double-quick. They're tired and cranky. Particularly the ones who didn't get the awards they expected. Easily enraged. Like handling eggs with boxing gloves. But a huge rush when you pull it all off.

I was growing up (a bit) and had matured my personal transport into something more dignified. English, even. I leased a tricked-out custom-blue Jaguar, with the personalised number plate UK PAPI (the last bit is Latino for 'sexy old guy'). I was, as on the *Monster* tour, earning more than I could spend – hard as I tried. And I was in the best shape of my life – working out early evenings in an exclusive gym. My juice was incredible, my appetites insatiable, my energy inexhaustible. It needed to be. I was living a Jekyll and Hyde existence: businessman by day, cholo by night. Generally my lives were kept separate. But how long could I keep it up? Longer than you'd think.

I was still young.

MUSCLING UP

Like most young guys in their twenties, I was into my body. I worked out in a gym most evenings. But, like most young guys in their twenties, I was impatient for results – the kind of results you'd see in a gym mirror.

Because of my high-risk sex practice, I was going religiously, every six weeks, to the Gay and Lesbian Center in Hollywood. More often if I had an itch, bump or drip.

It's a world-leading organisation – supported by philanthropy and the city – located at the east end of Sunset, where it meets Hollywood Boulevard. The Center has legal-aid departments, a refuge (gays get battered by their partners), assistance with handicap parking and concession cards and a big pharmacy.

I was so frequent a client I was on first-name terms with the staff. It was like my local Starbucks. Not that in Starbucks you'd expect the barista to go poking with a Q-tip in your throat, mouth, urethra and rectum (all places that clap bacteria could lodge, depending on orifice). I had particularly good relations with a young Hispanic on the staff. Good-looking, smart as paint, my type. His job was simply to draw my blood. This is a period when the results took a week to come through. Sometimes longer. Nowadays it's a finger prick and minutes. I go back the following week – negative, thank God. I see my phlebotomist walking through, white-coated. We make eye contact, then conversation, then we swap numbers. We went on to date.

He told me, shamefacedly, he'd secretly checked my results before the first date, 'just in case'. Strictly against regulations. He could have got fired for peeking. It was way above his pay grade. We had some good times before it fizzled out but we remained good friends. Again, breaking the rules, he would tell me my results over the phone: a major no-no. You sit there and, if the result is negative, it's instant counselling, more tests, and prescriptions.

Felipe was useful in other ways, important to me at the time. You could get steroids and testosterone at my gym – any gym in LA, come to that. But I never trusted the guys selling it in the locker room. And I certainly didn't trust their needles. Testosterone and steroids are widely prescribed for people with HIV. They build you up. 'Bulk' you up, if you're working on your body. Thanks to Felipe (and some gratuities), I got fortnightly injections of hormone and Deca-Durabolin. The results were immediate.*

A while later I was dating this guy, Frank. He'd had unprotected sex (not with me) and was terrified. I got in touch with Felipe at the Center for a quick test. Frank proved positive. After the phone call from Felipe, I had to break the news to him. Are you going to leave me, he asked, unhappily. There was no way out of it. I wasn't in any position to be a lifelong carer. He was just eighteen and had had relations with two guys – one unprotected. I took him to the Center to get looked after. It was early days in HIV treatment, but guys who would have died ten years earlier were surviving. Then, amazingly, Felipe came out and huddled us in a corner. He'd got the initials wrong – so many Hispanics have the same kind of name. Frank was clear. I didn't see Felipe after that, and my muscles normalised.

FIDEL AGAIN

One night, around 4 a.m., my phone rang. I kept it permanently on ring in case there was any emergency at work. I pick up and there's a wholly incomprehensible hysterical

* There was a downside. The amounts I was taking played hell with my temper.

babble at the other end. It's a young Latin voice, but I can't work out who. I know a lot of young Latinos and I'm dazed with sleep. Gradually the gibberish becomes sobs, then broken words. It's Fidel. 'Cesar's gone!' he keeps saying. 'He's gone, gone.' Arrested? Overdose? Run off with a boyfriend? I can't get any sense out of him.

I jump in the car and drive to Rosemead, where they're now living in a much larger house which belongs to the mother's partner. Fidel and Cesar now have a cabana to themselves, alongside a toxic swimming pool that should have been closed as a health hazard by the EPA.* I went inside – there's dirge music and candles around Cesar's mattress on the floor. No Cesar. But there are pictures of him on every inch of wall. Fidel is on the floor, weeping uncontrollably. He keeps saying he's gone but adds the word 'dead'. When that hits me, I burst into tears as well. They're family, my family.

There's a knock on the door – Rosa. I go into the main house. Everyone's hysterical. Inconsolable. I stay till morning, doing what I can. The next day I take ten days off work to comfort Fidel and help out the family. The elder brother comes by bus from Arizona and arrives a day later.

Latins grieve quite differently. It's passionate – none of that Anglo-Saxon tight lip. I order daily food deliveries (the mother's boyfriend keeps in the background – although he helps out financially); Fidel eats nothing. Over the next seven days the family goes from house to house where they're known. I handle transport. In every house there's a huge photograph of Cesar on an easel. There are occasional

* *John.* He means Environmental Protection Agency.

priests and it's all very physical. And real. I cry with the rest, hug with the rest, and pick up a share of the expenses.

The family has been given a plot in the Montebello Forest Lawn. There's a vigil before the burial and an open coffin. Gradually I work out what happened. Cesar had an Armenian friend, Jakob, who lived in the same complex and who they'd known for years. Jakob looked gangster and may well have been. He was, ostensibly, straight. But who knew. He was handsome. Fidel and Cesar liked their weed and drink – not excessively; they didn't have enough cash for excess. What Cesar earned went straight to his mother. Fidel could neither read nor write, and was still an illegal immigrant. Job prospects were not good. But they were honest, in their way. Crystal was becoming popular with young Latins and they'd dabbled. They knew I was super-against alcohol and any kind of drug.

They'd party with Jakob, who was not in the slightest against drugs. Cesar had a major crush on his Armenian friend and was clumsy – too obvious – in expressing his affection. On the night in question, he and Jakob had been partying heavily in Jakob's bedroom. Jakob had a gun, bought on the street. Allegedly what happened next was 'accidental discharge'. Cesar was shot in the face – above the upper lip. It's hard to picture any 'accident'. He died instantly. The mortician did his best with the wound. The family wanted pictures of him lying there, which (having borrowed a good Canon camera) I took. It wasn't easy.

For the funeral I arranged flowers and cars and white clothes for the family. Cesar was a huge Jennifer Lopez fan: white was her signature colour. There were music tracks at the reception after the burial. I took the shovel to drop in some of the last earth. The mother and children were prostrate on the grass in grief. Fidel wouldn't let go of the coffin and his fingers had to be gently prised away. As we all left, the mechanical diggers moved in. Fidel and I waited an hour, to place flowers on the fresh dirt. I often went back to the grave on Cesar's birthday.

Jakob was arrested. I never found out what the outcome was. The police weren't interested in that kind of ethnic-on-ethnic Saturday-night crime – too much of it. Fidel didn't even follow the court case. Nor did I. All I knew was that this lovable, innocent young kid had been killed by being gay, using that damned drug, and the universal access to guns in LA.

JACK A BIG SHOT?

After a while, I began to think – it happens as you come up to thirty when the great countdown approaches – what do I want that, for God's sake, I don't have? I could have stayed at Dav-El and made VP double-quick and had a big salary for life. But I would never have made it to the top of the firm. There would never be a Jack-El. I was too restless. You won't find too many CEOs with ADHD. It's not that I'm inattentive. It's just my attention doesn't stay in one place for long enough to make the most of where I am.

And, I have to say, once you got the hang of it, work at Dav-El was a yawn. Just another day. It's 1999 already? What happened to 1998? I wanted a bit more fizz. Where to find it?

Inside myself, I knew the answer. Time to take some risks. I had always admired another big player in the LA limo business, CLS. It stands for Charlie's Limousine Service. So who was Charlie? Interesting story.

Charles Horky had begun with a rag and bucket and one car, aged nineteen, in 1980. He didn't even own all four wheels. Just two. 'I met a guy back then who suggested I go into the limo business,' he recalled in an interview. 'We started with one car and the deal was that if I could make something out of it I'd own half the business. He lost interest after three years, I bought him out and I ended up with four limos.'

Charlie was rocket-propelled. A few months after getting control (I don't, for a minute, believe that 'lost interest' story; the other guy was 'removed'), Charlie was employed at a Budget outlet located at 3rd Street and La Cienega, opposite the then newly opened Beverly Center. It's just up the street from that Larry Flynt building I was talking about. His first serious job had actually been for Flynt Publications 'as a double-barrelled shotgun-carrying security guard' at his boss's Bel-Air mansion, while it was under construction. Charlie with a twelve-gauge was someone a trespasser wouldn't want to meet.

In ten years he had a fleet of five hundred cars. He was unusual in liking standout German vehicles among the Lincoln Town Car fleet. Favourites with Charlie were the S-Class Mercedes sedan and BMW. He locked down deals with five-diamond hotels, airlines and corporate clients. He *owned* the entertainment business when it came to limousines – it was his core income. Everything was done face to face. He planted big CLS footprints in Las Vegas, New York and San Francisco.

He was film-star handsome (still is good-looking) and a lover of rodeo. He rode the professional circuit. Few CEOs, in my experience, can handle a brahma bull. It would be fun to see some of the pompous bastards trying. He was a high-roller. Rumour was, he once lost a million dollars on a poker hand. It enhanced the aura of glamour and recklessness.

From his rag-and-bucket days, Charlie was fanatical about the outside cleanliness of his vehicles. They had to be so clean that the driver could shave in his reflection from any part of the vehicle. CLS limos glistened along the free-ways, boulevards, avenues and streets of LA. It was exciting to be near Charlie. But not too near. Guys who made that mistake are now in prison. (One of them, I read, killed him-self a few months ago.) Charlie lived close to the edge. And, too often, over it. 'CLS?' people would chuckle. 'Cocaine Limousine Service.'

And after a toot, what? Charlie also realised that a lot of clients who touched down in LA, away from spousal over-sight, wanted what is coyly called an 'escort' as well as a good (and discreet) chauffeur. Off-the-leash pleasures were provided. Hotels had to be alerted – back entrances made available for discreet entrance via the service lift. It was arranged and charges (what did Heidi Fleiss's girls charge? $1K an hour?) were tactfully invisible on the corporate bill.

It was one of the trademarks of CLS that Charlie himself was always available on the phone. He massaged his special clients – had 'things to remember' dossiers on them ('How's your daughter doing at NYU, Joe?'). It created top-tier loyalty. It was Charlie who realised limo services could fly. One of the smartest things he did, once he had the money (or could persuade the banks to lend him fiscally unwise amounts), was to purchase a couple of Lear turboprops. CLS took to the air. By the end of the nineties, he had top-of-the-line Gulfstreams. A Vegas high-roller could fall out of his satin sheets into a limo, be loaded like Louis Vuitton luggage onto a private jet, and find himself eating at Spago LA before going on to the clubs, not having walked more than fifty paces.

I put out a feeler. I'd been noticed as a rising young(ish) fellow in the industry. I was called for interview. It took place in the Polo Lounge of the Beverly Hills Hotel. None of that over-the-desk, 'take a seat, Mr Sutherland' stuff.

Charlie had his right-hand man, Joey Henriques, with him. I was nervous. They were an awesome couple. I was suited and booted. They were fuck-it casual. It was the biggest interview of my career so far. I began with a mistake – dropping names of clients I'd secured for Dav-El. Talking my CV. Horky interrupted me, in a voice which could be heard not just at the next table, but over most of the lounge. 'I don't give a *fuck* who you know or who you *think* you know.'

I took the point. He didn't give a fuck who I knew. 'At CLS,' he said, 'I don't need you to bring me business. I can do that, for fuck's sake. I need you to look after my clients. And, congratulations, you've got the job. Joey will work out salary. Don't fuck up.' We finished the meal with small talk and I left. Outside I let myself shake a bit.

I didn't fuck up. Far from it. I worked my way up and by the age of – what was it? Twenty nine? – I started in sales as local (if you can call LA 'local') manager, then rose to senior VP, sales. All the while CLS was growing explosively.

Charlie's Limousine Service, the firm that began with a guy with a rag and bucket, was the classic American success story. From time to time, particularly when I was working for CLS, a thought crossed my mind – I know enough about the game to buy myself in and go limo to limo with the big operators, starting niche-sized, as Klein and Horky had with a couple of vehicles. Screw the rag, bucket and peaked cap, I'm halfway there already. I was, by now, hooked up with every high-end hotel in the city. I was well liked – smiled in, parking valet to manager, wherever I went. True, I had to over-tip the valets and comp those managers with limos for their personal use whenever they felt they needed it for some reason, or event (lubrication, never bribery). They reciprocated with suites, whenever I might need them. Bank VPs liked me. I could have raised business loans for at least a couple of limos, a crew, an office front. From where I was, I could, could I not, have built an empire, given luck, just like Charlie?

But by now I was getting to know myself. I am, by nature, a 'player', not an 'owner'. So far I had been a lucky player. Wisest not to push that luck. I am, by nature, a chronic commitophobe. I didn't own a car (I leased), an apartment (I rented), or a permanent (i.e. anything over months) boyfriend. I sure as fuck didn't want to own a firm and I didn't trust myself owning one.

Anyway, it was a hunker-down-and-wait time. The

industry was still reeling from the 9/11 shock. A lot of rich limo gravy was skimmed off by those two jumbos. For a long while, no one wanted to fly – particularly business class. They were nervous about airports – particularly LAX. It had been rebuilt for the 1984 Olympics and total-car transportation. It's got nine parking structures, each a hundred feet from baggage claim, itself a few hundred feet from the gates. And more kerb space than any airport in the country for white-zone stopping. Terrorists wouldn't have to hijack a plane. They could park a van packed with explosives in each of the structures, drive down Sepulveda, make the triggering cell phone call and disappear. LAX Apocalypse. Or simply leave a car yards from the crowds checking in and deplaning at, say, the high-profile Tom Bradley terminal, and take off in a second car. It takes twenty minutes for the ticketing and towing and by that time the terminal could be blown to bits, the terrorists miles away, melting into their ethnic communities.

People saw these awful scenarios after September 2001 in their minds' eyes, when they travelled via LAX. I saw them, for God's sake.* There were other bad things. Firms, strapped for cash in the double-whammy 2008 and post-9/11 slumps, suddenly found the 'internet conference' suited their business needs very well indeed. Christ, we might have had to go back to doing funerals, where our business started. We were, of course, left with the local entertainment

* They are building a new LA airport, where the cars park half a mile away, and, after check-in and security checks, passengers will be brought to departure gates by bus. Thank you, Obama, on behalf of the LA limo industry.

industry (feeling the pinch as well), hotel business (ditto), and, God help us, student proms. I laugh hollowly when I see they've taken off in the UK. Of all the things the US has given the world, that is, by a mile, of least use to the human species. The limo industry hates those tuxedoed kids. They leave pecker trails all over the leather and they puke. It's a rite of passage. A good time for the little fuckers (too often, literally). A nightmare for the firm-maintenance teams.

And they're dangerous freight. Legal drinking age is a ridiculous twenty-one in the States. Underage drinking is universal – the Mormon kids, for some reason, are worst of all. With a load of boozed-up teenagers mooning their asses against the back window, waving bottles, flashing their tits out of the sunroof and shrieking like banshees, you're facing police stops and monster penalties for encouraging juvenile delinquency. Both the driver and, up the chain, the firm, are 'responsible parties' contributing to the 'corruption of a minor'. As if the little fuckers could be corrupted more than they are.

And, worst of all, at the end of the 'night of their lives' the promenaders don't tip. Tipping chauffeurs is an art. It has to be done with the grace of a paso doble and with the implication that money doesn't really matter – but here's a load of it just the same.

I used occasionally to see Phil Spector in that tarpaper-and-corrugated-iron shack, House of Blues, on Sunset. Who could miss that freak hair? Worzel Gummidge goes to Hollywood. On the night he killed that poor girl, Spector dropped a cool $500 tip in the restaurant he'd been eating in, Dan Tana's in Santa Monica. Not a special restaurant.

I knew the place, and places like it, but I never left that kind of money on the table (for a $55 bill!). Twenty per cent, that's it.

Kids out on their prom night are tight-fisted but not the worst tippers. In my experience, rappers are. The bling stops cold when they have to dip their hands in their pockets for whitey at the wheel.

Every now and then, I'd take on a driving assignment myself. Why? It could be that a driver had suddenly been taken sick, or some other emergency. Or I was just curious. Or bored. One I particularly recall – at least, as regards tipping. I didn't have any drivers immediately available for a night-long job. Anyway, there I was. Jeeves the 'was there anything else, sir?' English butler. I stood by the driver's door, tall, black-suited and servile as they went – carrying enough bling to buy their second Caribbean island – from club to club, drinking, slanging, wenching. Having a really good time. My 'gratuity' as dawn broke? Sixty bucks. They could have spotted me six hundred and not felt it. My theory? It was 'up your ass' for all those years in the plantation. Pull that rope, tote that bale. I could be wrong. They weren't the kind of guys you asked about things like that.*

It was real-world fun, though, putting on the black suit and taking the wheel, leaving the office behind. You got to meet interesting people as they really are. Britney Spears,

* I told my father this, shortly after it happened. He remembers it; I, oddly, don't. A piece of my brain blasted away by crystal, I suppose. I asked him what the name of the rapper was. He vaguely thought 'D' something. A bit of his brain eaten away by alcohol, I suppose. True story, though. He says.

not one of the great conversationalists of the time, was oddly lovable. She carried with her that aura of innocence – the world was very strange for Britney. One time I picked her up in a two-car motorcade from Ocean Drive in Santa Monica to take her to Ryan Seacrest's show on Hollywood and Highland. Easy drive.

The really cool thing about the Seacrest show was that it was free entrance on the day. Britney was topping the show and would have a huge turnout. The sidewalks were heaving with wristbanded freebie kids who'd been waiting for hours, having little parties among themselves in the queue, getting in the mood.

Opposite the studio is a large Gap clothes outlet. Another attraction for young fashionables. As we're pulling up to the complex, Britney saw the seething mob queuing all the way down the intersecting boulevards.

'Oh my, oh *my*, what *are* those people *doing*?' she asked in that cute Southern accent. She honestly didn't realise.

Her bodyguard replied, 'Didn't you know, Britney? Blowout sale at Gap.'

And, I swear, she believed him. Her eyes swung across to the store and she nodded. Got it. When she'd finished with Seacrest, I dropped her at *The Ellen DeGeneres Show* in Burbank. A big PR day for her (she'd just released an album) and a charm-filled day for me. I loved having Britney in the car. As I say, an aura thing. Not all stars have it – about 0.005 per cent of them, I'd say.

One of the most interesting talkers among clients, when he was in the mood, was Ryan Seacrest himself. I'd first driven for him when I was at Dav-El and he was doing his live show, midday Monday to Friday. He requested me as a driver, which made me feel an inch or so taller. He didn't quite clock that I wasn't a driver by trade – I was doing it as a personal courtesy to him. He later asked me to be his regular driver, which would have meant most days a week. I politely declined, muttering 'timetable difficulties'. I was running operations at one of the biggest limo companies in the world, for God's sake. True, I wasn't pulling in twenty million, which is what Ryan would reportedly get when he moved on to *American Idol* (crap show and beneath him).

I always made sure, though, when I wasn't driving him, that Seacrest got our star chauffeur, Arthur Belmontes. I'd given Arthur his job and instructed him in chauffeur expertise. Arthur was a retired LA sheriff. He'd gone out early with a knee injury. Police pensions are generous. But Arthur was bored. He was a genius behind the wheel – he could weave through jams like an eel and knew every surface street shortcut. All done ultra-cool, with light, but smart, conversation. When it was welcome. And, as an ex-sheriff, it was serve and protect when he was at the wheel. Everyone wanted Arthur, having ever had him once. We still exchange on Facebook. He still seems grateful, although he's so far up the hierarchy of Ryan Seacrest Productions that he could employ me.

As I say, I routinely horned in on that Seacrest drive. I liked the cross-seat, over-the-shoulder talk, when it was appropriate. So too with Kiefer Sutherland (no relation). I was, on such occasions, breaking chauffeur etiquette by conversing with a client; but, what the hell, with our names we Sutherlands must have been well within the six degrees of separation. I found him unfuckingbelievably nice to his driver (which is what he, too, took me to be – not a moonlighting manager on his hour off). I told him we'd stayed in the same hotel when I was touring with REM. When I picked up my messages I asked for those for 'the famous Mr Sutherland. Not.' That old *Wayne's World* joke. He smiled.

I could never quite work out, though, why – he was uber-rich – Sutherland lived on Vermont Avenue in the middle of what most (even those who lived there) called the ghetto. The police call it Death Alley and Ghettoside.* I took the other Mr Sutherland from that dark place to the same H&H studio as Seacrest. On one occasion he tipped me an embarrassing $100 for a ten-minute drive. Well, not that embarrassing. His contracts were in the eight-digit range.

Who, then, are my top three back-seat celebrities? Kiefer, and Ryan. Oh, and Britney. It would be fun to have them in the same limo.

LOVE IS NEVER HAVING TO ERASE YOUR TATTOO

'What's that great big black bar across your chest?' my dad asked me. 'I know you like tribal tattoos. What the hell tribe is that, the Blacktits?'

Good joke. We were stretched out, at sunset, in the tenth-floor rooftop Jacuzzi of Renaissance Tower, my current address, downtown spread below us, evening lights blinking through the summer heat haze. He hadn't seen me upper-body naked for a long while.

* *John.* See http://homicide.latimes.com/post/westmont-homicides

There was a lot of black on my torso. And I'd done a number of cover-ups on tattoo errors. I'd been obsessed with using my skin as artist's canvas ever since getting my first tattoo (wholly illegal), aged thirteen. I had no idea what picture I wanted – just 'my' mark on 'my' body. I told my mother I wanted some money for a piece of art, for my room. My friend Sarah Upton came with me to a seedy parlour round Elephant and Castle. The kind of place where every tattoo comes with tetanus, free of charge. I picked a flying swallow (hideous) from the template designs on offer (customised tattoos would come later). It was on the right arm, high up, easily covered by my shirt when necessary. No one was bathing me, aged thirteen. The swallow (long gone into the black) was soon partnered with a rose on the other arm. Then a dragon on the chest. The fourth, my biggest mistake, was a yin/yang thing I got over my back, recklessly, from a parlour on Venice Beach. Thank fuck I couldn't see the abomination. I was as addicted to the needle as a heroin addict is to his works. I covered up most of them with 'tribals'. I was getting close to Papuan by the time I was thirty-five.

What my father picked up on was the erased name of a friend and lover. I'd fooled myself the relationship would last as long as my skin. It didn't and it was another bleak (and amazingly expensive, hugely painful) trip to my favourite tattooist, an Asian guy, by Hollywood and Vine. Delete's a hell of a lot easier on the keyboard than on your chest.

The LAPD does free tattoo removal for gang members who want to go straight. I don't think they have a broken-hearts department. The gangs themselves, I'm told, use oxy-acetylene, no anaesthetics, for patching dropouts if they catch them. Or maybe it's something I saw on *Sons of Anarchy*, one of my never-fail get-me-to-sleep programmes. I like to think Jax looks a bit like me. Or vice versa.

I was running out of room on my chest for these trial runs with life. But I had clean skin on my inner arm for the Valentine tattoo of the name of my life partner of today, Jeison. I intend to go to the grave with it uncovered.

I've just mentioned drink and there's an awkward thing to get out of the way here. I had stayed drug-free and bone-dry sober for fourteen years. I had risen, rung by rung, in the chauffeured-transportation industry. My life was very comfortable. I was, by most measures, an LA success story. My success, for what it was worth, was in large part sobriety-generated. I fell off the wagon (full litre of vodka, glugged down like Mountain Dew – although I hate the taste of alcohol) in 2004. It coincided with my parents' divorce. I could tell you it was a reaction – but I was thirty years old and had made an independent life from them a whole continent away. We were a networked, not a nuclear family.

The net would be just a bit looser from now on. But it was still there.

As with everything in my life, at some level I willed my relapse. They'd changed their lives. I did the same. We both took the risks that came with the change. But for the next ten years my life was going to get very risky indeed. But not immediately. That vodka was the only booze I swallowed for a year.

It was ominous, though. I was falling victim to what AA calls 'screwy thinking'. I'd decoupled (I love Gwyneth's word) from the fellowship and deluded myself into thinking I'd been misdiagnosed. Addict? Me? Christ, I've been around drugs, drink and using friends and lovers for ten years – clean as a whistle. And the fact that I could drink a bottle, death-sentence-Russian-style, and then not touch it, confirmed the delusion. Fool me.

EMPIRE-CLS

Charlie Horky was always teetering just this side of legality. Or financial prudence. His vision was magnitudes bigger than his bank balance and what the banks, overawed as they were by his charisma, would loan him. Or, more importantly, what the law allowed. He overdid it. A venture capital company had to be brought in to pump in emergency finance and new structures. They bought a minority interest, then – when the state of things became evident – they took over as majority shareholders.

This was 2004–5. Charlie was allowed to own and run CLS Nevada. That meant Las Vegas. The jackrabbits and coyotes in the desert didn't need limos. Vegas suited him down to the ground. He tripled the firm's size and beat all the opposition, but with what turned out to be bad money. And he took too many risks. Even for Las Vegas PD, who are tolerant about human vices and those who supply them. Their city, after all, got fat on human vices.

In June 2014, Charlie, as CEO of CLS Nevada, and two top aides agreed to plead guilty to what the Las Vegas *Review-Journal* called 'a multimillion-dollar racketeering conspiracy involving prostitution, drug trafficking and fraud'. It was a federal indictment. His drivers were sprinkling ecstasy tablets like M&Ms into the back seats and allowing full-on sex, with escorts, to keep the client happy on the way to the Strip or the chicken ranches (brothels) in the desert, where they could lose what money the tables had left. What is it those billboards say as you drive into Vegas? 'Don't ask how much you spent, ask "Did I have fun?"' Charlie Horky offered more fun on wheels than any of the other operators. And, till the Feds caught up with him, it worked. They're not fun-lovers.

Scorsese could have made a movie like *Casino* out of the Horky story. And Charlie, God bless him, could have vied with De Niro for the privilege of playing himself on screen. He looked that good. With the necessary Joe Blasco touches, of course.

Charlie is still in his early fifties. My guess is that he'll bounce back. Christ, he may end up owning the prison bus service. I hope he does come back. I admired the man for what he did for the limo business. He blew life into it. Life was duller when he left LA.

NEW BROOMS

After Horky left for distant Vegas, the money men set out to put the business he'd left on a sound financial footing. It was well worth saving. CLS was running around seven hundred vehicles in different parts of the US, with LA at its heart. We were gradually recovering from the 2001 shock. But a firm hand was needed. David Seelinger was brought in as CEO to put Humpty Dumpty back together again.

Seelinger's a limo-industry legend in the making. He'll be up there with Klein, I would guess, at the end of his career (which is still some way off). In person he's un-LA. Chicago-born, young David S. dropped out of school in ninth grade and went to work in a service station. In six months, 'I was running the place', he recalled in an interview. Sounds like bravado. But if you knew the man you'd believe it. Running places was the Seelinger forte.

He grew up, as he himself recalls, an out-of-control teenage addict – drugs, booze, food. He wanted to swallow the world. (Again, if you knew the man, that too was in character.) 'In 1985 I hit rock bottom. I weighed 350 pounds, had lost everything, and ended up in rehab . . . After I got out, I moved in with my family and started my recovery process.' (Recent PR shows an elegantly trim man exuding power and authority.) Now in New Jersey, he took up work as a chauffeur with a baby limousine company. 'I only lasted about four months as a chauffeur,' he recalls. 'I had a very bad sense of direction.' This was pre-GPS. They were about to fire him and get someone who knew the points of the compass but he pleaded with the owner, Alan Lehrer: 'I'll do anything else you want me to do – I really just need a job.' He was put on 'dispatch' – operations – and was instrumental in growing Lehrer's firm from four to a hundred and fifty cars. Under him, Empire became a major player. And fast.

They opened a branch in LA on 9 September 2001. Empire LA lasted two days. Other limo companies went under after 9/11, but Empire survived and kept growing.

In 2004, the money men approached Seelinger. Empire and CLS merged – the biggest ever such merger in the chauffeured-transportation industry. And at the top of it was David Seelinger. The new firm was called Empire-CLS, not CLS-Empire.

At the time I was director of sales for CLS West Coast. A hub position. I loved it. When I took over the position, hotels had been neglected. Several were on the point of walking. Charlie had let things slip – other things, personal things, apparently, were on his mind. I enjoyed rebuilding the hotel connections. I would breeze into five-diamond establishments to be greeted like a friend, not a salesman. I made time to gossip. Salespeople should never seem to hurry when hustling. I handled big entertainment events with the easy skill of someone who'd been doing it ten years. I scooped in new top-end clients, not by sales talk but by the sheer superiority of what I could show that CLS offered.

I met David Seelinger the night he arrived in LA. He moved into a bungalow in the Beverly Hills Hotel. I was invited (summoned) to dinner with him and a bunch of directors. It was a power dinner, not a 'getting to know you, Jack' occasion. All change. Next day there was another meeting, on the thirty-second floor of CLS's corporate office at Sherman Oaks, where the 101 and 405 meet. Great views. But my eyes were clamped on the new boss.

He entered like General Patton in that movie to meet his staff. Very much 'his' staff. It was well done, and very un-LA, un-laid back. With him was Randy King, who'd been acting manager, commuting from Vegas. He'd been Horky's general manager there for years and done that job, and the acting LA job, well. But the set-up was wrong. In a crisis you could have an absentee manager, thirty thousand feet, out of phone contact, flying into a Burbank traffic jam on the 134 freeway. Seelinger and King had a closed-door meeting. I, meanwhile, was pacing my office area on the thirty-first floor, wondering what was coming my way. How up-to-date was my resume, if I had to sell myself?

Seelinger came out and summoned me downstairs to a common-parts area out of general earshot. Had Randy thrown me under a bus, I wondered. My mind was racing. Had I fucked up? You know the feeling. 'Randy's going,' said Seelinger. And then the magic words: 'I need you to take over.' Take over what? Operations. I'd been offered versions of the job before and turned them down. There's a yawning gulf in all industries between sales and operations.*

I was made for sales, all that front-line stuff, face-on with clients, fancy dinners, lots of out-of-office driving, your 'own man', no one looking over your shoulder at your computer screen, schmoozing on expense account – even if, for the far-sighted young fellow, sales meant lower salary and prospects. But Seelinger had clinched the deal with three little words. 'I need you.' I nodded and finished my coffee.

Downstairs I saw Randy in the lobby. We didn't speak. What could I say? But I suspect he was relieved. I went and got my boxes and moved into what had been his big corner office. Stunning one-eighty-degree views. It was all happening so fast.

* *John*. Could Arthur Miller write a play, *Death of an Ops. Manager*? Think it through.

On my second day as general manager – operations, I was driving to yet another meeting with a couple of other top execs. We were in a luxury SUV. They're big vehicles, but they jam you close enough to smell other guys' aftershave. Out of the blue, one of them asks me, 'Jack. Are you gay?' Another three little words. Normally it would mean nothing to me. It was small talk. He could have as easily asked, 'You smoke, Jack?' or, 'You miss England, Jack?' And I would normally have shot back something smart-ass like, 'Fuck, yeah, but you'll have to wait till we get out of this van if you want to blow me.'

Instead, I said, 'No.' I said, 'I'm not gay.' Why did I say that? Because, in an odd kind of way, I was thirteen years old again, denying myself. My nerve had cracked. There was so much tension. So many guys were being let go. That sad sight – men, who a week ago were 'businessmen', turning in their car keys, parking permits and BlackBerries, carrying cardboard boxes with their pathetic-looking belongings, security – men who yesterday bowed and scraped to them – checking to make sure there was nothing in the boxes that now didn't belong to them. You feel the guillotine blade on your own neck when you see that, day in, day out. And you say, or do, something stupid.

'I just wanted to know,' the guy added. Nothing to him. It should, of course, have been nothing to me. Then the conversation turned, casually, to other matters.

After ten minutes, I blurted out, clumsily, 'Yes, I am gay. I'm sorry for saying I'm not. I just wasn't expecting your question.'

I handled it so clumsily I still kick myself and moan when

I think of it. Being gay or straight wasn't the issue. On virtually my first day in the job I'd demonstrated, conclusively, to a vanload of blabbermouths, that Jack was weak. Word would get around. About the weakness, that is. Everyone close to me in the industry knew I was gay – no big deal. It wasn't talked about not because it was a big secret but because it didn't matter. There were a lot of us around. But I felt like a carpet had been pulled out from underneath me. And, of course, it did get out. There were snide jokes – 'You a friend of George Michael, Jack?' some bastard asked, all innocent. There are always little pockets of homophobic pus waiting to erupt, wherever you work.

I did the new job well, I believe. But I felt like shit. My new position was so demanding. Every week new budget figures were issued, requiring cuts. Friends carrying those sad cardboard boxes in the lobby. And I was the guy doing the cutting. Empire was tightening the firm up: cutting away all the Horky fat. Liposuction with an axe.

SEX ADDICT

I couldn't let myself drink or smoke weed. But addiction is the cunningest thing. It will point itself like a garden hose at any of your bodily appetites it finds available. Look at my father, who's just at this moment looking at me. He's been sober thirty-three years. Not so much as a rum baba or brandy snap. But I've seen him drink twelve coffees, doppio strength, in a day. He probably sneaks more when he thinks those who care about him, and his blood pressure, aren't looking. He's got one in front of him now.* Tell me that's not addiction.

I couldn't use what I would loved to have used: max-strength California-certified medical weed by the ounce at night, and the occasional litre of gulped vodka by day. I simply couldn't do this job, which I'd never wanted, fogged up to fuck. I needed a clear head. If only for self-preservation. My addiction found its outlet in sex. I was gay. So I'd be the fucking Godzilla of gay. Beware, Los Angeles. A monster's coming.

Normies, as AA/NA calls them, find sex addiction amusing. Particularly English normies. Michael Douglas is honest enough to admit his addiction in public and those English tabloids giggle their balls off. Wrong, wrong, wrong. It is, believe me (and I've been through all three), more destructive an addiction than drink or drugs. (Coffee I'll let pass.) And it fucks you up just as badly.

It's not that warning on the Viagra packet about 'should your erection last four hours seek medical help'. Priapism, that's called – easily cured in any ER. One needle prick to the prick. It's the obsession that does the damage. SA is a mental disease. It squeezes out everything else in your mind. It's like a forest fire in the head. And the worst of it is, it never ends, like ordinary sex does, with climax, conquest or empty gonads. When Jagger came up with 'Satisfaction' ('I Can't Get No') he was creating the anthem for sex addiction before the disease became commonly known about and taken seriously.

* *John*. True enough. Don't think my higher power is going to worry too much.

With me it started gradually, in the usual highway-to-hell way. (I love, positively love, *Final Destination.*) One or two nights a week, I'd be cruising around Dodger Stadium Park, MacArthur Park, Griffith Park. Quick, anonymous sex in whatever dark bushes were convenient. Sometimes without speaking more than a couple of words about position and preference. If no one was available in the wild, there were streets in downtown LA where rent boys hung out. No satisfaction. Just an ever-growing appetite for more.

I would cruise at night, sometimes having as many as half a dozen sexual contacts. Then back at dawn, short nap, quick shower, dark suit and tie (custom-cut), and meet the morning as the operations manager of a multimillion-dollar enterprise. Not every night (I wasn't a full-blown sex addict – yet) but regularly.

After one hectic episode in the parks by night with a young, nameless guy, I went to the Four Seasons (the stars' hotel of choice) to make sure everything was right for a big thing we were handling that day (the Rolling Stones, as it happened), and there, at the desk, was my night-time partner. He too, it seemed, had his Jekyll and Hyde selves. Discreet front manager by day, sex maniac by night. A quick flash of looks fixed it. No talk, no names. Strangers in the day.

The addiction grew. It was now every night, all night. Designer suits by day, jeans, plain T-shirt and scuffed sneakers by night. A few hours' sleep. Parks, parties, boulevards, wherever action could be found, bought or swapped. Genital contact, not necessarily to climax – 'play', gays call it. As many as twelve playful encounters a night.

I would be trembling all the while like a crack addict. Sometimes a third person would cruise by, hoping to make the one-on-one play into a party. I'd snarl, look big, and frighten them away (unless they were young, skinny, and Latin, when concessions might be made). I wasn't into orgies. One on one. And never enough ones. Me always in the driving seat, in control. Some nights I would drive sixty to a hundred miles, park after park, far into the boondocks. The driving became part of the high. I was a sex vampire on wheels.

There were day parks and night parks. I played both. There was no Grindr, or adam4adam, in those low-tech days. You could set up meets by cell with 'party lines'. But that meant joining a call queue (there could be fifty ahead of you) and often driving across town, only to find your guy had gone. Or, worse, he was waiting, a hundred pounds heavier, twenty years older and a whole lot uglier than he'd led you to believe. I wasn't exactly choosy – but I wasn't desperate. Yet. It was easier to take your chances and cruise. I got expert at setting things up by cell phone. There was no law against driving and talking at that time.

Elysian Park, at nightfall, was a favourite hunting ground. But it had a downside. The rangers would drive around at dusk, loudspeakers announcing they were closing the park up for the night. It was the funniest thing. You'd see forty to fifty guys, like a herd of deer with a forest fire behind them, running out of the bushes to the parking lot. Literally running.

Of course you couldn't fence off a city wilderness area like Elysian Park, and some fellow vampires, who'd come by bus or cab, stayed on. But the rangers could lock in any overnight cars in the lot, ticket them, tow them, and have the owners explain in court how they were fanatic owl- and raccoon-watchers, your honour.

I galloped to my car with all the rest.

Nowadays when, as I heard someone say in a meeting last week, I can barely crank out two wanks a week, I can barely recall the adrenaline rush of those mad months.* Towards the end of the run, your standards lower. One more, one more. If that 'one' was someone I wouldn't have let near me when sane, so what? Do it and move on to the next, and the next.

This impossible life was animalising me. I was getting aggressive, violent at times. Two or three times a week I'd get into ugly quarrels and even fights. Some with dangerous people, and life-threatening. One example sticks in my mind. When I needed a break from cruising the parks I'd rest up, before going home or to work, in quiet sex clubs and saunas. There were a lot of them round West Hollywood in those days. One night I was kicking back in a sex club in Los Feliz (since closed, I notice, last time I drove past – no loss to the human race). There was this Samoan in biker gear, around 300 pounds, none of it blubber. He had arms three times the size of my thighs. I'm big (six-two, around 180 pounds at that time, muscled), but not Giant Haystacks big. This guy was.

Every time I passed the Samoan man-mountain, he

* I understand it better, though, thanks to the previously mentioned bible of sex addicts, Patrick Carnes's *Out of the Shadows: Understanding Sexual Addiction*.

smirked and pinched my bum. I exploded every time. I hate, absolutely hate, my buttocks being touched. My arse is 'exit only'. No fingers, no tongues, no fruits, no vegetables (forget your farmers' market stuff), no toys and no willies. It's off-limits to everyone except my proctologist. I'm total top.

I was fuming all the time and, on the third bum tap, I really exploded. So what if the Samoan Hulk was three times my size?* Nine tenths of the time, if you act insane, nine tenths of people back down. Even bikers. No one with any sense tangles with a rabid dog – so act rabid. After the third tap I said, with my nastiest snarl, 'Come outside, you fat ugly cunt' – pointing to the small back smoking area. My full bravado act. This, unfortunately, was the tenth time. I look round, as I'm going out, and this human tree trunk is actually following me. I'm fucked, I realise – not literally (though some of that is going on inside) but homicidally.

I decide to brave it out. It doesn't wash. Before I can say anything, Samoan Drago is hitting me with sledgehammers, just like Dolph Lundgren in *Rocky IV*. Every damn punch blacks me out. I've probably still got the brain damage. He got in at least five clear shots. I fell into a water fountain; he picked me up and threw me, like a sack of wet shit (which was how I felt), into a corrugated-iron fence. It clanged so loud people inside heard it. I was on the ropes and he was still coming in. He might well be, I now realised, one of those guys who comes to clubs like this not for sex, but for a fight. His idea of a night's fun. That pinching was just to

* They're a big race and warlike. They star in sumo wrestling nowadays. The Irish don't. Not that we lack fighting instinct.

get my temper up. Or, who knows, he'd suffered some racial abuse and wanted payback. I wasn't in a position to inquire why he'd decided to kill me.

I did manage to get a few hits to his head and decided to wrestle. A few more of those punches would finish me. The noise had by now brought out the guys at the counter and some customers who broke us up before his bear hug snapped my spine. I managed a brave final snarl. But the shit had been beaten out of me. I still put on a 'let me at him' act, for the spectators and personal pride. But inside I was relieved.

The management weren't at all worried about me getting beaten to pulp. They just didn't want ambulances and police cars rolling up and crime-scene yellow tape round the premises. The next day my ribs and kidneys gave me hell. I pissed blood. My face looked bad. Shades the size of saucers wouldn't stop people noticing and drawing their conclusions.

And I was getting very concerned. If it went on like this, I'd get killed, arrested, or so badly injured I'd spend the rest of my life in a wheelchair. For what? Sex that meant nothing to me, except that I always wanted more of it than I could get.

Other things concerned me. I've always had something of the hunter in my sexual make-up. I tended to go for quiet, slightly submissive guys. But there were a lot of strange characters wandering the hills by night, and in the dark you could never be quite sure who you were hooking up with. They did not display their ID. And even in the daylight they'd often have fake ID. Every so often the LAPD, or morality vigilantes, ran sting operations – putting out bait for the potentially dangerous characters they knew were out there. Like me, they might think. There was no good way out of the underworld into which I was falling.

One thing was clear, I wasn't going anywhere professionally. I knew I was at the end of my time at Empire-CLS – but, what the fuck, Empire-CLS was now destroying me. Or making me destroy myself. I booked myself into rehab. There was no objection: Empire-CLS knew I had a problem. They only had to check on my desk computer use. One of those high-priced places where stars go, on lawyer's advice, before their court appearances, around Malibu (Dreams, Imaginings, etc.) was an option, as was the Betty Ford clinic, if I wanted to go out of town to Rancho Mirage. (Funny names they choose for these places.) I chose somewhere quieter and, it turned out, better – for me, at least.

Las Encinas is an establishment of high reputation (and high price) between Pasadena and Santa Anita racetrack. The setting is old Southern Californian. Wooded grounds, Craftsman, Greene and Greene-style buildings.* It looks like a 1920s upmarket 'sanatorium', the kind of discreet retreat from the public eye where film stars and writers like F. Scott Fitzgerald dried out in the Prohibition era, no one knowing. Check out the website. Almost worth having a drug/drink (or sex addiction) problem to enjoy the amenities Las Encinas offers. And, as they say at the end of AA meetings, 'it works'. Or it always has for me.

* *John*. This is me talking – I visited you there so often it felt like I was an inmate as well. You don't know Greene and Greene from the Häagen and Dazs.

My presenting symptom was uncontrollable sex addiction. But I'd got a diagnosis for deeper, underlying problems three weeks before I checked in – bipolar, ADHD, obsessive-compulsive behaviour, the works. I was started on medication: Seroquel, Depakote, Strattera – the strong cocktail. Bipolar, my main affliction, was only recently being recognised as the destructive thing it is. And only now were antipsychotics (Seroquel, in my case) being cleared by the FDA for general prescription. They maxed out the dose, initially, and then measured the right amount and mix by the increase or decrease of my shambling, dribbling and mumbling.

At Las Encinas I had one-on-one therapy with a Dr Robert Miller.* He confirmed his colleagues' earlier diagnoses. Miller was a practitioner of EMDR (Eye Movement Desensitization and Reprocessing). There was a lot of hypnosis-like 'passing' with the hands and the recall of early, deep-buried, traumatic memory. It sounds pure Svengali but the daily sessions worked like a charm for me. Miller was very good. I didn't get as much from the twelve-step groups this time round. They'd been lifesavers at Ingletraz. But nowadays I could game them. I knew the moves too well. EMDR was a whole new game. Fascination helped the cure along.

After a month at Las Encinas, I was on the road again. It helped that my father was teaching at nearby Caltech and could visit daily.† I went back to Empire-CLS, where I was now senior VP, sales – West Coast. That highpoint only lasted a couple of months more. I was pulling in a large salary,

* No protocol issues about mentioning him – he advertises in the *LA Weekly*, and elsewhere, as Californian practitioners are free to do.
† *John*. Great fun.

which I wasn't, as things now were, worth. I was let go on the pretext that the company was in financial straits. It was politely done on both sides.

8: LIMOUSINING WITH SIR RICHARD

On leaving Empire-CLS, under a cloud, I called Robert Partovi, owner/president of a new limo company, Ridewell, who knew me of old from Dav-El and CLS days. Under Partovi, Ridewell brought new ideas to the limo industry. I knew that industry inside out by now and I fit in, now that I was myself fit. I was appointed at around $100K p.a. take-home (plus the full benefits range), and all running expenses paid for my Jag. I too was riding well. The new medicines, after I got the dosages right, kept me rock-steady. I was happy again.

I had bought, sometime earlier, a house in Eagle Rock – not Beverly Hills (yet, I told myself) but upmarket. Being me, I'd over-extended. I was never the Prius-and-affordable-condo type. Jaguar and mansion all the way. The house had a deck overlooking distant downtown with an eight-person Jacuzzi and barbecue area big enough for parties. I remodelled lavishly: $50K on oak panelling, custom oak doors, Bose speakers in every room, flat screens and walk-in wardrobes. Shit, I paid $800 for one (one!) wall bracket to hold up the bedroom TV. Without three of those brackets the wall would have caved in and killed me and whoever was with me.

The house wasn't my only new expense. I was now in a live-in relationship with a young Latin, Juan, a wannabe dancer. It was my first 100 per cent commitment: the first time in my life I felt there was something in life more important than my career. Juan was beautiful, lithe and charming, and, it later emerged, somewhat difficult. A hopefully-up-and-coming dancer. He cost a fortune and it was never enough. When I gently pointed out, for example, that Coffee Bean was advertising for wait staff he'd give me a cute smile and I'd melt. 'No, carry on with the dance lessons, babe. What do you owe this week?'

I was madly in love with him. Mad's the word. Part of the madness was my increasing use, getting dangerously close to dependence, on weed.

This is the story of how that happened.

California had (via Proposition 215) legalised 'medical marijuana' in 1996. Happy year. One Sunday me and one of my Ridewell colleagues, Cathy, had worked our arses off on an RFP (a bid for business). It was aimed at a multimillion-dollar account. Back at mine, when we finally got it done, she asked if I would mind her having a joint. I knew she was a careful, legally carded pothead and she never let it affect her work (as it hadn't today). Go ahead, I said, be my guest.

As she took her relaxing drags the sidesmoke faintly touched my nostrils. Those drug-thrilled days in South Pasadena flooded back. (Why do smells do that?*) I was thinking screwily. I'd drunk vodka, I thought, and then not drunk it for a year. No problem. I could control weed just the same way. And it was just as legal as booze. Screwy thinking won.

* *John*. I'd say read Proust, but what's the point.

I shared the joint Cathy companionably offered, according to smokers' etiquette. I remember to this day the feeling when it hit. Not a stupid, silly, stoned feeling but comfortably high. That overused word, 'mellow', was what it was, as we enjoyed the Jacuzzi, watching the sun go down, us getting high.

After that afternoon I left it alone for a month. But Juan was another pothead and little tubs of the stuff were always lying around. Over the years I'd got to know marijuana well. There are two varieties – sativa and indica. There were a huge number of differently graded, and powered, brands in the Los Angeles dispensaries: they were like the candy counters in 7-Eleven. And there were, as accompanying instructional leaflets directed, any number of ways of using: smoking, roll-up or pipe, baking into cakes, moulding into hash, injecting liqueur chocolate, water bong, hi-tech vaporiser. You could even, with the right preparation, stick it up your arse as a suppository.

Getting the 'card' was a formality – but sometimes a comic act. Juan had got his after three minutes' conversation with a gay doctor on his coffee break in Starbucks. (I never quite believed he hadn't offered something else.) The back end of the gay magazine *Frontiers* was full of ads for 'doctors' who could help, along with those for DUI lawyers, escorts, laser hair removal and – the latest party gimmick – naked plumbers.

I picked out a half-page ad with an address on the residential side of Beverly Boulevard, where it meets La Brea. When I got there it was less upmarket than its address – a grotty mini-mall, over a mailbox outlet and a liquor store.

From the outside, the 'surgery' (Americans don't use that word) had barred windows – usual enough in a high-ish crime area – but spray-painted gold, in front of purple velvet curtains. Not usual.

Entrance was via a buzzered, CCTV-lensed security cage. Banks have them. Once inside, everything, including the walls, was gold, with purple cushioned chairs. Very camp – satirically so, almost. There were ten or so people sitting, silently, on the chairs; an odd assortment – young Latins, old weathered hippies whose ponytails were long gone but fondly remembered, smart white girls, regular working guys and me, in my Ben Shermans, at that time my casual dress of choice.

I filled out the paperwork. I could have entered insomnia, bipolar, depression as my 'condition'. Instead I went for back pain. Not true – but I had horrific operation scars. A $70 'consultation fee' was required upfront. No socialised medicine in America. There was a peep-show cubicle informing you about the health-giving medical properties of marijuana.

When I finally got to see the doctor she turned out to be young, pretty and Persian. She was wearing pink scrubs and matching pink high heels, blending into the décor. The consultation lasted all of a minute and a half. She saw the scars, winced, and signed the form which I could present outside for my 'card'. Open Sesame! But another hundred bucks, please. With the card you were, potentially, a state-licensed junkie. No limit on purchase if you dispensary-hopped. The Great Rock Candy Mountain was yours. An utter fucking sham.*

* I think they may have tightened it up a bit recently. Last time I was in LA I noticed my old 24-hour dispensary was closed up.

That evening I celebrated with three friends from South Central. We smoked to oblivion, while I cruised back to Eagle Rock in UK PAPI. Behind the tinted windows it was like a Cheech & Chong movie. Feelgood fog. We were stopped by the cops. (I was driving too slow – mellow's not always the mood for freeways.) I threw open the sunroof and a plume of smoke shot out. The patrolman couldn't not smell it. He was a rookie and unamused. Do you have any marijuana in the car, he asked? Yes, officer, I said. He was going to arrest me. Twenty minutes later his sergeant arrived. I waved my card and showed the branded legal product. Apologies and on your way, sir. The rookie was furious. But if you'd arrested every pothead driver in Southern California you'd have needed drunk tanks the size of the Rose Bowl. It was sensible. The thing about weed, unlike booze, is however much you take you never get paralytic: higher than high. Cokehead drivers, on the other hand, are lethal on freeways.

Looking back, my thirty-third birthday, 2007, was a high-point of what had been some good years. Gene La Pietra was behind it. You hear cringe-making 'Happy Birthday' outbursts in LA restaurants, even the best of them. Clubs generally don't do the 'Happy Birthday' thing. Certainly not Circus & Arena. Gene made an exception. 'We'll make it a special night for you, Jack,' he told me, when I went to his office to say I would like a small private event at Circus.

Small it turned out not to be. The entrance, when I drew up, had massive poster boards. My smiling mugshot on them. There were flashed pictures of 'Jack' on every one of the club's big TV screens, on all four floors. Lasers scrawled my name across them.

Gene never hung around the club at night. He gave me a big hug, a big kiss, and told me, as he said goodnight, that Irwin, his general manager, would take care of it. Enjoy.

I'd drawn up a guest list of eighty names (my idea of 'keeping it small', you'll understand). They got free, specially inscribed wristbands ('Happy birthday, Jack'), giving entrance to a velvet-roped VIP zone with finger food and Dom Pérignon on the tables. The champagne gurgled merrily down eighty celebrating throats, and after an hour, I myself was slugging straight from the bottle, like a MacArthur Park wino.*

More, more, more was the call of the night. More kept coming. Non-stop. There was a vast 'photo cake' of me – snaps from three stages of my thirty-three years pasted into the icing. I was blown away by what Gene had done for me. I'd originally estimated three grand for the party. But the flood of champagne (at $200 a bottle) meant, if I was in any condition to count, the damage would be 'more, more, more'.

The party was over. The club was closing. How much? I stammered to Irwin. All those zeroes floating before me, I was, momentarily, stone-cold sober. Financial shock will do that. I calculated $20K, minimum. Visions of myself eating at IHOP for a couple of months. Irwin handed me an envelope. I opened it. A clean sheet of vellum paper, with 'Happy Birthday, Jack' handwritten by Gene on it.

Indeed it was. I tipped everyone from the busboy to the

* I told my father the other night that I calculate I drank nine bottles of fizz. He thinks it physically impossible. Who counts after the fifth?

valet, and my straight, sober friend Jerome drove me home in UK PAPI, a very happy thirty-three-year-old.

It was in the best job I'd ever had, and it would probably have got better. But I left Ridewell. Why? Two words give the reason. Richard Branson. Same way that Charlie Horky drew me to CLS like iron filings to a magnet – it was the man behind the empire. Hero-worship.

My worship had deep roots. As a young child – with homes in London and Los Angeles – I'd done a lot of transatlantic flying on prehistoric carriers like BA and PanAm. 'Flag' companies. The first time I flew Virgin Atlantic – I must have been twelve years old – it was like a new world. This was what jumbos – wide-bodied passenger jets – were really destined to be. Those early, mid-eighties Virgin Boeings – now he prefers the patriotic Airbus – had extended legroom in cabin and sultanic luxury in what Branson, mischievously, called 'upper class'. (Another touch of mischief was the virgin pin-up on the fuselage.) These weren't flagships – they were fun. The crew looked as if they'd been picked from Central Casting and they were trained to delight the eye as well as serve. There were individual TVs – and things really worth watching and listening to. And it was competitively priced. It all made you feel good. Branson had sexed up transatlantic travel while maintaining quality and contriving to offer much more for less. It wasn't just brand-marking and advertising. Anyone can hire Usain Bolt for a TV ad. An iPod with wings, sneerers call the first Virgin Atlantic airliners. They were much more. No one, flying Virgin, was made to feel a cheapskate – not even in 'cabin class' (never 'economy').

The old 'nationals' saw themselves as ocean liners in the sky – 'Steward, bring me a brandy and soda, if you'd be so very kind.' After Freddie Laker's Skytrain and Reagan's deregulation, most passengers were simply battery chickens in the sky. Self-loading luggage. Humiliated every step of the way. Branson realised that something new, something dignifying, was needed. And fun. Fizz in the mix. Virgin (the name said it all) returned 'frills to flying', the *LA Times* commented with a snide compliment.

What Branson offered, to my knowing adult eye, was limousines in the sky. Those TV sets on the back, the iPod culture, the little treats in the glove compartment (a toothbrush! No condom? Aren't we a mile high yet?), that sense of being pampered by the cuties in red. (Who, when the word 'Virgin' is mentioned, doesn't remember that outrageous rip-off of *Catch Me If You Can*?) These weren't iPods with wings, they were Lincoln Town Cars with wings.

Branson, I'd picked up from trade gossip, was good to work for. And the closer you worked, the more you liked him, apparently. I knew at least one person who was very close to him. His original US driver. Moguls, celebrities and big shots generally like, in every city they have business, to have their 'own' chauffeur. The same 'Home, James, and don't spare the horses!' man at the wheel. These assigned drivers are treated like kings by the firms that employ them – they're half chauffeur, half PA, when their man or woman is in town. Branson had built up a particularly good relationship with his (then) assigned San Francisco chauffeur, David Lipschultz. An extremely nice guy. Now higher up the chain of command.

Some background. Virgin Atlantic, by the mid-1990s, had two or three international flights a day to San Francisco International. Thanks to Branson's frequent-flyer clubs, the 'upper class' front ends of the planes were getting fuller all the time. David sold Branson (who likes to chat on car journeys – chat everywhere, in fact) on the potential for chauffeured transportation with his, Branson's, brand on it. Virgin Limousines was duly founded in 1995, as an SF-specific airport-to-city service for upper class passengers.

It was one of the innovations of Branson's upper class package on Virgin Atlantic that you got complimentary chauffeured travel from home to airport and fast kerbside checking, never having to lift your bags once. They treated you like a prestige paraplegic.

So Virgin Limo SF had this exclusive San Francisco business. David made do with two or three cars, borrowing more when and if the need arose. On start-up, the head office was David's own downtown apartment. Small, neat and profitable. But why not grow? More so since Branson (himself restless) had long been thinking about Virgin America – domestic flights within the US. He was itching to take on JetBlue and Southwest.

David, a far-sighted guy behind the charm, got permission to use the Virgin label to raise money for growth – specifically expansion to Los Angeles. Most importantly, to get the Virgin Atlantic account. It would be a tough market for a newcomer to break into. People hadn't thought Virgin could take on BA. Branson did – and won. David needed a man behind the evolving master plan, someone with a big book of business (industry contacts).

I heard rumours in 2007 that Virgin Limo were intending to expand into Southern California and were looking for someone who knew the ground there. I fit that bill. As I say, I knew David and his then vice president, Butch Henke, to chat with. We'd all three met at trade shows and got on. We'd jointly handled the Rolling Stones on their trips north and south.

Anyway, on spec, I sent a CV to David. No pre-call. I got the callback next afternoon – direct. I was at the time in Chicago with RuPaul. David and I went on to have a cell-to-cell talk. He outlined his vision – Virgin Limo LA. And he wanted me on board, leading the attack on the big Southland operators. Of course he was also attracted by all the LA names I had in my business book. By now I had strong connections with companies in the entertainment industry and other clients requiring big limousine usage. He was an unknown face in LA. They were on the starting blocks for launch in weeks, I gathered. Perhaps things would start ticking over as soon as a fortnight.

I'd just made a mega-deal for Ridewell Las Vegas. I was in good standing with the firm. But I made one of the few unethical decisions I've made in the chauffeured-transportation business. I stayed with Ridewell, as VP-sales, drawing my salary, knowing that, when the time was ripe and the price right (for me), I would jump ship. I felt bad about it. I'd always got on well with Robert Partovi, who treated me better than well. It was all the more embarrassing because David, under pressure from outside, kept on having to push back the Virgin LA start date.

I eventually told him, 'Listen, I can't keep working under

false pretences for Ridewell. It's making me sick.' The ethical thing would have been to quit, but my house and car (and, God help me, Juan) expenses would have killed me in a couple of months.

David came back with a holding offer: 'All I can do is start you as director of sales in San Francisco, until the other thing, in your town, gets going. Come up and live here for a few weeks,' he added. 'We can also get to work on the new business. Grow the brand.'

I agreed. Rashly. The San Francisco operation was tiny, compared to Ridewell, and sales potential up there would never be massive.

But I was dazzled by that one word, 'Virgin'.

I resigned from Ridewell as graciously as I could and went north. Juan came with me. We found an apartment. Friends took care of the LA house. This was early-to-mid 2008. I'm not a Bay Area guy. There was a lot of 'And who are you?' but by sheer hustle I got a five-diamond client, the Fairmont Hotel at San Jose. I'd stayed there with RuPaul. We both loved the place. I installed myself with a front-of-hotel desk and a little fleet of five limos, connecting with San Francisco International. The hotel gave me use of a complimentary suite. Bit by bit, sales grew. By now the central Bay Area operation was running an on-the-road fleet of forty-plus on a good day. The Virgin international airport connection was getting stronger all the time.

But all this was in San Francisco. Nothing definite in Los Angeles. Yet, yet, yet. I was getting a bit tired of that word. My initial salary was pitiful, $60K (raised, after complaints, to $80K). Out-of-town accommodation was covered but I had to shell out expenses on my empty house in Eagle Rock and for my own personal transportation. I discovered, after all these years, that keeping a $100K Jaguar on the road was surprisingly expensive.

What kept me bright-eyed was that hero-worship of Branson. When customising the package with Virgin, one thing I took care with was to secure health coverage from the new firm. As a newly appointed vice president, I bumped it sky-high. I had chronic back problems and, after my last (it wouldn't be) rehab at Las Encinas, I wanted that safety net underneath me. That was, it would turn out, the only wise thing I did.

I was using quite a lot of ecstasy at this point. I'd been introduced to it by Juan. (It's a favourite drug with dancers; makes them prance like crazy.) Over weekends I would relax with handfuls of it and medical marijuana. Ecstasy, I discovered, was a great aphrodisiac. It releases a tidal flow of dopamine, one is told, and the resulting sex is mellow and long-lasting. Juan and I once videotaped a three-hour session under its influence. (I still had some gear, and two cams, left over from my Tallwhiteboy days.) It was controlled intake. But literally ecstatic. No day-daze. At least, not work days. And San Francisco, I discovered, was a relaxed kind of city. Hangover from the hippy era.

I had a different pedigree and didn't entirely know how to use the northern city. On one Sunday I ran out of marijuana – a *Panic in Needle Park* situation. I drove all the way from San Jose to Los Angeles in a new Escalade that Virgin had just acquired (from LA, ironically). I was coming down from ecstasy and some alcohol. And tired. I was driving solo. I tried all the old remedies to stay awake and alert: plucking nose hairs, singing to music on the radio turned ear-shatteringly loud. Nothing worked. Fifteen miles outside SF I fell asleep at the wheel, going a legal seventy, and was woken up by the rattle of the 'blind driver's braille' – those rumble strips they put, along with camber, between the fast lane and the concrete dividers, which I scraped. My angels saved me. The Escalade veered out of my control. The right-hand wheels flew a foot in the air off the camber and fell down with a crash loud enough to wake me. If it had been a Town Car, it would have flipped and – chances are – I would have died on the highway. The quick death I wanted – but not for another half-century at least. The Escalade, thank God, was unmarked, although the tracking was fucked.

The reason I'd been recruited was for the coming battle for LA. But one thing which hadn't been made clear to me – or, more likely, I hadn't sufficiently listened to what was being said – was that the funding wasn't there. Yet. Yet. Yet. There are three hundred or so Virgin-branded enterprises in the US. They share that magic word. But they don't necessarily put money into any business but their own. They are corporately independent.

So no help from Virgin Group America could be expected. Sir Richard uses the Virgin brand brilliantly – but he doesn't himself always invest to the hilt in enterprises that he sells the brand to. He often leaves that to outside investors who want to ride along with him. Many SF investors couldn't see the point of putting money into an LA firm, and in LA, some thought, the limo marketplace was already saturated.

My two months in SF became eight months. There was strain on me, and breaking strains on my personal life. Juan was getting very bored. And, when bored, he was untrustworthy – more so with the ungodly hours I was having to put in at the office. Things were increasingly tense.

THE MAN

The upside of all this hassle was the prospect of (eventually) getting close to the man himself. Sir Richard. It happened during the launch of Virgin America. This was Branson's baby. He'd had to battle for airport slots and locations. Resistance had been ruthless. The American airline industry intended to do what they'd done to Laker's Skytrain and the BA–Air France Concorde. Kill him. But Branson finally pulled it off. An arterial Virgin network between major US cities. It took him three years' tooth and nail struggle.

There's a good account of how the firm was launched on Wikipedia. What it leaves out, though, is how brilliantly the man mounted a publicity campaign round himself – 'Bransonising' the whole show. It was egocentricity with wings. VA was got off the ground, literally, with inaugural flights to every major city to be interconnected by the airline. The first of all were New York to San Francisco and another, simultaneously, Los Angeles to San Francisco. 'Virgin's maiden flights.' Sir Richard made a lot of that. Saucily. They happened on 8 August 2007 – only hours after he got final permission from the Federal Aviation Administration to start operations.

The wow factor was to make San Francisco International the setting for Branson's astronaut-style splashdown – the guy is obsessed with space travel. Both in-flying planes were loaded with celebrity and press. *Wired* was particularly impressed with the 110-volt outlet electrical sockets. A 'geek-friendly' airline, they declared. They meant it as praise. Other journalists, less geek-oriented, commented on the welcome extra inches of legroom and the 'iPod that flies' music offerings.

Branson personally captained the JFK–SFO flight, walking up and down the aisle, jollying the press. A whole gate at San Francisco was dedicated to his arrival. Fire trucks on the side of the runway spurted a watery corridor of honour for the landing plane.

And then, to the amazement of the thousands watching, Sir Richard threw open a cockpit window (who knew they had them?) while the Airbus 320 was still rolling (had they attached a safety belt to his ankles?), smiling that trademark smile, and waving a flag.

Virgin brand-holders all over the world shat themselves when they saw that photograph. Their firms were wholly Branson-dependent. If he went (a fall from the cockpit might well have killed him) they would have been splattered on the tarmac with him.

He deplaned, still smiling, to five hundred employees loyally chanting, 'Bran-SON! Bran-SON!' He was greeted by the mayor and hugged, then taken to his hotel, me in close attendance. This was how I met him, for the first time. He was immensely courteous. Dressed in blue jeans and button-down shirt. Understated to the point of 'don't give a fuck'. I, like the others who would be close to him, was warned not to wear a tie. He didn't like them. He's been known to call for scissors, apparently, and cut them off. (Mayor Gavin Newsom, a famously dapper guy, was spared.) I carried his bags to and from the car trunk – fighting him off. He always carries his own, given the chance. It's not affectation. It's him.

Over the next few weeks, Branson did a series of headline stunts and visits to the big places he was opening up in. I was his on-site transportation manager at the major West Coast locations: San Diego, Seattle, Las Vegas, Los Angeles. It was a tight schedule. I would meet him, take him to the party which had been arranged, handle his transportation, troubleshoot, and get him back for the next morning's plane. All close-up and-personal service. I was Jeeves to his Wooster – except that Wooster has never been Branson's style. I would conduct him onto a plane – eight upper class seats, always some empty (and his aircraft, for God's sake) – and he would defiantly sit in cabin class, not even by a window, aisle or extra-legroom emergency exit. He was (is) so low-key. Not for show: just him. The closer you were, the clearer the key he chose to strike was.

It was done with humour. On one morning flight, return SFO to LAX, with not many media on board, there were the usual complimentary mimosas, champagne and bagels. And, without making a big show of it, Branson welcomed and directed oncoming passengers at check-in, issuing boarding passes. One young girl, carrying a guitar case (as common in Southern California as briefcases on Wall Street), he stopped.

'I'm sorry, I can't allow you on board.' Her face falls. He continues: 'The only way I let you onto my plane is if you promise, halfway through the flight, we break out your guitar and you get the whole plane to join in a singalong.' Which she did.

During the flight, Branson did the trolley-dolly delivery up and down the aisles. It sounds corny but there was something sincerely Branson about all this. And something real about his vision of what air travel could and should be.

Las Vegas, 10 October 2007, was the craziest. And again pure Branson. He decided to do yet another death-defying publicity stunt. The defiance wasn't as successful as usual. He had this 'brilliant' (trademark Branson word) idea that he would jump off the roof of the Palms Casino Hotel in Las Vegas, suspended by an abseiling rope and tackle, dropping 407 feet to the sidewalk.

Three hundred members of Virgin Group America were shitting themselves all over again at the prospect of their primary owner splatted on the Strip sidewalk. And it damn near happened. I had the car standing by, while he'd done a cautious rehearsal jump a few hours earlier. (God knows what the punters thought if they lifted their eyes from the slots – a public hanging?) Everything perfect. He descended at snail rate.

For the real jump, Sir R. was wearing a tux as he stood on the top parapet. 'Jump! Jump! Jump!' shouted the idiots on the ground, hoping, against hope, for a disaster to remember. They nearly got it. He made the jump, smiling – teeth visible a mile away, as usual. No problem. But then there came a huge gust of desert wind, out of nowhere. Not unusual in Nevada, but this was a bad time for it to happen. It slammed him against the hotel wall. You can see the agony on his face. It's all on YouTube (though his press people kept the worst of it out of the next day's papers).

The scraping descent, against the wall all the way, meant more agony. He reached the bottom, limping but still smiling through the pain. At the back, his tuxedo and trousers were shredded to the skin. He could have died. 'Bare-ass Branson Dodges Death', is how YouTube cheerfully labels it.

I helped escort him back to his accommodation, where he received in-room medical attention. 'Branson in the ER' would have been quite the wrong headline for the launch of a new airline. He smiled and was courteous as ever through the pain. But he couldn't talk. It was gallant – no other word fits. He made the star party that night.

GOODBYE, VIRGIN LA

I loved the man and would have worked for nothing. But that wouldn't be required. I saw a great future for Branson, me, David and the firm. We'd managed, by hook and crook, to get the LA Virgin Atlantic account (Music Express, I recall, was the main opposition). By now the money was promised (not yet in hand) and my own revised contract on paper. I would continue getting my bare-bones salary package. Small feed. But I would also get 1 per cent of all gross revenue from the LA limo operation, which I would be running. Virgin LA would, Sir Richard agreed, have an exclusive on Virgin Atlantic upper class custom. It was getting bigger at LAX all the time. One per cent doesn't sound very much until your calculator tells you what that's worth on the then-projected years and millions. And, in that flagship position, I'd be at the centre of one of Sir Richard's operations. We spent months on budget arranging and roll-out plans. Everything approved and stamped. I was psyched up. Marijuana and ecstasy were well under control – just weekend maintenance dosage.

Virgin Limo LA should have worked. We'd got the structure in place and I'd recruited a good team. The brand was all-conquering. It had all the necessary promises for the cash a medium-sized infrastructure would need. I had lots of ideas how to get an edge on the established big operators – I was itching for the fight. But there was delay after delay. Endless meetings which bored me witless. I wanted to get out there and sell, not 'strategise', whatever that meant, other than not doing anything. It got to me. On one occasion I told David to stuff his vice presidency up his arse – I'd rather work for McDonald's in a Ronald suit. I simmered down. But I felt something bad was coming. It was in the air. You could smell it in late summer 2008. 'Earthquake weather', they call it in Los Angeles. Butch Henke picked up the signals and moved on to Avalon Transportation.

If I'd foreseen the frustration, I would have thought twice about leaving Ridewell. But I was now a VP, and there was always that pot of gold at the end of the rainbow – Virgin Limo LA. Me as mini-Branson. It was not to be.

A week or so before the great November 2008 meltdown, Morgan Stanley had warned Virgin (as I was later told) that they should hunker down for something very bad coming. It was an early storm warning. Batten down the hatches. Pull money back, do not put any out. If we hadn't delayed, all might have been well – but we had been forced to delay. The end-of-the-world recession was precisely synchronised with our roll-out. Perfect-storm catastrophe. End of the World as We Know It.

In a day, that fucking day, in November 2008, our $2.5 million in the pot shrank to $250K. The projected forty-five-car fleet became two, then one. I might as well have been pulling a rickshaw from LAX to Sunset Boulevard, for all the good my 1 per cent would do me. No one's fault – certainly not David's or Branson's. The operation has got back on its feet over the last few years. It was always a good idea.

CRYSTAL SOLUTIONS

The sub-prime thing hit me like a bullet between the eyes.

The banks, who'd brought this disaster down on the country, lost their nerve. I'd taken out an interest-only mortgage on my house. It was spacious and I had two paying-guest friends. For two years the $4K monthly payment was nothing serious. I was distracted by my day job and had signed all the mortgage papers like the dizzied wombat I always was when confronted with long documents. They called in mortgage debt, which, overnight, doubled. I was never a bad bet for the bank, earning well as I was, on target to earn better, with thirty-five good repay years in me. If they'd given me some elastic they would have got their money back over time. But all they cared about was saving themselves. Time was the one thing, along with new credit, they weren't offering. Some middle manager with the axe on his own neck took one look, and that was curtains, at my shrivelled income and the $19K annual property taxes. I was underwater. The house was worth less than I'd paid. I tried broker after broker, but my salary against the half-million still owing on the house disqualified me.

The bank pulled the plug on me. No mercy. Unless I could come through with $9K p.c.m., they'd foreclose. It was enough to make you buy a gun and go postal. The banks had killed the property market then come in like vultures to buy what they'd wrecked on the cheap – and then, when the time was right (they could sit out the storm – too big to fail), they'd sell it on at a handsome profit to the next generation of suckers.

Wells Fargo, BoA, Union Bank of California – they're still around. And fatter today than ever. Three quarters of the 2008 residents on my lovely road, Mount Eagle, are gone. There were foreclosure signs on the lawns all over Eagle Rock. It was a real-estate holocaust. And these weren't reckless people, or never-should-have-been-given-a-loan-in-the-first-place residents. They were decent middle class. I, along with them, was fully fucked.

I'd have a few months' breathing space. Five at most. The banks were required, by law, to give their victims a chance either to sell and settle, or find the money elsewhere. But, to put it mildly, 2008 wasn't a sellers' market. I should simply have sent the bank the keys and moved out. But I couldn't. I kept draining what money I had, or could borrow, in a lost cause, like a gambler chasing his losses.

It was staring into this abyss that I became introduced to

crystal. My initiation took place in the Hotel Vitale, a five-star boutique hotel where I'd managed to land a contract for Virgin Limo. They gave me ten days' free luxury-suite accommodation as part of a deal seal.

I was very low. Juan, I knew, was two- (two? Who was I kidding?) timing me back in LA. The relationship was over. The house was lost, barring a miracle. The firm was in trouble. Budgets were sliced deep into the bone. I was still selling but with no hope of catching up.

I was ripe for some catastrophe. Which I got. I'd been chatting on adam4adam, on and off, with an Asian guy. I invited him over to the hotel for some relief-sex and oblivion. He came carrying crystal – which I hadn't asked for. Frankly, I was afraid of the drug. Afraid of the loss of control which I'd seen in other guys using it.

I wouldn't hold or smoke from the pipe my guy fired up. I agreed to one blowback (kiss and swallow). The cloud swirled down into my lungs and hit. It took me, in seconds, to a level I couldn't recall ever reaching before. Love at first gasp. As I grabbed the pipe and puffed, deep and long, I found myself totally without inhibition. Or, more importantly, pain. And jacked up to an incredible height of lust. I attacked the boy; wild, wild, wild. It went on for hours. I was hooked.

Crystal had been around for ten years as a major street drug. It started in Hawaii (where, I was told, they called it 'ice' – it's always been lucky in its street names). It was a perfect holiday drug and was brought back in holiday luggage to the mainland. Then the dealers moved in (no customs between Hawaii and LA, and lots of pleasure-boat travel).

The great thing about crystal was it didn't have to be imported across frontiers. You didn't have to grow it, process it in jungle factories and smuggle it – paying in blood, dollars and potential prison time all the way. You could 'cook' it in a trailer-park kitchen with stuff you could buy from the local drugstore (though they might look at you oddly when you asked for a hundred packs of ephedrine-laced cough medicine at Rite Aid). It could reach the customer via short, relatively safe, supply lines.

Crystal is an upper and a powerful sexual stimulant. It reacts in a friendly way with other drugs. Gays love 'tweak'. You can ingest the drug in various convenient ways. Least glamorous is the 'booty bump' – inserting a moistened lump as a suppository. A bit of a passion-killer, some would say. You can smoke it or snort it or 'slam' (inject it) or take it heated in a small glass 'pipe' (which would, in the months to come, be my intake of choice).

I hope, for your sake, you never take crystal. But this is how you do it, American-style (it can be different in the UK). You get it, as the name suggests, as crystal. You melt the jewel-like stuff in the bowl of a glass pipe, with a cigarette lighter (blue flame in the UK), watching it all the time as it turns into pure, watery liquid. In Asia, I would later find out, they go to huge trouble with twisted foil to make a sharp narrow flame which heats the drug to a higher temperature.

However you do it, once it's all melted, you gently turn and twist the pipe, coating the bowl's inner surface. You cool the bowl down, with a damp cloth or towel. It re-crystallises, turning white. Once it's hard, you reheat the pipe with a lighter, till it's a clear liquid. Then roll the pipe so it touches the whole of the hot inner bowl surface, creating pure, white smoke. You pull on the pipe.

How do you do that? There are three methods. Some say don't inhale (Clinton-style) but channel the fumes through your mouth and nose. The membranes pick it up. Others prefer to suck the fumes down deep into the lungs, like a cigarette, then exhale. The third option is to hold it for as long as you can in the lungs, as with marijuana (my preference).

An old wives' tale claims the stuff can crystallise, a third time, in your lungs. Fatally. I've never known anyone that happened to. You'd be dead before the ambulance could sound its emergency horn. It's a risk I was willing to take.

So that's how you do it. And PLEASE DON'T.*

LOWER AND LOWER

You can't do crystal on a regular basis and not have anyone notice. There were office rows. They accused, I raged, things deteriorated. Last chances came and went. One of the very worst things over this awful time was that, as addicts do, I smashed – was it deliberate? – every important relationship in my life. Most painfully, as I now look back, that with Ru.

I was still accompanying him on trips and doing bodyguard work for him. It was, as it happened, my body which

* After spelling all this out I was blubbing and had to go to my NA meeting. What I had to get off my chest was that I still want to use. But I can't. And won't. *John*. I went to the meeting along with him.

first attracted his sarcastic notice. Always to this point in my life razor-thin, I was now putting on a ton of weight. It was the mix of my medication (mainly that damned Depakote, which blimps you up to Goodyear size) and weed, which I was now smoking every moment I could. And when you smoke that stuff in the quantities I was doing, you eat like a locust.

I acquired the strongest strain available from the LA medical dispensaries. To get the maximum effect, chasing that increasingly elusive high, I smoked it, carefully ground up, either through a water bong or using a hi-tech vaporiser. It was insanely strong. I'd wake up in the middle of the night, or at seven in the morning, and devour a tub and a half of Häagen-Dazs and anything else super-sweet that was lying around. It didn't lie around long. Hence me and Mr Goodyear. I was lacing the intake with handfuls of ecstasy and the occasional litre of vodka, which didn't help. The pills make you incredibly soda-thirsty, the booze has thousands of calories. One fat bodyguard: more body than guard.

Ru, of course, suspected what was going on as buttons flew off my jacket, giving up the lost struggle to get round my now fifty-inch chest. He was, as always, razor-slim. Flaco y Gordo, I heard one Hispanic waiter whisper. The crunch came at Santa Barbara, where we were staying at a beachside hotel. In other circumstances it would have been blissful. I'd driven up from LA to meet Ru there in UK PAPI, smoking so much it was like a Cheech & Chong movie behind the tinted windows. I speeded a bit, but was getting smarter – paranoid-smart – and avoided the highway patrol checks. This was not a time to be caught DUI.

Ru was doing a club gig, but during the day we could pamper ourselves in the hotel spa and massage parlour – they're a Santa Barbara speciality. I added extra marijuana pamper for beyond-total relaxation. That evening I was so stoned I lost track of time and came to consciousness with the awful discovery that I'd missed the luxury bus taking Ru, Joelle and entourage to his performance – he was bodyguardless. Lucky it was Santa Barbara, not Detroit. They'd banged on my bedroom door, waited a minute or two, then taken off, arranging for me to be picked up later, wherever I was. (In fact I phoned ten minutes later and they swung back for me – not good.) I'd always prided myself on being on my game. Now I was a total fuck-up. Permanently comatose, losing it. Ru could see it, but said nothing. The temperature was lower between us.

I managed to patch things up with the usual excuses. The next performance was at Las Vegas. I decided not to carry marijuana on me when we flew (it's easy enough to get in Vegas), but I had eight ecstasy pills, wrapped in cling film, secreted in my world-famous foreskin as travel comfort. Wrapped, if you're curious – I wasn't a street junkie, for God's sake. It was a domestic flight, but there was always a chance security would do a spot check. I didn't want to embarrass Ru. (If the papers got on the story – RuPaul's bodyguard carrying drugs – they'd assume it was for him.)

We had adjoining suites in Vegas (the Venetian, was it?). I spent time, again, in the spa. As bodyguard, the promoter picked up my tab. I was bored – Ru didn't want my company. He'd gone to bed early. I went on adam4adam and put in a request for a young Asian, and when contacts were thrown up, a secondary request for crystal, more ecstasy, and weed. A few yards from where Ru was resting, I embarked on a night of Party and Play, P&P. Another guy joined in later on – making it a threesome. Hotel rooms in Vegas are state-of-the-art sound-insulated – for obvious reasons.

The next morning we were flying back to LA. Ru and I by ourselves, Joelle back to New York. The two of us barely made it to the cut-off. The atmosphere between us was now frosty. No talk. Then, catastrophe. In my drugged and exhausted daze, I confused the two-digit flight and gate numbers. I took us to the wrong check-in and sat there, after the posted departure time, assuming that there was some delay. Happens all the time on domestic shuttle flights. We sat there over an hour before Ru (not me) realised the mistake. Megafuckup.

I felt utter sweat-soaked shame. Ru's face – one of the most eloquent faces in the world – wasn't showing anger, it was showing disappointment. Nothing was actually said, but thereafter we went our separate ways. The most important friendship in my life was over.*

LAS ENCINAS

Within less than a month I was crystal-crazy. I made what was my most deliberate suicide attempt, back in the house that was no longer mine. I had surrounded myself with thunkingly depressive music – Pink Floyd – sinking deeper and deeper. No mere cry for help this time. Real thing. I

* See my personal endnote for how things now are.

left a phone message for my mother and father in England, thanked them, said it was nothing to do with them, I loved them. Then smashed the phone.

I drank a bottle of vodka and gulped what would, surely, be a fatal dose of my antipsychotics (I'd just got my monthly Rx 100-pill refill): glug of booze, ten pills. Then again. After the tenth round, I began to slip into a coma. My last conscious thought – 'This is it.' I burst into tears. But I wasn't frightened. If anything, I recall relief. Semi-conscious I stumbled to my home office and collapsed on the floor, where, thank God, one of my housemates, Jen, returning early from work, discovered me. It was around five o'clock in the afternoon.

Jen called for an ambulance. Juan called in friends (one of whom, I suspect, relieved me of my personal jewellery and watch. Why not? I wouldn't need them where I was going). The ambulance came and took me, siren going, through the evening rush hour, to Glendale Memorial, where they pumped out my stomach. I was still unconscious.

It was touch and go, but they saved me. For what? My parents, who'd aged ten years after that phone message, called close friends to go and report on me. Which they did. 'He's alive, in critical. He may still die.'

When I came round, surrounded by tubes (and by now in acute withdrawal), belly pumped out, I was blind. I'm in hell, I thought. They'd strapped me to the bed, like that girl in *The Exorcist*, because I was convulsing so violently. And screaming. My friend, Flaco, a thin transsexual, took a video – Stephen King couldn't have done it more terrifyingly. Gradually I surfaced. I was transferred to Kaiser, out of intensive and into recovery and counselling. On the conveyor belt back into the world I'd so wanted to leave. I persuaded everyone to put out the cover story that it was accidental overdose of my prescription drugs. Assuming, that is, you can neck fifty Seroquels and a litre of vodka by mistake. Happens quite a lot on busy days.

After a week or two I was straightened out sufficiently to put my affairs in order. But I was finished at Virgin Limo. It was return-the-BlackBerry time for Jack. I was un-Bransonised, and I'd come so near. Fucking bankers.

But I still had a month or so's health coverage and booked myself into Las Encinas, my personal Hotel California. The house, waiting for the bank repossession notice on the door – over new locks and barred entrance – I left in the care of the friend, Jen, who'd been unfailingly kind to me and, you could say, saved my life. Only her Korean god knows why she was so kind to me. Juan and I were finished. He would eventually go to New York. His Skype in the following months showed a top-of-the-line computer. He still emails, noncommittally, from time to time. I'd been madly in love with him.

I was the Wildman of Encinas when I arrived. Raving. Off my face. They put me in their closed ward. You went there voluntarily – this wasn't a state hospital for the criminally insane. But once your signature was on the paper it was under 24-hour watch till you were judged no danger to yourself. I was dangerous to myself and the world. In my madness I pried open a window, ran along the roof, jumped from the second floor. What was in my mind? Escape? Self-harm? Drama-queen antics?

I dislocated a thumb. But I could limp in trainers without

laces (they were taken from you at night, along with recharger cords for phone and iPod), half a mile to Rosemead Boulevard, buy a bottle of vodka, glug it down between the store and the nearest trash bin, and limp back a little more merrily than I'd limped out. A point was made. Pointlessly. I could have calmed down and walked out of the front door, on voluntary discharge. It was closer confinement from now on. They had a kind of lockdown unit. I went there (again, voluntarily).

It was the first time in eight months I'd been sober. Gradually I came down and gave up the 'Escape from Las Encinas' dramatics. It was a long way down. I was jobless, I was carless, I was partnerless. I was less than zero. Less in life you could not be than me at that point in time. Among my souvenirs from the last few wild months was a slew of STDs. I had so many antibiotics in my body I didn't crap right for weeks. (The medicine kills all the flora in your gut, I learned.) I hope I never go back into rehab. But Las Encinas (whatever it cost) was the best of the three incarcerations (including Ingletraz) I've had. They put me back together again a second time. I recommend the place if you need to be put back together.

LITIGATION GOLD

I had unrealistic hopes of getting my job, any job, back. I raised a $10K loan from the bank. It added to the money problems. I had to pay back quite a slice of the money I'd borrowed when I was still loan-worthy. And employable.

(My name was now shit in the chauffeured-transportation industry. Word gets around.) But I did have a source of income. Call it litigation gold.

I realised, early in my career (from conversation with a lawyer friend of a friend), that if you play your cards right, you can get a little back of what the medical and insurance industries scam out of the American population. I had car accidents. No one, living on the road as much as I did, could avoid them. There are so many bad drivers around as to make good drivers' lives hazardous, however good they are.

My first back trauma, however, wasn't on the road. In the days before flat screen, TVs the size I wanted were the size of (American) refrigerators. 'We gotta move these refrigerators / We gotta move these colour TVs', goes the Dire Straits song. Not for the feeble. At this time (we're talking mid-to-late nineties), I was muscled. I worked out most early evenings with free weights, had a trainer, and was taking fortnightly injections of growth hormone, Deca-Durabolin (steroid),* and testosterone, illegally, of course, from a transsexual friend who worked in a hospital and could raid the locked drugstore. For money. It was the real stuff and made you feel like an angry David Banner about to go Hulk. But with lifting heavy household goods, it's not muscle but technique that counts – that 'snatch' which the best weightlifters have. I ricked my back. It would never be what it was again. Add painkillers to my illicit drug intake.

The first car accident was when I was at Propaganda driving a truck through a quiet residential area of Hollywood.

* Probably the most dangerous drug I've ever used.

A four-way intersection meant a stop. Not what they call a 'Californian rolling stop', but one which rendered the vehicle static with a little back-jerk. I stopped then started. I had right of way – first-arrived vehicle. I was in this massive five-tonner, high above the road. A brand new Camaro crosses my path illegally. I smash into him, turning his bonnet to tinfoil. Repairable, though. Less repairable was the genuine whiplash (from the jammed-on brakes) which had jolted my neck and shoulder out of position.

At Propaganda, you were self-employed. No personal insurance (though the truck was something else – it was straight off to the shop for loving repair). There were chiropractor's bills and a few days' loss of work. Quite a few. And, of course, you always go back to work before you should, which means pain. Worse, I'd sustained physical damage. Permanent, as it turned out. On wet days I can still feel it, and my neck mobility is impaired.

A lawyer friend (I was getting to know the value of that kind of friend) advised suing the other driver's insurance company. I did, and got $50K for pain, distress and loss of earnings. And a useful lesson. If you're hurt, attack – always attack – with lawyer friends snarling either side of you.

The second accident to car and spine centred on my beloved Jaguar. I'd had a string of them. All leased. I started with an entry-level X-Type and graduated, as the salary rose (with my ego), to an S-Type, custom-designed for me, newly shipped from the UK. Crate-new. Much admired on the road. The last Jaguar I leased was an XJ8L. This particular marque was preferred by the Queen of England and her prime minister, I was told. But good enough for me, despite that.

The first X-Type I had was an utter lemon. It spent more time in the shop than on the road. Robert Partovi (who would later employ me at Ridewell) had a lawyer friend who specialised in warranty claims. He invoked the 'lemon law' for me and negotiated a full refund, plus compensation for the familiar peripherals (loss of earnings, etc.) – around twenty grand.

The big earners, and the most painfully earned, were my four later back surgeries. The basic spinal injury was the result of a car accident – other driver wholly at fault. But he had a friendly witness. So friendly, indeed, that he had the same surname. Not, as it happened, a common one. A succession of lawsuits followed, evidence from a crew of doctors – all on contingency (no win, no fee). They'll do it if it's prima facie a winning case. This was a winner from the start and yielded me, at the end of it all, many tens of thousands more.

While I was in treatment (chiropractic and orthopaedic) for that injury, I sustained another spinal trauma when a car rear-ended me on the freeway, two days after had I picked up my repaired car from the first accident. It meant medical bills and a back operation (general anaesthetic, deep-cut surgery).

There followed a complex sequence of suits – one against my own car-insurance company. I came out from that with about $150K. I also came out of the hospital with MRSA. They make you sign disclaimers before treatment to avoid malpractice suits. This was just that – malpractice. Dirty hands in the OT. The pain was unbelievable. I'm insensitive to most painkillers – and the antibiotic they used, in piledriver amounts, to wipe out the MRSA screwed up my hearing, which has never entirely recovered. I looked into a lawsuit but was advised against taking on Big Pharma. They have better lawyers, and more of them, than you can ever afford.

The spine was now herniated. A third and fourth operation were advised to replace lower discs L4/L5 with titanium bracing – cap and bell. If it went on this way, I'd be like the Tin Man in *The Wizard of Oz* and never get through the security arch at LAX without the 'Anvil Chorus'.

For this last operation they had to go in through my stomach, pushing the organs aside to reach my lower spinal column. I came round from what was major surgery with a predicted nine-month recovery time. The pain had, the surgeons discovered, an unusual origin. I had double the number of nerve endings on my vertebrae. The doctors had to make another, larger incision and deaden the agonising nerves. I was a patient of great interest to medical science.

It wasn't over. Five days after what was a fast recovery, I spent the whole day with Ru. That night I was struck by spinal cramp which got worse and worse. Agony – my old friend by now. Late the next day, I couldn't stand it any more, and Ru drove me, and my father, to ER. MRSA again, and extreme, constant pain – so acute that I seriously asked my mother (who'd flown in from London after a hysterical phone call) to mercy-kill me. She stormed at the medical staff to give me more morphine. It did, as usual, too little (except for constipation – on an internally bruised stomach). The pain got worse. The huge barrage of Vancomycin (one of the few antibiotics supposed to work with MRSA,

I was informed) was doing nothing. The hospital feared I would, as I sincerely informed them, strangle myself with one of the wires surrounding me. 'I can't fight it any more,' I told my mother.

There aren't too many patients in the intensive care unit on suicide watch. There were twelve-hour nurse shifts round my bed for three days. 'Pain-management doctors' were coming and going. I was pumping my morphine PICC line continuously. I was catheterised and pissing pus.

Those awful days were an interesting insight into how the American health industry generates its phenomenal income. Every day, while I was thrashing in pain, a psychiatrist would pop his head round the door. 'Do you want to hurt yourself?' he would ask – keeping his distance (I was, after all, infectious). Whatever the answer (yes, no, fuck off), he was gone in five minutes. I looked at the eventual bill landed on my insurance company – $400 a pop for my shrink's daily 'consultation'. He was better paid than Michael Jackson, and about as much good to me at that time.

Oddly enough there was one post-operative doctor who did help. They called her in from Venice Beach (just down the road from the hospital): an obviously lesbian, crop-haired, fifty-something physician who'd evidently picked up her skills in the hippy era. You expected her to come in accompanied by a few bars of the Beach Boys' 'Good Vibrations'. At this point I didn't give a fuck. They could have called in a witch doctor – not that this woman was much different. She was 'alternative' and came twice a day. She employed strange 'manipulations', making, all the while, grunting noises. My mother and I exchanged glances: 'Another whack job.' Dr

Warthog. For the first time in weeks I managed a feeble laugh. Then, the strangest thing, relief flooded through my body. My angels, holistic voodoo medicine, or just the passing of time, I felt better. On the mend.

I couldn't sue the hospitals, whatever damage they did. I'd signed away that right.* No signature, no treatment. But what I went through added, legitimately, to my pain/distress claims on various insurers and responsible parties. It was hard-won money, and I would rather have had the healthy spine I was born with, but I grossed around half a million – after everyone took their cut, about $250K. Probably more. Tax-free. It was all racking up. Unfortunately, it came in dribs and drabs. The last drib as late as 2013. More of which later. Take my word for it – there are easier ways to earn money.

* The hospital I was being treated in, those awful weeks, has since been closed. 'Filth', someone told me, was a reason.

9: ME, MICKEY ROURKE AND BAD TIMES

How did I put myself back together again and come to work for Mickey Rourke? A long story, which I'll keep as short as I can. You can pad it out, if you need to, with a Google search for Mickey Rourke + 2009. Plenty on record.

I'd been out of the PA business for years and, to be honest, I was not as young (now mid-thirties) as the sharpest in that line of work need to be. Not to mention the titanium where my L4 and L5 vertebrae used to be. I was no longer the guy who could fireman's-lift Bill Berry without an ominous twinge of the spine. I was no longer the eager beaver who'd worked for Stipe.

This would be my own forlorn comeback. The last time I'd take a PA job on. Gloriously and disastrously, as it would turn out. I'd left my high-paying jobs in chauffeured transportation, left my foreclosed-on house in chintzy Washington Heights. (Fuck the bankers who fucked the country and double-fuck those that wouldn't refinance my mortgage.) A friend, Albert, told me they needed a crane to get my eight-man Jacuzzi off the back deck, with its view over downtown, to auction. I hope it went to a good home.

The sheriff's notice had given me fourteen days, the last six of which I spent in a despairing weed stupor. I left Mount Eagle Place with my freshly installed titanium back (cost to my insurer, $450K), carrying my $1,800 Tumi briefcase that I treated myself to when Branson made me vice president. Inside the bag: a change of clothes, passport, and a photograph of my grandmother.

I hitched an upper class berth back to the UK on Virgin Atlantic. Aromatherapy at thirty-nine thousand feet. A last taste of what I'd left behind. In front of me, eight months of mother-care and overdue grandmother time. She, poor woman, didn't have a lot of time left. And I, for once, had all the time in the world.*

It all went serenely, until the inevitable disaster. As usual, self-inflicted. Riffling through my Tumi I discovered, idiot that I was, that I'd left my green card among all the clutter in the house – unpaid bills, etc.

My alien resident's permit had swung away into oblivion with the eight-man Jacuzzi, the five thirty-inch wall-mounted flat screens and a wardrobe of clothes which had cost me enough to retire on, if I'd had the sense to put the money into IRAs. That little plastic rectangle may, in fact, have been more valuable than everything else I lost, threw away or had stolen. Including the jewellery I left.

You can get thousands for a valid green card in Tijuana – especially one, like mine, which had no ten-year limit. And which had, dating back to my misspent youth, a picture of someone who looked as Mexican as Oscar De La Hoya. They didn't bother to counterfeit them south of the border. The scam was simpler. There's such a tailback at the port of

* *John.* You'll get a day or two off purgatory for what you did for your grandmother over the next months, Jack, if there's any justice in the afterworld.

entry, where Mexico meets the I-5, that if you're driving a car with California plates, and luck's with you, the immigration guy or gal just looks at the card, not even checking the picture, and waves you through. You then get someone legit to do the return journey, hand car and card over to the next customer. That one green card is a revolving door to riches beyond the dreams of campesino avarice.

Getting back home – the US – without that card was, I would discover, harder than getting a visa to Tibet. Trip after trip to the embassy in Grosvenor Square and calls to their £2-a-minute premium phone line got me nowhere. I now had no American address. No job over there. No family members resident. I hadn't filed a 2008 tax return. And I owed.

It would have been easier crossing the Rio Grande with the indocumentados, except, at this stage, I probably couldn't have come up with the cash in hand for the kind of coyote who wouldn't cut your throat to save himself the trouble of cutting the fence. They didn't take American Express.

I finally got the stamps, and letters, that would get me over the yellow line at LAX. They're nice guys at the embassy, but they don't hurry. They know you'll wait. And wait. And wait. I had, in various accounts, a stash of about $150K from the medical malpractice suits I'd brought. That was all that was left from the near-half-million which had been fallen on by chomping chiropractors, electrotherapists, epidural needle merchants, the IRS, and, biggest chompers of all, lawyers. My titanium vertebrae, full-body brace and that nest egg were all that was left of my litigation gold. There was a final chunk to come my way, but my lawyer warned me it would be two years. And have his teeth marks all over it.

The insurance companies were increasingly resistant to Mr Sutherland's never-ending claims and the lawyer needed me back, to sign settlement papers, draw up affidavits, and undergo the necessary physical examination with hired physicians. Then it was get in line for our day in court and pray for no delay motions from the other side.

I hired, over the phone from England, an immigration lawyer ($2K, up front) and flew back Virgin upper class. Victoria Beckham, looking diamond-flawless after an eleven-hour flight with kids in tow, was behind me in the immigration queue: in the no-hassle VIP and aircrew lane, probably. She, it turned out, would get through a hell of a lot quicker.

The INS officer gave me grief – I'd been away for more than six months, which put me in the 'residency abandonment' category. The bastard chose not to look at the dates on my embassy documentation. Just dates of egress and ingress. They have absolute power at that desk. No appeal. Get one whose girlfriend's just dumped him and you're likely to find yourself on the next plane back to where you came from. You should, if you're sensible, play it very cool, standing there, looking into the iris-recognition lens. But I still had big anger issues – the last rehab had helped, but not fixed them. I was dumped, raging wildly, into the tank for four hours, until there was a change of shift and a more sympathetic officer. Welcome home, Jack.

I'd planned a ten-day trip. Just to sign medical settlement papers and immigration forms to get my new green card.

Then back to the UK to hunker down for a couple more months, till my money finally ran low and I landed a job. With cars, probably. I'd cross that bridge when I came to it. I wasn't anxious. Something always turned up.

I got it badly wrong. My immigration lawyer coolly informed me I needed a no-exit stay in the US for six months. Leave during the application and it's five years. If you're lucky. It would also help greatly to get an employer and since I would cross the 15 April deadline, file an up-to-date tax return. And I should get a bona fide address to register and receive the dispatched card: no PO boxes or parking lots.

LA was now my Devil's Island. (Remember to look at *Papillon* again for hints.) What, seriously, to do? I couldn't apply for a long-term job with a big firm, without 'status'. Federal law, even with Obama in the White House, was getting tough on that. But, as I say, in this kind of jam it's not what you know, but who you knew. I reached out to David Unger, a big shot at International Creative Management (ICM). He would be, this time round, my 'who you know'.

I'd known David since he'd left college. We'd both worked on the bottom rungs of Propaganda Films' music video department, back in the early 1990s. In Southern California, in that line of business, twenty years is two lifetimes.

When I first befriended him, David was textbook-smart, frighteningly so, but green. He'd barely taken his mortar board off before starting his career in the entertainment industry. I, at the time, was an intern. He had been brought in as an assistant to Rhea Rupert, director of music video. I helped David where I could (not that he needed much). He was long-time grateful. I met up with him, meaningfully, in 2006, when he was the rising man at ICM. I myself was earning big at Empire-CLS.

We had lunch, I remember, at the Boulevard – prestige eatery inside the Regent Beverly Wilshire. The hotel was a client of mine and I rather enjoyed swaggering a bit for Unger – now very big in Hollywood. (You may know the hotel – it's where they filmed *Pretty Woman.*) Unger was duly impressed by the VIP treatment and courtesy meal. We'd both come up in the world.

It was one of those useful catch-up lunches. He put some high-end chauffeur business my way. Then he told me Mickey Rourke was a client. Mickey's latest film had been *Sin City*, that Rodriguez graphic-novel adaptation. Out of the blue, David asked me would I be interested in PA-ing for his man. When I told him, ballpark (plus a bit over – everyone does it in Hollywood), how much I was pulling in from CLS, he changed the subject and we concentrated on the petits fours and reminiscence about the Propaganda days.

Now, three years later, I was holed up, for economy, in a $80-per-night motel near Burbank airport (earplugs at night) with a rented C-Class Mercedes. I was ashamed to be seen on the Sunset Strip. That awful question – 'WhatyadoingJack?' My dad visited that summer and I wouldn't even meet him at the Sunset Tower, where I'd hooked him up, but arranged the encounter in a nearby Starbucks lot. He couldn't work out what was going on – I looked clean, and in great physical shape. If he'd been streetwise – which, God bless him, he isn't – he could have worked it out from the very un-Jack C-Class Mercedes.* I was scraping bottom. Not quite panhandling with a hard-times piece of cardboard but, from where I'd been, very low. I was getting by on advances of future settlement money.

Who, I wondered in my little Burbank Gitmo, did I 'know'? I riffled through my mental Rolodex and came up with David Unger, one-time boy wonder and now well on his way to master of the agency universe. I phoned him, direct line, and told him my dilemma. 'I'm banged up in the US for six months. Do you have any clients who need an assistant of my proven calibre?'

No CV, application or interview required. 'Leave it with me,' he says, and gets back next day. Always a good sign in Hollywood. 'I've got the perfect gig,' he tells me: 'Neil Patrick Harris.' Harris is a lot bigger in the US than in Britain.† He made his name with *Doogie Howser, MD* and the Harold & Kumar stoner-comedy films. I didn't much like his stuff, but I admired Neil personally as a gay guy who'd bravely come out publicly. He was, apparently, between contracts. I'd be perfect, short-term. Details to be worked out.

All set. But the next day I got yet another call from David. 'I know I hooked you up with Neil,' he said, 'but I'd rather you took on Mickey Rourke. He could use someone with your skills.'

I never got even to meet Neil Patrick Harris. It might

* *John*. I did wonder what the hell was going on. Jesus, I drove a five-year-old Ford Fiesta in England.

† *John*. His film-stealing performance in *Gone Girl* has recently made him big in the UK. He seems to love playing madly hetero characters. One sniffs sarcasm.

have worked. Who knows. I took the Rourke gig. It sounded exciting. And so it turned out.

THE MAN

Who, then, was this person I was going to be touching-close to for the next six months? Let me, looking back on those eventful 2009–2010 months, sum Mickey Rourke up as best I can.

One of the stresses in a PA's life is that they see what lies behind the image. No man is a hero to his valet, they used to say. Most PAs would nod to that. But the gap between public image and the real thing is closer with Rourke than most anyone else I've worked for ('with', 'under', 'alongside' – take your pick; I've adopted more ass-in-the-air positions than a porn starlet in my PA jobs).

Even to the valet/PA there's something truly heroic in Rourke. In *Barfly* he played Chinaski, that drunken down-and-out genius whose main recreation in life was getting into fights when words failed him. Mickey's a moderate drinker (nowadays) but he had lived a life not entirely unlike the barfly's for the best part of fifteen years, after having tasted superstardom. Five hundred dollars a week was a good week in those bleak years. And he wasn't, by his own account, 'moderate' in his intakes.

You'll note the yawning gap in his Wikipedia entry. Only his agent, David Unger and one dog (he had five when I came into his life) kept faith with him. For six months I polished the shrine to his beloved late chihuahua Loki, complete with memorial statuette, and kept the candle burning there day and night.*

Then, just like the fighters Rourke most admired, the comeback. Or was it? At the end of *The Wrestler*, when 'The Ram' jumps off that corner post, is he going down, or coming up, 'the winner!!!!', for the last time? Ali versus Foreman, or Ali versus Holmes? Aronofsky did it perfectly. The enigma of Mickey Rourke.

Deep down my belief is that he's in that classic tradition of actors who don't buy Hollywood but every now and then let Hollywood buy them. I'd look at him in a film, when he hadn't been putting his all into his performance, and think of that other 'Irish' star, Robert Mitchum's, sour verdict on his craft: 'Making faces and speaking somebody else's words isn't a job for a man.'

Rourke should, if there was any justice in the film world, have got an Oscar for *The Wrestler*. Six months before I was employed by him he explained, to the entertainment press, why that would never happen: 'I stupidly once said acting wasn't a job for a real man. I threatened producers, raged at directors, forgot my agent's name. I really burned my bridges. And a lot of people have long memories.' Telling it as it was didn't get him any votes from the academicians. Living dead, most of them. I saw a Joan Rivers joke in the reports of her death: 'The people voting for the Oscars are so old I haven't seen one voter with a tampon in her purse.' And the men? Beyond Viagra – but, as Mickey Rourke says,

* It was also a shrine to his brother, whose early death devastated him. All this is on the public record – often rather sneered at. I wasn't inclined to sneer. I love dogs. More than humans, sometimes.

with elephant memories for any badmouthing of their precious selves.

What's 'real' manhood? The answer vibrates off Rourke's screen persona, when he really is putting his all into the part. You feel fists in the words. Often, at the most memorable moments, they're his words. Like Brando, and Welles, he ad-libs and improvises his best on-screen monologues. The *Body Heat* cameo, or the monologues, wrecked Coney Island in the background, in *The Wrestler*. It's the Irishness in his blood.*

What would be Rourke's idea of a job for a man? No prizes for that. A 'fighter' (not a boxer, or a pugilist). He tried twice and won an impressive number of his fights. But he had, in common with other boxers who come forward in the ring all the time, taking punishment to hand more back, to weigh up physical mid-career risk, dementia pugilistica. You go punchy. After a couple of serious concussions, his doctors solemnly advised retirement. Which he did. Ruefully.

And then, having hung up his gloves and saved his brain, he had to make do with being Mickey Rourke, the film star who could, perhaps, had life dealt him a better hand, have been a contender. Like Terry Malloy (Brando's Irish act in *On the Waterfront*, hugely influential on Mickey's acting style). Stardom, for someone like Rourke, will always be second best. Hollow manhood.

One last thing. He's instinctively generous. I'm not thinking of madnesses like those six Cadillacs which he bought (for cash), then gave away. Or the $60K worth of his clothes

* *John*. Please, spare us that Irish-blood stuff.

that he gave me (we're of a size) while I worked for him. What I mean is small 'kindness of stranger' things.

I'll give one example. We're walking back from some nightspot, in New York winter. He needs the air. Bitter cold. Mickey sees some dirty, homeless-looking guy, apparently semi-conscious across the sidewalk. New Yorkers are stepping over and around him like he's a large dog turd. Maggots in the Big Apple. Mickey takes off his coat, puts it under the guy's head, then kneels down and starts reassuring him that everything is going to be OK. He stays by his side, keeping him calm. He instructs me to call an ambulance. He waits by the man's side the entire time until the paramedics arrive, sirens ringing. They realise the Good Samaritan looking after the homeless guy is the legendary Mickey Rourke and start whispering amongst each other. They've seen everything but this is something. Mickey makes sure the guy's on his way to ER. Then he shucks out his coat with a quick flick and puts it back on. He lights up a cigarette and we continue our way home.

Nothing else was said about it. It was so nonchalant. There were no reporters around, and he'd forget having done it next day (though I bet the guy remembered, if anyone believed him). Why did he do it? Like they say of the frog and the scorpion, it's his 'nature'.

They say it about all of the stars but it's truer about Rourke than most. He always has time for fans. He's courteous to anyone serving him and is a generous tipper. On the other side, he can be surly with the powerful and the rich – emphasise 'can'. I admired the way his roles fitted his character. Tough, uncompromising, but only hard in the ring.

Rourke did lots of things like helping that guy in the street while I was with him. Not – lest I overdo the violins – that he couldn't be a royal pain in the arse, as well. But, Christ, that's what the PA arse is for. Ask any of us.

THE MEET

The background to my future employment was as follows. Mickey – riding high on his *Sin City*, *The Wrestler* and yet-to-be-released *The Expendables* and *Iron Man 2* roles – was scheduled to do a film called *Passion Play*. He would lead opposite Megan Fox, herself riding high on the just-released gothic-horror comedy *Jennifer's Body*. Great, underrated film. Bill Murray was going to drop in for a while and play a villain. Mitch Glazer directed. A top team.

It was new ground for Megan and Mickey – a tender love story. They wanted to establish themselves as actors with depth. (Mickey is, in fact, much more versatile than his tough-guy persona suggests.) The film would, sadly, be a flop. Mainly because of criminally bad editing, in my view.

The on-screen connection between Mickey and Megan was intense. Things really flamed between them. Bill Murray (the villain) was something else. Ever since *Ghostbusters* I'd been a see-every-movie fan of his. He's only got one on-screen character: Bill Murray – laid-back, terrific timing, ironic, like he's over your shoulder, laughing with you at that guy Bill Murray.

Off-camera, he was the same. Funny as fuck and easy-going. There was this one day on the set when he hired the largest mariachi band I have ever seen. All-female and sexy. Blowing their little hearts out. Christ knows where he found them. Christ knows what he paid. They were wearing the costumes Steve Martin, Chevy Chase and Martin Short wore in *Three Amigos!*: all black with silver stitching and matching sombreros. Cute.

Bill had me ('Would you be so kind, Jack?') open the door to Mickey's star wagon without knocking (always dangerous) and these chicks poured in one by one, playing to burst your eardrums. I was pissing myself with laughter. Murray's best-ever comic moment for me. He did the same in Megan's wagon.

How had Mickey taken it? He was laughing too. Thank fuck for that.

Mitch Glazer was cunning about the first scene in the movie, in which Mickey and Megan meet. He insisted they must not meet off-screen, to create on-screen surprise. Everyone had to be very careful to keep them apart. They mustn't even catch sight of each other.

The film opens with Megan in a travelling circus, held, for some reason, in a glass display box, with the light dimmed. Mickey comes in after crossing the desert, having just had his life saved. (Is it a dream?) He stumbles into the viewers' side of the booth and pulls the switch cord down to throw the light on beautiful Megan Fox, who looks angelic. She then stands up and actual angel wings slowly unfold. My Christ – she is an angel. Mickey didn't know that was coming. It's on his face. (You can see the scene in the YouTube trailer.)

That woman's beautiful on screen. The lens doesn't 'like' her – it's crazy about Megan Fox. Even a gay male like me was blown away when I saw that angel stuff on playback. I asked Mickey about it and he said it's a gift that some stars have. Call it the Marilyn Effect. Off-screen you wouldn't have known her from Lucille Ball.

I repeat: *Passion Play* is a great, undervalued movie, destroyed on its early showings by crap editing. It's been cleaned up. Give it a try.

But all this was far in the future, and confidence was high in September 2009, when my Rourke stint began.

I headed down from Burbank to the ICM offices for a client preparation meeting with David. The meeting was epic – almost two hours of me taking notes – and by the time we were done I had what looked like an encyclopaedia's worth of notes containing everything that a PA might have to know, and the world shouldn't know, about Mickey Rourke. I wouldn't have been surprised if Unger had asked me to eat it after reading.

One thing really impressed me. Mickey did not use long-term PAs – not his style. Fine, of course, given my own current timetable. It might be another problem that he had problems with LA. He'd made no friends, ten months earlier, telling an English reporter who asked him whether losing in the ring, or losing your reputation in film, was worse. The second, Mickey thought: 'It's way, way worse. It's so much worse. Especially if you're living in a shithole town like LA, a town that's based on envy.' The Hollywood ('shithole') welcome mat, as you might say, was permanently furled for Mr Rourke.

Mickey, I learned, was flying in next day from New York. With a dog. A fluffy white-haired Pomeranian. It was a gift for a girl he had a crush on – Anastassija ('Ana') Makarenko. A stunning Russian model. Over the months I was with Mickey he would date Ana, then they would become a couple.

I made sure his arrival at LAX was silk-smooth. I arranged gate clearance (I'd had contacts and greased palms at LAX for ten years) and I met Mickey as he deplaned – if I didn't know the face behind the rock-star shades, there weren't too many passengers cuddling Pomeranians.

The luxury Empire-CLS chauffeur-driven SUV was waiting at the kerb. Luggage all taken care of. I made sure that his favourite magazines (boxing, male fitness, style) were in the rack at the back, with Badoit (it was daytime, no alcohol) and Marlboro Lights. He probably needed a refreshing drag or two of his preferred brand after the five-hour flight. Then me alongside the driver, no peeks in the rear-view mirror, everything by the book as the Town Car glided, noiselessly, to the Four Seasons Beverly Hills – his favourite hotel, as David's dossier had instructed me. Dog food and bowls on a rug – spare lead, and poop bags and dog blankets, if he hadn't brought them. He hadn't.

He and Unger met that afternoon for a catch-up. I'm, at this point, in security mode. On all-round defence for gawpers, snappers and paps. The enemy. When required, I switch to discreet valet mode. Tricky – I haven't seen him undressed yet. Always an awkward moment. And, of course, I'm a bodyguard as well. Not that I'm in his class (he could take me in seconds, and three like me), but better I face charges for any manhandling than him.

In short, Jack of all fucking trades. And, God help me, I'm enjoying it so much. I feel like a teenager again.

As valet, I unpack his bags, wardrobe and steam-press and dry the close-to-body items. His travelling clothes will be dry-cleaned by morning. He has, I note, an extraordinarily colourful wardrobe for a straight man. He's going a bit cowboy at the moment. As I get his things in order, it becomes clear to me he has a wholly incompetent houseboy in New York. He hasn't packed necessaries. Sharp phone calls and express delivery of said items by courier express, next day by noon. Latest.

I may have to do something about that houseboy. A few hours later, Mickey gives me a pay rise. I share an elevator with Hugh Grant. This hotel is Celebrity Central. I was breathing oxygen again and basking in starglow.

Mickey's not in LA for long. He's here to catch up with David and win Ana's heart. The dog helps. My initial impression of her? Beyond beautiful in the flesh, tall, lovely husky voice with a lot of deep Russian in it, no cosmetic aid required, and very, very warm personality. And so beautiful. Put it all together and I could love her myself. Nothing will happen, over the next months, to change that first impression.

From the opening, Mickey let me do a lot for him. As long as I didn't get in his way. I felt like a cornerman, between rounds. Occasionally bustlingly in charge, irrelevant during the action. It was a crazy week in LA, but normal for him, apparently. One high point was a big boxing match between the Ukrainian man-mountain Vitali Klitschko and local Hispanic hope Chris Arreola (aka 'The Nightmare'). If you look at the YouTube highlights, you'll see me alongside Mickey. Looking good. We had ringside seats, just along from Schwarzenegger and Stallone in the same row.

The Governor, Sly and Mickey knew each other from *The Expendables*, which was due for release.

I had a special interest in that fight. I'd had a warm-up myself, months ago, with Arreola's little (i.e. 220 pounds) brother, nicknamed Risky, at Circus & Arena. He'd picked on my friend Albert. I was very wasted. Alcohol, ecstasy, marijuana. Violent-intoxicated. I couldn't remember anything as I sat in Kaiser's ER the next morning, waiting for the X-rays (fractured rib, bust-up hand, and a lot of very painful bruises). The whole thing had been caught on CCTV. I had been berserk. If it meant anything (it didn't), I was holding my own when security pulled us apart. Berserk can sometimes beat pugilistic skill. (Risky, I suspect, sparred with his brother in training.) Gene La Pietra, after giving me a private view of the video in his office, was not pleased. Watching that video hurt more than my injuries.

Klitschko steamrollered Arreola. It was an ugly fight and the referee stopped it in the eleventh round on a TKO. The local boy had guts. To be honest, quite a few were hanging over his Everlast waistband. I'm not sure Mickey wasn't rooting for him. Me, remembering my bruises, I was all for the Ukrainian.

Later that week I met another of the *Expendables* team, Jason Statham. He got not merely my attention, but my instant worship. He rolled up to the Four Seasons patio in an impeccable Audi R8. The valets were fighting like cats to get the keys. There were only a couple of the vehicles on the road. Prospective owners were paying surcharge to get their early deliveries. Audi gave it to him, I believe, as a reward for the S8 sedan which was his car in the *Transporter* movies. The car, with Jason Statham in it, was freeway product placement.

That car, the R8, was the real star for an old limo-hack like me. I went schoolgirl on it. The *Transporter* movies I could take or leave. I never quite got with the *Expendables*, either – the guys looked so damn different off-screen. Except Mickey, who played old, tired and beat-up (brilliantly) in the first movie, and ducked out of the others. He was more into real-life tough than Rocky/Rambo stuff.

After our crazy week, Mickey and I went back to New York, where he had the whole floor of a building in the fashionable Meatpacking District (where they filmed *Sex and the City*). I'd guess thirty thousand square feet in all. Size of two basketball courts and looked even larger on a clear day.

When we walked through the door I realised my first job would be to move the houseboy on. It wasn't the forgotten-suitcase business. That could be forgiven. The place looked as if it had been burgled. There were heaps of dog shit, fresh, caked and prehistoric. The rooms all had running hot and cold dog piss all over the floor.

Mickey went nuts. He'd have to go. He was also, bottles revealed, a full-time drunk. So, with the lightest of hearts, I sent the ex-house manager on his way to AA and oblivion. We now, of course, needed a new houseboy. Another came and went. I then suggested a young gay guy I'd had friendly intimacies with in LA. He was an ultra-camp Mexicano who'd modelled himself on Lady Gaga. And taken her professional name as his. Gaga was sweet, and I liked him. All intimacies stayed, fondly, in the past. No bonking the underlings. Rule One.

Surprisingly, when I told Mickey there was this West Coast Latin drag queen hoping for the job, he responded favourably. Ramrod-straight as he is, Rourke is very comfortable around gays. (Had Unger sold him to me on that ticket?) You don't have to be Sigmund Freud to work out why. Gays offered no physical threat in a world which was, as he saw it, full of physical threats. Gaga was flown out and was perfect.

This may be the place for a round-up of the howling Rourke pack. They were all over him when he got back – he looked like a mountain of seething fur. Gang-raped by canine love.

There was Ruby, a timid rescue dog – miniature and who-knows-what breed. I liked her the most. Max, a Jack Russell terrier, had a mean streak. He once drew blood from Mickey's lip. Very few two-legged animals could have done that and walked away whole. I myself was a bit nervous round Max.

There was a hugely obese black pug, whose name I've forgotten and can't be bothered to Google (let's call him Jabba the Pug). Mickey loved him. There was a Pomeranian, Mr Friendly, brought in to keep Ana's dog company. There were others, whose names and breeds I've forgotten, though if I try hard I can recall their rear ends. I saw a lot of those. Anus city.

Presiding over the living, excreting canines, the statue and shrine of faithful chihuahua Loki, who'd stuck with his owner over the bleak years. He was Mickey's personal Greyfriars Bobby (that Victorian Scottish terrier so faithful to his dead master that he visited his grave every day for fourteen years. Bobby's got a statue as well). The living hounds also got unconditional love. I witnessed Mickey pay $25K for a heart operation on Mr Friendly. You could have bought a castle in Pomerania for that kind of money.

And, completing Mickey's animal kingdom, Sunnybird the white cockatoo. He was played by a trained bird actor in *Iron Man 2*. Mickey insisted on his pet getting in on the act, although it does, I think, play out rather unconvincingly in the screen narrative. Sunnybird had a big thing for me. I fed it. Easy enough to get a bird's love.

Harder to get an employer's respect. As the weeks slipped by, I tactfully assumed a management role. Negotiating Mickey's appearances at, say, a Las Vegas fight night or a club. The fees, with photographers in attendance, were high. Particularly if you could get into the glossy 'in town this week' pages. So now there were two other trades for all-trade Jack. Night chauffeur and (unofficial) impresario. Not in charge: just helpful when necessary.

I used to thank God every time Ana came to town. A furlough for Jack – they wanted to be alone. It was no secret that Mickey was madly in love. The gossip mags were full of it.

When we had to, we two went to 'shithole' LA. He was getting his wardrobe for *Passion Play* done by industry costumiers. He was fitted, I carried.

It was knackering. I kept myself relaxed, after the day's toil, with maximum-grade marijuana. The supply was very NY. I made my connection via one particular late-night relief bonk on the fire escape (I did quite a lot of that – for relief), while Mickey was sleeping. My guy gave me the number of a quasi-commercial supplier who, in thirty minutes, would scooter the stuff to your door like Domino's Drugs. No risk whatsoever to the receiving party.

He'd come to the door, open his zippered sample case. Row upon row of MJ in plastic vials, $40 a pop. A narcotic smorgasbord. It beat the LA medical marijuana clinic any day of the week. And that (every day) is how often I was, by now, calling on Drugs R Us. I was occasionally doing ecstasy. Nothing, by my standards, hard. Just maintenance dosages. Mickey never knew. I think. Or he was either tolerant or indifferent. Drunkenness was something else. He didn't like it. I never touched the stuff.

Everyone was getting antsy. Ana, pursuing her own career, was often out of town. The funding for *Passion Play* kept falling out, and production was pushed back. Mickey, meanwhile, was training for the part – getting back to his fighting weight, as he had for *The Wrestler*. An MMA cage fighter was recruited. (Pretty guy – I had a huge, hopeless crush on him. But being near a star somehow drains away all your own sexual appeal.) Mickey loved it – a new kind of fighting.

He was also taking trumpet lessons: the hero of the film, Nate, is a small-time jazz musician, riddled with addictions. As I saw it, Mickey had no problems in those directions. Nowadays, I repeat. In the past, he had done enough to keep the *National Enquirer* headline writers busy day and night, week in week out, years on end. Broken, messy marriages, and an obstinate, wholly mysterious refusal to evolve his career. He spurned directors who offered him plum parts (as did Tarantino on *Pulp Fiction* – a movie that would have fitted Mickey like a glove. Willis got the boxer's role and enjoyed a huge career boost). And he'd gone off the rails, big time, when his little brother, Joey, died of lung cancer in 2004. That was still a painfully sore thing with him.

They'd both been beaten, as children, by an ex-cop step-father from hell. 'I come from a violent background,' Mickey would explain. And he wanted revenge on that background. But by 2009, as far as I could see, violence had burned down, leaving something interesting and, I have to say it, rather lovable. Now in his mid-fifties, he told a reporter, Chris Sullivan, he felt he had reached a new phase: 'I'm not angry with anyone now. I'm just grateful for this second chance with my career.' *The Wrestler*, he added, 'was a gift from God'. Scar tissue, of course, remained, on his personality, in his heart and on his face. Most of it was boxing, part of it cosmetic. 'I went to the wrong guy to put my face back together', was how he put it. False economy, but he was happy to live with it.

After the first six weeks I felt proud of doing what Unger had wanted. Protecting Mickey from Mickey, was how he put it. And protecting him from the vultures forever circling for a 'story' – fuck truth.

At last, four months on, production started on *Passion Play*. We took off for New Mexico, leaving Gaga to look after the apartment – now, without its human occupants, one of the bigger dog kennels in the Western world. It was December. And witch's-tit cold. Till we got a house (on top of a snowy mountain), we stayed in Santa Fe's best hotel. Mickey had the presidential suite.

There was a small disaster. Jabba the Pug (still forget the pooch's name) had a fatal heart attack while he was being bathed. Gaga phoned me, nervous as fuck. I too was so nervous I phoned David Unger, long-distance, to ask how I could handle it. 'Just tell him,' he said. So I went to the table where Mickey was eating with Mitch and the other guy in the film, Rhys Ifans. They were talking scripts, sets, shots and business.

I drew Mickey aside and broke the news. As I did so I my eyes moistened – not fake. I was worried for him, not the dead dog. He took it calmly. I felt foolish. Eyes dried.

Mickey and Ana wanted to get back to New York for their first Christmas together. He said I could take off to London, but I stayed. I wanted to help make their holiday special. Particularly for Ana. Mickey had told me, when I started to work for him, 'Treat my friends and family as if they were me.' He wanted her parents flown in, from Germany, as a surprise present. They'd never been to the US. I arranged visas and the guest suite – even down to German and Russian channels on the cable flat screens.

Things happened. They always do. It all went to pieces for me that terrible Christmas – on 23 December, to be precise. We were still in Santa Fe, but preparing to leave.

Driving Ana back from the set, I got a phone call from Albert in LA. BJ, he told me, had passed away. HIV, massive amounts of crystal meth and alcohol are what I assume did it. We had been on and off for almost five and a half years. I was not prepared to be monogamous. I was far too popular on the Latin gay scene to commit to only one guy. He had accepted my terms. My way or no way. Bastard that I was. He wore a gold-and-diamond ring I'd bought for him until the day he died – he could have traded it for crystal. Most terminally hooked addicts would have done, to get that last big hit.

After we broke up for the last time, BJ and I would meet up a few times a month. He contracted. I still remember the day he told me. The whole world around me just stopped. Frozen frame.

For the first time in my life, I realised what 'heartbreak' means. He'd left me for another man, and I could handle that. But not HIV. That was a different level. From then on, every time we met for a catch-up, there were always the same two things we talked about. The first was whether everything was good with his HIV status. It was always the same response: everything all good and the doctors were happy.

The second thing was, 'You dating anyone?' Again, he always had the same answer. 'No. I am single and will stay single. I am just waiting for the day that you come back to me. I am here waiting for you, whenever you're ready.'

I always used to jokingly ask for the ring back as we were not together any more, and he would say, 'But some day we will be.'

He'd been trying to phone me for weeks. I left his calls to my answering service and either never picked up or kept it super-short. 'BJ, I'm with my client – I'll call you back.' Too busy, I told myself. He must have called me about eighteen times in the three weeks before he passed away. Not one conversation or callback did I manage. Too busy with My Client. I cry now when I think about it. I'm not sure I'll live long enough to forgive myself. Albert told me he'd refused medication. AIDS was no longer a killer. For BJ, I was the killer.

I fell apart.

I was scheduled to drop Ana at the house in Santa Fe, then drive to Albuquerque to pick up Mickey from the set.

I didn't. I went to the liquor store and bought a litre of vodka, which I glugged, from the bottle, in the car. Before the alcohol hit, I managed to get the car back to the hotel, on autopilot. Ana confronted a PA who was slurred, blurred and snottily hysterical. Some assistant.

I go to my room and wreck it, Ozzy Osbourne-style. Ana, good woman, nurses me, comforts me and takes me to their suite. She arranges to have Mickey picked up and driven back by one of the crew. I, by now, can't stand up, let alone drive. He comes back. Righteously angry. 'I need you to get through this,' he says. Yes, I promise (but what do a drunk's promises mean?). Then, God help me, I pass out on a bed in their suite.

When I wake up, remorseful, in the morning, I have one hour to pack their stuff. 'Don't fall apart on me,' said Mickey. 'Be a man.'

Running on PA reflexes I get it all done, pack the bags, have the cars brought up, and we make it, by minutes, to the VIP line in the airport. Saved. It's the first of a series of last-minute crises.

Everything, as I've arranged, is ready and decked out in the New York loft for Christmas Eve. Ana walks in, sees her parents, and breaks down with sheer happiness. I leave them to their happiness and go to my room, call up adam4adam, and arrange, on the stairs, to meet an Asian guy who will bring a pile of crystal meth and the necessary paraphernalia. I sneak him into my room. Chemsex all night. No satisfaction.

I'd done crystal half a dozen times or so, when working for Virgin. This, however, was suicidal-intense, not dabbling.

Hits and orgasms hours on end. I didn't want satisfaction. I wanted oblivion. And death. In that order and the sooner the better. None of this comfortably-numb shit. I had to be out of my head and my thoughts. There was not one minute that I was not high on something.

One of the things about crystal is that you don't need sleep. It was a small mercy that night. The exhausted parents had gone to their bedroom, which I'd decked out with overnight candles. The father had, as he fell asleep, pushed a satin-cased feather pillow onto a candle. It ignited, flared, and soon was a bonfire. I smelled the smoke before the alarms went off, flung open the doors, and stamped out what could, in a few minutes, have been a funeral pyre. Unfortunately, while performing my fireman heroics, I was barefoot. The crystal anaesthetised the immediate pain, but I couldn't walk comfortably for days after. I'd bought enough crystal for a few weeks (hugely stupid; it made me liable for an 'intent to distribute' charge if I was found with it). One of the things about that drug is that you don't need to take it every hour, like coke (though quite often you do). And it doesn't intoxicate you, or make you falling-down stupid, like vodka. You can function. If anything, for a brief time, you're faster and more competent than ever. A further benefit is that crystal has no detectable odour. Makes it easier to disguise.

What it does, of course, is accelerate your life to warp speed. You want to know what you'll look like in twenty years' time? Buy a mirror and three months' supply of crystal. 'Meth rash' is worse than leprosy. I've had three teeth drop out during the time I've been doing this book. I'll need more implants than Katie Price if I ever want to eat rare steak again. Not that you worry about food when you're using. The amphetamine in the drug kills appetite and replaces it with its own expensive energy. By the time I'd been doing it for a couple of weeks, living on coffee, Mountain Dew and fresh squeezed orange juice, I had a twenty-eight-inch waist and a face that looked like one of the Native Americans at the end of the long walk to Wounded Knee. It's one hell of a diet plan, believe me. Forget Atkins. Trouble is, it doesn't just take the fat off your bones. It takes everything.

There's a picture of me shadowing Mickey at the Golden Globes in Los Angeles that January. He was presenting the Best Actor award, which he'd won the year, before and was dressed in outrageous cowboy style (check it out, Rourke + Golden Globes + 2010). I look like I'd been vacationing in the Valley of Death. But I was holding on. For now. Just. Running on fumes. Literally – fumes from the crystal pipe. I took two hits during the show.

After a wonderful break for my employers (not me), it was back to New Mexico for the main shoots in the film. Mickey and Ana would fly down south. I was instructed to drive his luxury conversion van, ahead of time, packed with mountains of gear – including four dogs, the cockatoo, and Loki's shrine.

The luxury conversion van wasn't an ideal vehicle. In fact, the dealer I leased it from, when I said where we were taking it, muttered 'death trap'. It was no good in snow (no four-wheel drive) and the mansion was on an ice-bound mountaintop. But Mickey was adamant about the vehicle. I was to get there first and set everything up. It was a five-day drive, at least. Mickey gave me three. Stars don't wait. I knew that well enough. And their wish is your command.

It meant eighteen hours a day non-stop at the wheel. Motels on the highways weren't dog- and cockatoo-friendly. They'd freeze to death in the car so Gaga and I were forced to smuggle in the animals each night. Thank fuck Mickey likes small dogs and not Rottweilers.

To top it all, the eastern seaboard is currently being battered by storms. Gaga is supposed to be my co-driver, except, with the overload we're carrying, and dangerous driving conditions (and, to be honest, maniac me), he is too frightened to take the wheel. He minds the dogs. Most of the trip his eyes are closed. Puffing my crystal meth pipe, and steering with my knees as I fire up every hour or so, I make it. Though that damned hill, even with the chains on the tyres, damn near defeats me.

We have just two hours to do the impossible. I get the house keys, me and Gaga unpack, steam, press and sort the clothes, settle in the yapping, squawking menagerie, get household essentials (and a sack of dog food) from Kmart, and warm the freezing house for the couple's arrival. Scented candles are lit, incense wafted.

I meet them at Albuquerque airport. What was it George Bush said? 'Mission Accomplished'.

It couldn't go on, of course. I was spiralling. Mickey was on the edge of really fire-the-bum anger. Rightly. I'd wake up of a morning, with the larks (are there any in New Mexico?*),

* *John*. Several varieties. The famed horned lark (*Eremophila alpestris*) would seem to be appropriate here.

then strong coffee, run a deep bubble bath. While my bath was running, I'd still be in a deep comatose state from the triple dose of my prescribed antipsychotics. That, combined with copious amounts of the strongest weed I could get my hands on, was the only way I could override the meth and get in a few hours of sleep. I would then grab my best friend, the meth pipe. Which I had meticulously prepared before I went to sleep the night before. It would be loaded with an extra-large amount of crystal, ready for the first hit.

Normally the first hit is the most amazing, as the warm rush starts to swirl though your whole body from head to toe. But being so doped-up on my meds, it would take me at least ten to fifteen huge-mega-hits. Then, all of a sudden, at about hit number eleven: what I was waiting for. I would throw in a few more hits just to be on the safe side. Then I would grab my breakfast – a huge glass of fresh orange juice and my second cup of coffee – and sit in the super-hot bath in a candlelit room with about four incense sticks burning. This was always my favourite part of my day – all alone apart from Sunnybird, who would be perched near the edge of the bath.

I would sweat my high off in forty minutes, keeping the bath boiling. Then I would take a warm shower, decreasing the temperature until it was freezing cold. The cold water would induce deep moaning – if any one overheard me they would have thought I was having a crazy sex session.

Then a third cup of java and my second helping of breakfast – another large glass of OJ. A few good hits of the meth pipe and then I would prepare what was needed for the day of shooting and fix Mickey's breakfast and coffee.

I'd wake him up, deliver his breakfast, then load the van.

After that, I'd be pretty much ready to go. Two more puffs on my meth pipe and I'd be 100 per cent awake and able to deal with another day of hell.

While Mickey got ready, it was time for the glass weed pipe and a few big puffs of the green, so it wouldn't be too obvious that I was jittering. We had a long drive to the set. In my business briefcase were all of Mickey's necessities. In my velvet red bag (which I was always spraying with cologne), my necessities. My stash, weed and weed pipe, which were in four separate zip-lock bags to hide the scent. I also had a bag of meth to top up the pipe, which was inside my designer jacket pocket. Be prepared, as the Scouts say.

There's no problem getting crystal in New Mexico (think *Breaking Bad*). And with meth the only non-liquid I was ingesting, perhaps I would actually starve to death before the drug did for me. I wouldn't, at that point, have minded. I blame my addiction and despise myself for my actions at this end phase. I made trip after trip to Albuquerque, or into Santa Fe, on invented reasons, simply to buy crystal, consciously provoking Mickey, who was constitutionally inclined to be kind, into firing me. I was writing my own last act. I wanted the freedom of a lost soul. I got what I wanted. Mickey Rourke is kind, but he's not a saint.

It reached, as they say, a head. I'd arranged for Mickey and Ana to go to a natural spring spa, an hour and a half away. After they'd gone, I made off to a nearby Albuquerque motorway motel – totally anonymous, unquestioning kind of place. I took their Jacuzzi suite and set up a meeting with a guy who could deliver, along with himself, enough crystal for us to party and enough to keep me going for a week. It started with the two of us but as the high got stronger, so did my desire for more guys.

'Let's do a threesome,' I suggested as I lit the meth pipe.

Time slid by without my noticing. When I did look at my phone, it was blowing up. A barrage of missed calls from Mickey, Ana and Gaga. Where the hell was I?

It was the first time in six months I'd deserted my post. It was Sunday – supposedly (but very rarely) my day off. I said I'd return next morning. No, I was told, return now. I had to do what I was told. PAs always do. There was a major storm brewing up. I drove through it. How I made it, I have no clue. Mickey was, understandably, also storming. Against me. I walked out on him and drove, back through the storm, to the Albuquerque motel. I was high, emotional and driving wholly illegally under the influence. And smoking in the car. I should have been locked up.

Ana reaches out – I must, simply must, come back. No, I won't. I'm partying. Ana demands that I get back by 9 a.m., and I agree just to get her off my back. At noon I look at my phone and again there are too many missed calls to count. I then realise there are six of us scattered around the suite. Where did they all come from? Who cares. I'll never see the parasites again. I have one quick play, then I hit the road to head back to what I know will be World War III. This is the first time I have upset Ana and Gaga; now it will be three against one.

I get back by 2 p.m. the next day. Mickey's not needed on set until 4. I can handle that. He's taking a nap. Gaga is wailing. Ana looks at me and sits me down. For the first time since I've known her, she's angry. Incredibly angry. I shrug it off, driving up the temperature. 'Just fire me,' I say. In other words, put me out of my misery. She does. I thank her and go to my room and start packing. Then the sleeping bear comes out of hibernation. For what comes next, read the preface.

It all ended very sordidly – not least the six different STDs I'd picked up along the way. But not (yet?) the big one. All the colours of the urogenital rainbow. I was a walking bacteria farm. There are other things at this point I don't want to share, can't share, even with my ever-forgiving father, who's putting all this down on paper. (He's looking at me very sadly at the moment.)

DARKER STILL

I managed to get myself together (Ana, bless her, helped discreetly) and limped back to Los Angeles. A fuck-up – certified by the world's expert on fucked-upness.

There is, I discovered, always more room at the bottom. I could have gone back to London and some kind of R&R. Instead I embarked on a five-day binge, the longest I'd ever gone on. No sleep, no food, just drugs and sex, sex and drugs. I'd booked into the Bonaventure – that space age-looking downtown hotel with the outside transparent elevators. I chose it because I'd never done enough business there to be known by the front-desk people. I took a suite so I could have 'guests'. And discreet deliveries of what I needed. I never went out – I looked like what I was, a fucked-up mess. If any of this sounds glamorous, or 'heroic' (James

Frey-style), it wasn't. It was squalid and shitty. In this spiral into the depths, I'd also given up taking my antipsychotic medication and the bipolar mania/depression cycle was spinning wildly and ever faster.

Most of my income and savings had gone to New Mexico dealers. But I'd come by a bit of family inheritance and other dollops of settlement money. I was afloat. Just. Don't, by the way, believe all that *Breaking Bad* crap about the wonderful 'Heisenberg' product: outside the American big cities it's scrapings from the bottom of the barrel. Like everything else, crystal follows the dollar. And the money is where the best-dressed people hang out. You want good stuff – go to Manhattan, or Beverly Hills.

Then the worst thing of all happened. On the second day of the binge, my mother phoned and left on the voicemail the news that her best friend – of whom I was very fond – had died. Some cruel cancer or other. Then, on the third day, she phoned to tell me my grandmother had passed away. The wonderful old lady had simply come to the end. No pain, just terminally finished with life. She'd lived enough. She was the kindest, most loving person I'd known in my life. I was her first grandchild – and she'd made me feel special. I should have been there. And where was I?

I slammed the phone down both times. Said nothing and rushed to the bathroom for the pipe. What I wanted was erasure. What I got, as before, was total exhaustion. My body, dammit, just wouldn't let its owner die. Yet. BJ, my gran, and Yvonne had died, but I was still in the land of the living. Or hell. I couldn't tell the difference at that point.

Miguel, ever-faithful but never entirely trustworthy, spent the last two days with me. He himself never touched drugs. 'You've got to get out of here,' he said. He packed my bags, cleaned up the room (orgies are not tidy affairs), and got me cleaned up as well. I could have cried, and did. And I got a few hours' sleep.

I should add a word on the relationship between me and Miguel, whom I have never seen since that awful time. It was complex. I saw him and loved him as my little brother. I had been, in the past, over-protective of him. I would have given my life for him and came near to doing so a couple of times. But our relationship was messy. We were best friends and, at the same time, lovers. This deep relationship had continued for years and gave me the funnest time I had of LA life. Miguel and I were inseparable. Today we're separated. And I'm truly sorry for all the pain I caused him.

Foiled in my attempts at self-destruction by self-abuse, I called Virgin and put my last remaining dollars into an upper class ticket back home. I booked a chauffeured car for the airport. I told check-in I was recovering from a recent back operation (it would also explain the way I looked) and I was wheelchaired on and off the plane. I had them pull out the bed as soon as I was aboard and swallowed a dangerously high dose of my Seroquel. While you're a passenger in that condition they treat you like a 200-pound Fabergé egg, till, that is, you hit that arrival line – then velvet turns to burlap and you're just a sack of ex-passenger. That's unfair, I know, to an airline which had been good to me. But it's how I felt.

'Get me orange juice,' I croaked from my wheelchair at my father, waiting, as always, at Heathrow. There was shock and horror on his face. I vomited the orange juice he brought me and burst into tears. He drove me back to my mother's flat. We didn't talk.

HOME. WHERE'S THAT?

I wasn't recovering over the next months, but I was staying alive. Seroquel helped, but cured nothing. It wasn't designed to. It's a keep-the-show-on-the-road drug. Over the following weeks I cleaned up, in a roundabout, month-clean, weekend-lapsing kind of way. Go to any LGBTQ-NA meeting and you'll find a few people in the group who get through life that bumpy way.

It's the loveliest of drug names, 'crystal'. It makes you think of the first fairy stories you heard, your parents reading to you in bed: the Snow Queen, a splinter of icy crystal in the eye. The reality is different. There are people who can 'use' drugs – everything from coffee to crystal. Recreational users. I'm not one of them. I'm an addict. Addiction is hell on earth. It's like smoking your own crucifixion. As I say, I survived to suffer on. For what? And for how long, oh Lord, how long? There is no 'why' in addiction. Explaining it to a normal person is like putting a GPS on a horse. Different planets.

There's an added complication if you go to a gay/transgender NA group. It has to do with the different natures of addiction. Crystal has this strange – unique, in my experience – property. Scientific reports I've read online say it has to do with pleasure receptors in the brain. With 'Tina', as she's called in London, sex is like 300 per cent plus of normal experience. Not only does the drug extend physical performance (for days, if you're in top shape and take the right dose), it heightens pleasure to levels you can't believe. Until, that is, you've been there. Then, God help you, you'll never not want to have that sexual high again. And again.

Miss Tina does not, like alcohol, give you blackouts (or brewer's droop, as my father's generation call it), nor, like heroin, does it send you into a semi-conscious, nodding-off doze, isolated. It makes you hypersensitive. Like experience is being burned on your brain. Unforgettably. Your penile brain remembers, as well. It craves, like an alligator jaw in your pants, for more. Sign on to Grindr, or look at any of the places that advertise hook-ups for gays, and you'll see something like 'Only chemsex, please.' Crystalfucks.

That's the upside. The downside is, when you're not chemsexing, it's less than 10 per cent of normal pleasure. It's not that you can't, with the right stimulation, get what you have to up, in, and out. It's just thrill-less. Hence that pattern I mentioned earlier: month off, weekend on. My problem, always, was that I couldn't – like some lucky addicts – keep to the more-or-less-stable-weekender pattern. I spiralled down, as the dosage spiralled up. I managed, by a heroic effort, to get by with vodka and marijuana (considerably stronger, I discovered, than what I'd got used to in the US. Skunk was a world-beater).

I kicked crystal but I needed something to kill the pain and remorse. I regained consciousness every day (after horrific dreams), staring at the ceiling, praying this would be the day that I died. Then I'd get angry at God. If there really was a higher power I hated him, her, it or them. Then guilt, tears and rage – against myself. Why didn't I just take a dignified farewell? I'd plotted over recent months any number of suicide plans. One was the *Thelma and Louise* exit at speed (though I might want something better than a clapped-out Mustang). High window in five-star skyscraper hotel onto a deserted night-time Sunset Boulevard was another possibility. A thousand dollars on the bed for staff inconvenience and whatever the 'Traumatic Scene Clean-up' service charged. (It's yellow-pages business in LA nowadays, no need to call in *Pulp Fiction*'s 'Wolf'.) The top-end Sunset Boulevard hotels looked high enough and smart enough and fairly empty at the back – looking south (I wasn't sure, though, I wanted to land on the dumpsters – I actually went into that mad level of planning). And, of course, overdose. That seemed, somehow, too 'gay'. Too Judy Garland. The Germans, I was once told, have something called 'autobahn suicide' (driving at high speed the wrong way into oncoming traffic) – but that means perhaps killing someone else.

I didn't do any of those things, much as I thought about them. I'd like to think it was because I didn't want to cause further hurt to the people I'd already hurt.

What could I do until the last payoff from the American insurance industry came in? One thing had struck me over my first few weeks – the almost copless nature of London. No prowl cars. No omnipresent blue line. Protect and serve had been outsourced, in London, at least, to the so-called 'security industry' – men in black at doors, standing everywhere that people drank, partied or clubbed. By night, central London looked like the invasion of the funeral directors.

Many of the security guys, as I would later find, were ex-military or police. It was a privatised army. I was now a drifter. Why not drift into the 'men in black' profession – at least for a while. I'd been instructed in close protection and security drills when working with Michael Stipe. All I needed, in London, was some basic training, introductions and a licence. If I chose to survive, dim visions were forming about starting my own close personal protection service. It needed its Horky.

I borrowed (call it that) four grand and got myself on the most reputable course I could find on the web. It mainly trained me in things I already knew or couldn't imagine finding a use for. But it was fun, in an all-guys-together kind of way. And good exercise. I particularly enjoyed the live firing ('Look at me, Mum, I'm Rambo') week in Slovenia.

I liked the company, if not the tiring and all-too-familiar barrack-room homophobia. I kept that side of me out of it. I've always been more the Ronnie Kray style of gay than Stephen Fry. No problem. I could ogle the air hostess and joke about poofs with the best of them (some of whom, my eagle eye could detect, were doing exactly what I was doing – taking cover in the portable closet). On the course the only drugs I touched were Guinness and local raki. A lot of other ex-military guys had picked up a speed habit in the services (where it actually has a use in front-line night-time combat).*

* *John.* I read somewhere that the US military is the largest purchaser of Viagra in the US. *Jack.* They go into battle waving their erections??

Once I got my close protection/Security Industry Authority badge* I went to work, mainly in the West End hotels. It's a high-fluidity profession. For a night owl with good lateral vision, some physique and chronic ADD, it's a fun(ish) job. It pays about twice minimum and the hours can be brutal, but if you build up a decent reputation, there's always work enough to scrape by on. And the work uses up so many hours, and energy, it keeps you from thinking too much.

The night world of London is very different from LA or New York. And, given the general absence of firearms, safer – although there are, believe me, gay gangsters. Sinister bastards. Most of the job is glad-handing with some occasional 'bouncing'. I could make enough doorkeeping, and managing doorkeepers, to scrape by, and get rest, relaxing intakes of drugs (mainly weed, no crystal or MDMA), and relief-sex in the city's bathhouses. They allowed condomed sex, if you were wise. Bareback if you didn't yourself care. No hassle if you just wanted to zonk out. Naked, steamed-up, it was a bubble world where you weren't you. No one was anyone. Just flesh. If heaven exists I see it as a great bathhouse in the sky. I was holding on – just.

The main problem for me was ego – I was diminished: a little man. The world had become like one of those funhouse mirrors that throw back an image of you as a midget. What was I, AD 2011? Snow White's eighth dwarf, Druggy. He used to be Biggy, poor little man.

It hit me with my first job at Bungalow 8. (The London venue is closed now, I believe.) It was a classy chain

* Hostile environment, close protection, level 3.

of members-only clubs and I'd got the position through a friend. I'd been to high-end clubs all over the world and thrown twenties around like confetti, lording it. Here I was on £10 p.h. What, apparently, I was worth nowadays. Try running a Corvette (or even a fucking Subaru) on that. I could barely afford a night bus. Worst of all, I didn't, apparently, look out of place on it. I fit in. That hurt.

I'd been a couple of months dry and clean(ish). God, take me back to Arena, I thought every night as I put my dark suit and badge on and larged myself up to be your friendly, but hard if he has to be, doorman. What was humiliating was that no one seemed to want me for the more prestigious security positions I applied for. I applied for plenty.

In fact, I wasn't on the door at Bungalow 8 – I was even lower than that. I was in charge of the 'smoking area'. Regulations meant only twenty could be allowed out there to puff at any one time, though it could easily hold two or three times as many. No drinks were allowed outside and, since it was a residential area, noise had to be kept down. I was supposed to act as the warden. I was, I think, the most insulted guy in the West End of London over those weeks. Tell someone who's had a few drinks, is a member, to leave their glass, wait their turn, and talk quietly in a nightclub and the snot deluge is Niagara. 'You fucking 5p-an-hour loser,' they would say. The more polite ones. I would bulk up and say, politely, 'Regulations, sir, sorry.' It was humiliating.

I didn't have authority and I didn't get respect. One of the many times it got nasty was one night when a couple of B-list stars (you'd know their names)* came by, after the *GQ* Men of the Year Awards. The stars themselves were nice enough – insofar as they didn't notice me. Why should they? I was a lesser life form. A human microbe.

Their entourage, doing what they saw as their jobs (big fucking deal), could be ugly. Very ugly indeed when I had to stop one of the B-listers from going out into my smoking area ('Regulations, sir, sorry'). The star didn't mind standing awhile (he didn't really notice – he was surrounded by admirers and wasn't himself dying for a fag), but one of the three guys escorting him put his face about a millimetre from mine and said, 'Do you *know* who he is?'

'No, I don't,' I lied, just to needle him. 'Nor,' I added, in a low voice only he could hear, 'do I give a fuck. You've got your job, I've got mine.'

'Not for long, arsehole,' he told me, with a meaningful look towards the manager's office.

I couldn't, after a minute or two, without getting physical, stop them walking into the area, now well over the twenty-person limit. I, of course, was now in line for a bollocking. I went in and, just for spite, snatched my guy's drink from his hand and took it back inside where regulations said it should be. When he wasn't looking, I toyed with spitting in it. But didn't. I could have been seen. If I'd reacted as I wanted to react – physically or with a gob of angry phlegm – I would have lost my job and my badge. I'd be lucky to be taken on as a traffic warden, the lowest kind of slime on the London streets. Not that I was much higher. But I had some fragments of pride left.

* Email me and I'll tell you.

I read somewhere that Leona Helmsley, bitch owner of a string of New York five-star hotels, said that 'only little people pay taxes'. The tax-paying 'little people' who worked in her kitchens liked to dip their dicks in her iced water before taking it to her. Think twice, my friend, before you insult that busboy.

Truth is, that escort I'm badmouthing here was doing his job (and what was he getting? Twenty pounds an hour if he was lucky). I'd probably done the same kind of thing myself in my PA/close protection days and someone perhaps spat in my drinks or dipped their dick in my 7 Up.

I kept my cool, to keep my job, but the constant slag, slag, slag ate away at me like acid. My ego was shot. It was an education, of a kind – what they call a 'learning experience'. Most people going around their business and pleasure in a big city never realise how much contempt there is for the low-paid in the modern world, how much shit they have to eat and how you never get used to the taste. There's going to be a revolution one day. And which side will I be on? UK PAPI or doorman?*

UP A RUNG

Gradually I rose a notch or two. I was given an opportunity to work for the legendary Jeremy Joseph, proprietor of the premier gay club Heaven. His head of security was

* 'Expose thyself to feel what wretches feel,' says King Lear. A footnote not for you, Jack, but our more literate readers.

off, on holiday, for a couple of weeks. I'd got the post of artist security, I think, on the strength of my own profusely star-spangled CV, which I was throwing around everywhere. Jeremy was the only person who'd shown any interest. The first big name to deal with was 'The Hoff', David Hasselhoff, whose two daughters were featuring in the club entertainment. I could do the escort-the-star thing into and out of the club, onto and off the stage, second nature. I felt, momentarily, I was in a little time machine, back to my glory days. I did likewise for Joe McElderry and Leona Lewis (who was ostentatiously grateful and huggy). Joseph seemed to be impressed, and suggested I might stay on in some capacity, after the guy I was filling in for returned.

When he did come back, I was down to low-rung status again. 'Security'. One Direction were coming in that Saturday. I decided to quit, having briefly tasted something better than footache at the door. Jeremy was furious – there were, one gathered, complicated things going on with security firms at that time. Rumours were also flying about me: someone was slagging me off as a hopeless junkie. A security guy, I suspected, to whom I'd confided too much.

To scrape the mud off my name I wrote a long letter to Jeremy, telling him about my past, that I was now clean and sober (about eight months, at that time) and intended to stay that way. It didn't work. It might have done in LA, with Gene La Pietra, but not in tight-arsed London, with anyone. Word got around and I was, for a while, unwanted anywhere in Soho. The only places I could work for a while were Vauxhall and straight clubs. Back to square fucking one.

At last the last money from America came in. After the usual chunks had been torn out of it, the payoff came to something over £100K. Net. I could have settled debts with it, put a deposit on an apartment. Or simply saved it as a nest egg. Started a small business, even. I did none of those things.

At this point, when the cash landed, I'd been working for two months as 'head of night security' at one of the town's most exclusive, boutique, multi-starred hotels – I can't name it, you'll see why.

With REM, all those years ago, I'd stayed at the Hempel. This place was in the same class. But now I was down with the non-English-speaking toilet cleaners and bed makers. The job title was a lot grander than the job. I, alone, was the night security. A one-man 'team'. Six twelve-hour shifts a week, £7.50 an hour. Slave rates. I was, at the beginning, dry and drugless for a couple of months. Otherwise I would never have got the job. I could still put on a front, when I had to.

Every night I was hooked up with radio earpiece and radio communication phone, based in the control room with all-round CCTV screens for company when I wasn't making one of my five patrols a night. I was black-suited for when I popped up, front of the hotel, or when I might be called to the desk (e.g. 'Someone screaming in room 101, Security Officer, check it out').

The hotel underground was vast on several levels, cellars, store rooms, tunnels, pipes and hissing steam everywhere – I was the only human being down there. It was like Danny

Boyle's *28 Days Later*. Vampires would have loved the job. Wandering through the belly of the beast, the feel of it matched what I was feeling. Barely human.

After I'd got into the job, and had inspired some trust (I was good at the screaming-in-room-101 emergencies), I was keeping myself sane with vodka and marijuana. Discreet intake on the job, overdosing on my measly one day off. Maintaining. But, of course, it's a slippery slope. I'd been down it more often than an Olympic bobsleigh, and here we went again. Within a few weeks I couldn't get through the night without a toke on my glass marijuana pipe every hour or so. I smoked it, American-style, pure. I'd reversed by now: it wasn't getting me high, it was keeping me sane. That job was so boring. It was like a prison sentence in one of those new high-max penitentiaries where you never see another human being, just the eyeball in the peephole. Except I was doing the eyeballing.

Because I was one man, with a vast private space all my own underground, no one noticed. (I kept out of range of any CCTV in the parking lot.) I kept the job on, I suppose because I liked the solitude, after the windfall American money had fattened my bank account. It kept boredom at bay. Gave me something to do with my insomniac nights.

I could finally afford crystal, at the outrageous prices London dealers charge. I added it, judiciously, to the nightly mix of vodka and weed. If anything, for a while, my work performance looked more alert to anyone who cared to notice. There's a honeymoon period with crystal (like coke, I'm told – which is why so many young bankers use it), when you're 110 per cent on the job. Even at three o'clock in the morning.

Secure in the knowledge that, with my fat bank account, I no longer needed their damned job, I started playing games. I don't know whether it was a kind of revenge for the humiliation, or just madness. Or, as I say, out-of-the-skull boredom. One outrageous night, for example, I bought the services of two escorts. I prepaid for a room in the hotel, taxi fare, service fee (all night, good room) and tip. I watched them, on hotel CCTV, alight from their Addison Lee and be ushered through the door by the guy in stupid livery. And there I was, sitting in my Captain Kirk chair, down in the control room, whipping up an adrenaline storm and doing crystal. As the drug hit me I had that feeling all chemsex users know – I had to empty my bowels. Someone once told me it's the same with wild animals doing their flight, fight or sex. Sphincter relaxes.

I was deep into role play, something else many chemsex users will be familiar with.* I'd given them detailed instructions. They were to douse the main lights and use candles only. They were to strip to lily-white Calvin Kleins. Jockey. One was to stand, smoking crystal, while the other, kneeling, serviced him.

I would use my master card to sneak into the room and do a peeping tom, until I got fully excited and jumped on them, like a stalking leopard, for the kill, P&P. Fuelled by the ever-glowing pipe. I was like a film director (I'd worked with enough). And it was the fantasy, the scenario, which delivered the highest high.

I did this around five times. Then the crash came. It

* For chemsex and role play, see the appendix, Drugalog.

always does. I was wearing out, what with the drugs, the sex, the twelve-hour shifts, six-night working weeks, crystal insomnia. In my vast underground domain there was a vault where the hotel stored rollaway beds and cots, for rooms which, for some reason, needed them. I would unroll a bed and catch a couple of hours' kip. The earpiece would be my alarm clock. Calls squawked in, usually about three or four times a night from the upstairs desk. The staff never came down themselves. And if they did they'd need GPS – it was a warren. My underground kingdom. I felt like Gollum down there; probably, by this stage, looked like him as well.

It was cold, smelly (something you could never quite identify) and a creepy, down there in the bed storeroom. And, to be honest, I couldn't be bothered to put the roll-aways neatly back in the stacks. It all got a bit too much of a hassle. I couldn't sleep on any of the empty-room beds upstairs in the hotel, because it would rumple them and I've always been a duvet, not sheets-and-blanket, expert. But in the presidential suite (usually empty), which was three rooms knocked into one luxury apartment, there was a nine-foot leather couch in the lounge area, a few feet away from a wall-mounted fifty-inch TV.

Good enough for me.

This particular night, knackered, I took to my presidential couch and made the mistake of leaving the TV on – I've always found that the nightlong burble helps me sleep. I was on what drug users call a 'comedown' – chemical hangover. It's when most of them ('us') commit suicide. I'd medicated with a vast intake of marijuana, in one of my basement nooks.

It was a mistake. I'd taken a lot of naps in the past few weeks, but had always woken up when any radio transmit squealed in my ear. This night I was wholly dead to the world. Comatose. If al-Qaeda had bombed the place I wouldn't have heard it. Calls on the radio came in that night, for some unusual reason, thick and fast. My mobile was going crazy – I didn't hear. They could have been texting a corpse.

It was early morning when I came round and saw what was on my phone. I got myself up, put my shoes on, turned off the TV, plumped the cushions (thank Christ I hadn't drooled) and staggered down the fire-exit staircase towards the control room. On the way down I met the two day-shift security guys coming up, looking for me. (The presidential suite hadn't occurred to them as a very likely place.) One of them was fairly senior in the outsourced firm that handled security for the hotel. If what I'd done that night got out, they'd for sure lose the contract.

'What happened, for fuck's sake?' the senior guy asked – as well he might. It was not a friendly question. I looked like shit, I had no story, so I decided to be honest (as honest, that is, as an addict ever can be). It was sheer physical exhaustion, I said – plausible enough from what I looked like. They didn't give a toss about me, probably didn't believe me, but they had to protect that all-important contract with the hotel. An excuse was needed. And they would have to keep it to themselves (since their jobs, too, for Christ's sake, were at risk. That always sharpens wits). It was their responsibility to ensure I was doing my job.

The cover story they came up with was I fainted – who

knew why – on the stairs, where they found me, still semi-conscious, perhaps dying. They carried me to the control room, and put in an emergency call for an ambulance. I played the part. Rourke couldn't have played it better.

The ambulance arrived and carried me, playing death's door all the way, klaxon blaring, to the A&E. I was stuck in there for seven hours while they looked for something that wasn't there. I kept the pretence up until I finally discharged myself voluntarily and took a taxi home. Game over. Job over. Onwards and downwards.

The next chapter, be warned, is grim. And you won't like the Jack who's in there. I don't, either. Unfortunately, he belongs to me.*

* *John.* And, as you always forget, to your parents too. The drug dealers and pick-ups wouldn't come to your funeral and weep for you.

10: *WORSE TIMES: INDONESIA*

What did I go and do with the American money? I blew it. Simple as that. I cut out all relations who didn't use. Parents, family, friends. They would suffer, I knew. That's what they got for loving or liking me. I numbed any thought of them. They were lucky to have me out of their lives.* I moved into a glitzy five-star hotel on the South Bank. Good view of the Thames. More importantly to me, minutes away from my favourite sauna, in the Waterloo area. Can't name it, for reasons that will become obvious. I'll call it MFS.

I took, of course, the presidential suite. Nothing less would do for what I had in mind. Two entrances (for discreet arrivals and departures). Three mega flat screens all viewably placed, glowing and muttering 24 hours a day. In the master bathroom a Jacuzzi which could hold four grown men (I tested its capacity). Addison Lee cars on account. I rented a Range Rover when London got on my nerves. (I was still driving on a Californian licence – its six-month validity had long lapsed.) I'm surprised I didn't keep HMS *Belfast* at the dock ('Where to today, Skipper? Scapa Flow?').† It was surprisingly reasonably priced. The proprietor – a well-heeled

* *John*. We thought differently.

† *John*. I confess, I put that wisecrack in. Just to cheer myself up.

Indian, moving into the London hotel business – had spared no expense in fitting the place out. But he'd stinted drastically on service. In the West End my suite would have been close on two grand a night. Here it was a tenth of that. I was staying intermittently: a regular, not permanent, guest. Usually it was available, sometimes not. They must have known I was a mess but my money was as good as anyone else's. And, when there, I largely kept to my room(s). The escorts coming at all hours of the day and night were discreet. I didn't have the wardrobe for clubbing or high-end restaurants: two pairs of baggy jeans (getting baggier by the day – I was down, again, to a twenty-eight-inch waist*), one jacket, half a dozen shirts – all faded relics from my Rourke days. When you're high, mirrors never tell you the truth.

I had plans. All totally insane. This was how drug-fucked my thinking was. I'd always said, because of my sex addiction, I'll kill myself if I get a positive result. Why? Not self-pity, but to protect the gay community – with up to six encounters a night I would be an epidemic time bomb. Mr Ebola. I kept my Gaydar account very busy. But, to hurry things on – get the narrative moving to its climax, so to speak – I began to have consciously risky sex. I hooked up with guys on BBRT (the first two letters stand for bareback – the rest is irrelevant). I was deliberately playing with destruction the way I've seen crazies gamble at Vegas. It was *Deer Hunter*-style HIV roulette. I was often so off my face I paid escorts, or dealers, twice or three times. They accepted

* I'm forty-two and rising at the moment. A clean and sober Bunter.

my generosity without comment. Bastards. Vultures flock round a dying animal.

I recall, from the blur, one episode. I'd invited two escorts. Both crystal users, both of whom had forewarned me they were positive. One of them told me, again head of time (they were ethical vultures), that he 'slammed' (injected) and was it OK to bring the 'pins' (needles – what heroin users call 'works'). I had the crystal and Viagra on hand. Boots, I knew, provided free syringes but I didn't inject. It gave you a higher, faster high, I was told, but if you missed a vein (easy to do in the half-light of the drug world), there were tracks and infection. And it was more likely to produce the hideous meth rash.

The pins were clean and, for the first time, I slammed. It was, as promised, more intense. When it hit, there was this telltale little cough. It all got wild. At one point, all of us trashed, the choice was three recharged pins loaded with Tina, GHB laid out on the table. Whose was whose? Two were dangerous. Lousy odds but I took my chances. The fact was I wanted an excuse to off myself – and feel I was doing the right thing by staging it as an accident. Kismet, nothing to do with me. Beyond screwy. Past fucked-up. Crystal and G will do that to your brain while destroying it.

This went on for weeks. But still my results came up negative. It was, in a strange way, frustratingly good news. I craved my grand exit from the world. I didn't want the bullet to miss me. I'd even taken out an expensive life-insurance policy (my parents, and BJ's parents, the beneficiaries). I asked one of my later-life friends, Dr Christian Jessen (he of *Embarrassing Bodies*), how I'd dodged the bullet. He's a revered figure among gays for his work with the Terrence Higgins Trust. Christian says it's just luck of the genetic draw. But don't fool yourself that you're immune, Christian warned. It's a cunning virus.

It went critical with a fleeting moment of clarity (they were few and far between at this stage of my wretched life) after a three-day binge. I'd just been to the Mortimer Market Sexual Health Clinic.* Negative. I was furious. It must be wrong. I just sat there, saying nothing.

'Are you alright?' the nurse asked, repeating that the result was negative.

'Test me again,' I said, furiously.

Negative again. What the hell did a man have to do in this town to get infected?

Once I'd left the clinic I went crazy for an hour or two on crystal. Then to MFS. I'd meet escorts there in my long-hire private room. No. 9. I was a reckless tipper and I'd always prepay any escorts I called in to meet me there. You could pay for an hour or a whole ten-hour day/night. Rates were from £100–£150 short-spell, around £800 long-spell. Clock running all the time. Crystal, while on the subject of money, was around £60 a quarter gram, £240 a night's supply with company. Two grams would be necessary if there was slamming. I had large stocks of marijuana – mainly for roller-coasting (what goes up must come down before going up again) and for sleeping after the comedown. My partying

* It used to be a seven-day wait. Now it was a pinprick and a couple of hours in the waiting room (never on the phone). If they didn't tell you the result but called you into the consulting room, it was bad news and counselling.

was getting beyond hard. A death dance.

Death was increasingly the theme. The third night running in MFS, I met this young guy – early twenties, blond hair, skinny: not really my type, but I liked him well enough. The light's dim in bathhouses. We started playing. The usual cycle is sixty to ninety minutes' play, high on crystal, then a shower, time out, a couple of refreshing Lucozades, rest your cock for the next bout. You swap stories in the breaks from the action. On one of our intervals we had a long conversation in which he told me about his boyfriend. He himself sold G to keep the wolf from the door. The boyfriend was 100 per cent non-user. Virginal. He'd only been drunk twice in his life and had never even smoked weed. He was a fitness fanatic and drank great quantities of Lucozade during punishing workouts.

On this day he'd been out delivering while the boyfriend was at home. The home supply of G, a liquid, was stored in any old bottles that came to hand. You don't collect it from Boots – no warning brown glass. On this occasion it was a Lucozade bottle. While he's on his rounds – like a druggy milkman – he gets this panicked phone call. His boyfriend had, after press-ups, burpees or whatever, picked up the bottle without thinking and gulped a couple of mouthfuls before he realised what the foul-tasting liquid was. Lethal in that quantity.

'What should I do, what should I do?' he had screamed down the phone.

Throw up, dial 999 and get an ambulance, of course. But he was dead before he got to the hospital.

As we dressed he showed me photographs. The story

broke me up. I started thinking about BJ. It kicked off a depressive fugue. (I was getting to know psychology jargon well.)

I ran to a quiet corner and called the only escort I knew who didn't do drugs – Jackson. A totally white guy, unusual for me. Hugely endowed, with fairly strict rules as to what he'd do for money or anything else. He was the only repeat escort I used at the time. We'd had four or five dates. Why did I like him? Because he didn't treat me as what I was, a 'client'. He seemed to like me. Could've been an act, but I didn't think so.

I was in tears on the phone. He, amazingly, seemed genuinely worried about me. My hunch was right. He had friendly feelings. I told him I was going back to the hotel, where I'd get some rest with my Seroquel and weed mix. I'd been three days virtually sleepless. When I woke up, please could we go to dinner and talk? Yes, he said. 'Off-book' – no charge. I went back to my presidential suite. I smoked enough weed to tranquillise an elephant and drew a bubble bath, throwing in a handful of Lush bombs. I lit candles. Funeral parlour all the way. All I needed was the Wurlitzer. I'd lie in it, Jacuzzi bubbling around me, like a warm, wet corpse and get some peace, while the drugs oozed gently out of me.

But I don't. I begin to hallucinate – a full-on psychotic episode is changing the world around me. I've locked the maids out for days, there's so much paraphernalia around. I hallucinate they've broken in, a horde of them, all Indian midgets, all chattering like chimpanzees. I see them from the corner of my eyes, through the gap in the bathroom's paired doors. Then gangsterish guys, first one, then two, then four. Scuttling. And then a sudden horrible quiet. I start shrieking and jump out of the bath, stark naked. No one there (cunning little bastards, those Indians). I check both doors. Chain-locked.

I call an old, and very loyal, friend, Nick. I'm crying down the phone. He used to deal, but no longer. He's hard up – having trouble with the benefits Gestapo, he tells me. I wire him £3K. I crawl back into the bath. And then – epiphany. I start to think of all the times *I should have died* in my life. HIV tests. I've had guns pulled on me half a dozen times – and at least once a knife. I've been carjacked. I've driven in a condition where I was a car crash waiting to happen. But it never has. I've overdosed to near-lethal levels. I've twice attempted suicide. The second time the doctors said they never worked out how I managed to get back. I track it right back to the abortion of me that never happened, thirty-seven years earlier. Then it hits me – maybe the higher power, which I've been cursing every day for keeping me in this shitty life, has some kind of purpose. I've got guardian angels, must have.

I decide (all this in the bath, candles burning low) I want to live. I drag myself out of the tub and, at last, fall asleep, helped by too many Seroquel and too much weed.

The next day I have the promised lunch with Jackson at that neat little Asian fusion restaurant, The Hare & Tortoise, in Brunswick Square. I'm more or less functioning and enjoy the food and green tea. Get out, says Jackson. Leave this place. He'll stay with me, again off the clock. As a friend not a whore. Run away, he says. But where? I think back to my REM global-travel itinerary.

Through Facebook I'd reconnected with one of my best friends from school, all those years ago, in San Marino. She was Indonesian. Her father, who'd been high up in the country's airline, now had a luxury hotel, among other interests, in Bali. That, I decided, was where I was going to go. I had between £30K and £50K left of my spinal injury money.

I planned two weeks in my friend Sandra's hotel. Luxuriating and cleaning up. A week in Ubud. I'd got a yen for the place from Sandra Bullock's lyrical posts about its meditation spas and body-cleansing. Finally a week in Thailand, coming back to normality. I recruited Jackson to come with me, all expenses paid. I would, indeed, get out: holiday of a lifetime for him, escape from London hell for me.

INDONESIA: PARADISE

I book all our tickets, every segment; business class me, economy Jackson. Bali, Phuket, Bangkok, London. We're running up to my thirty-eighth birthday. I rent a Range Rover and check out of the hotel. I do a farewell round – family, friends. I'm only doing marijuana. Mildly stoned night and day. I present the picture of someone 'mellow'. Not crazy. I'm feeling OK(ish). Pleasantly numb. Decisions have been made. A new life awaits.

I've left my passport, among other bags of necessaries, with Nick. On the morning we're leaving, I drop by to pick it up. No answer at the door. Christ, you'd think for three grand he could at least stay in a couple of hours for me. But he's out and his partner Cornell's sleeping. Frantic phone calls. Finally Nick comes back and I get my stuff. I do ninety miles an hour, cursing all the way, along the M4 to the car drop-off.

When we get to the Singapore Airlines check-in (fucking hard to find at Heathrow), there's not a single human being present. We've missed the cut-off by five minutes. I call my travel broker. No transfer. We have to buy new tickets for the outward flight. What the hell. It's only money. We spend a less-than-presidential night at a nearby hotel. Next morning, it's off and away with our second tickets.

We arrive at the island, Bali. It's love at first sight, smell, touch and feel. Sandra's hotel, the Legian, is beyond five-star. A chauffeured limo drives us from the airport. We're lodged in the club villa compound – two butlers. A private pool. Costs are low in the Far East, but this must be a thousand-plus a night – even with heavy discount. Impolite to ask. I've been to many good hotels, but this is the best ever.

Over the next few days, Sandra – who's become a celebrated chef in her country (another triumph for good old San Marino High) – shows me and Jackson the sights of Bali. I resolve, one way or another, I'll stay here. Who knows, I could set up a close-protection business. Craftsmanship here, of furniture and ornaments in wood, stone and jade, is exquisite. An import/export business is a possibility. My mind is turning over. It's cheap manufacture here, but the mark-up in Oxford Street, or Manhattan, would be phenomenal.

Jackson wants sex, but off crystal, I don't. Can't. I need his help and companionship and appreciate it, but that's all. He's conflicted. So am I. We sightsee by day and explore the gay scene by night. I occasionally get annihilated on vodka. Jackson gets very angry when, one night, I invite an Indonesian guy back to the hotel. He's not attracted to Asians, sexually.

We've been there three weeks, soaking it in, me in a recovery arc, when Sandra's father comes down dangerously ill with dengue fever, in Jakarta. Then Jackson decides to go home, against all my persuadings. I'll never see him again.* I cancel (more losses) the flights I booked for the two of us and buy a bunch of new ones. But Sandra, God bless her, only charges us for room service and spa sessions. Two hundred dollars per day. My money is leaking away but not, at this point, dangerously. I've decided I'm never going back to London or LA. I hang with Sandra, in Jakarta, as her father recovers.

Disaster comes from an unexpected quarter. I've run out of Seroquel. Not easily available in Indonesia – and almost impossible to get it through customs from Britain. I self-medicate with marijuana and alcohol. Marijuana use is risky, verging on suicidal, where I now am. The law is ferocious. This is not West Hollywood or Old Compton Street. You can end up years behind bars for even small amounts for personal use. Not that I'd last too long in an Indonesian prison – though, I'm told by people who've been there, drugs would be easier to come by.

It's not just sleeplessness. The manic phase of my bipolar cycle kicks in, harder than I've ever known it. I'm crazily euphoric. Everything's perfect, I think. But I look like

* I hope it's clear I'm hugely grateful to him, if he's reading. I've changed the name but he'll know who he is.

someone cranked out on coke. I've got myself a nickname, someone tells me, 'Bula Gila', crazy white man. It fits. I go round in oversize clothes (I'm withering by the day) and a signature panama hat.

Sandra's polite, but keeps her distance. So does everyone else. I spend hours blasting crazy emails to the world. No answers. There are other problems. You can only get thirty-day visas in Indonesia. Either you have to marry someone local (not an option) or incorporate yourself as a firm. Which means capital investment. My money is now leaking like water out of an old bucket. I'm living in an apartment in a tower block. A Scottish guy has rented it to me. I'll pay him, I say, when some money from America comes in. He trusts me – we're white men east of Suez. I've loaned people money in the US over the years, and I call in those IOUs. Some of them send me something. Never enough to quite pay the rent. I invite friends to invest in the import/export company I'm planning to open. I'm going to be the Branson of Bali. No one's interested. They can smell insanity.

As my dreams crumble, crystal, once again, seems the only way out. It's cheap out there – but the penalties, if you're caught with it, are horrendous. After a long wait, Albert sends me $2K from the sale of my household furniture in LA – about a tenth of what it was worth. It's a lifesaver. But what am I living for?

There are the never-ending problems of being a foreigner. To get new thirty-day visas, I have to hop to Singapore or Lumpur and back. I could have got my import/export business on the books if, fool that I am, I'd kept a fraction of the money I had just three months ago. All I need is ten thousand. I send out more begging emails.* Again, no one answers. They can see I'm past insane and into train wreck.

When I can be bothered to eat, it's boiled pasta (two quick-boil packs) and tomato ketchup. A treat I'd loved as a child. Weight is dripping off me like butter. I push away Sandra and any friends who have any concern for me. Shame makes me an outcast. I arrange sex parties, taking a cut. I have sex with guys who like dominating a white man – kind of colonial revenge – and twice prostitute myself for money. My rate is a measly $40. I've turned down thousands, from some eminent people, in the past. How low can I sink? Stupid question. There's always lower.

I was, for several months, off my medication. I'd run short, then out, and it's not easy to get the stuff in Indonesia. And I was feeling good. I didn't need expensive re-prescription. I'd substituted my home remedy: marijuana, Guinness and vodka. As the Seroquel seeped out of my system, I went into permanent, non-stop, stratospheric-high mania. Planet Bipolarity.

I had this Indonesian friend, Cuki (pronounced 'Chuki'), who was mad about me. We had nothing going on – I have a lot of love for him (and he saved me innumerable times). Cuki was well off and well connected. I was burning through my money and on a manic, master-of-the-universe high. Why shouldn't I take over Indonesia's personal-protection industry? Lots of stars – Kylie, Madonna, Justin, etc. – did shows there. A huge market. It *needed* me.

* *John*. Indeed you did. Psychosis in every syllable.

My good friend Mawan was always willing to help. He set up a quiet, intimate dinner with the country's major concert promoter. I'd be able to pitch Jack. I arrived half an hour late.

What happened over the next ninety minutes I don't, thank God, exactly recall. I thought, afterwards, that it had gone perfectly. On the drive home, Cuki looked at me sadly.

'I don't know how you even got breath into your lungs,' he said. 'You spoke like someone who'd just inhaled a spoonful of grade-A China White.' A cokehead rhapsody. Total disconnect from reality.

I began, dimly, to wonder if I had, perhaps, a mania problem. Or perhaps it was the Guinness. Better cut back on that dark Irish stuff. Yes, that was it. Cut out the Guinness.

ME AND BOY GEORGE

I'd always been, and still am, a fan of Boy George. Not his music – him. Along with Elton and Mercury, he'd been the first superstar to come out. And I knew he'd been madly into drugs and then quit.

He was doing a DJ gig in Jakarta. I went there, first night, high on mania, chemicals and delusions that I could sell myself. Every star needed a bodyguard of my calibre, didn't they? Mr Security. I had previously loosed off a barrage of emails to Boy George and his manager. I had opened up a Twitter account to fire off a few more messages. Oddly, they hadn't replied. Hitches, glitches – whatever.

I went to the nightclub Boy George was playing – the

biggest straight club in the city. I was the only white guy there. Cuki and I placed ourselves at eyeball level, up close to the stage. Christ knows what Boy George thought of the pale, white, skeletal face leering at him through the dry-ice haze.

In the interval I barged in to ask him for a photo. (Cuki obliged with the camera.) He agreed.

'Are you somebody?' Boy George asked. I apparently reminded him of a promoter he knew, who might matter.

I drop names like hailstones: Stipe, Rourke . . . His face blanks. I'm not who he thought I was. Interval's over and he goes back to the discs. I'm nobody. An insane nobody.

What, I wonder in my madness, could possibly have gone wrong?

HAPPY PILL TIME

What they call 'happy pills' are big things in Indonesia. It's their equivalent of ecstasy – a club-experience enhancer. (On prescription it's an antidepressant.) Taken with alcohol, happy pills are euphoria-plus, of an oddly distinct kind.

It was in an upmarket straight club that I first swallowed them. The kind of place where Jakarta's rich, young and beautiful like to go. Cuki got me through the rope.

Inside I'm sipping vodka and cranberry. Someone offers me happy pills. Why not, I think. I could use some happiness. I neck a couple. Nothing. I take two more. Still nothing. Two more. I'm now six times over the advisory. At last, a little dribble of happiness. And then a tsunami of bliss. I've had every kind of high, but this is unique.

But now it's hit I don't actually like it. Not that I've got anything against happiness. But (perhaps it's the overdose) I don't like drugs which rob me of my self-control. That's the great thing about crystal. However high I am, I am still in charge of myself. Off my face, perhaps; never out of my mind.

Anyway, carried away by the pills, which I've swallowed like a handful of Smarties, I dance like a dervish. I'm half-conscious – then, suddenly, like a curtain falling, everything goes black.

I wake up, alone, in the dark. Where? Suddenly lights go on, burning my eyes. I'm in a fucking maze. Walls and passages all round me. What is this? Hell? My trousers are round my ankles, my shirt is off. My trademark hat is somewhere, not on my head. Two security guys are shaking me – none too gently.

I work out where I am. I'm in Jakarta's only legit gay club. Apollo. It has a maze layout – lots of booths, partitions, dividers, nooks and crannies. Lose yourself, find yourself. And a central 'dark room' area to see what develops. That's where I was, and where I am.

My memory banks are wholly wiped. First thing I do, as I stagger to the door, is what is called a reach-around. To make sure I haven't been raped. You don't want to know the details. I'm OK, that side. God knows about cock and mouth. I'll never know. Nor do I want to.

I leave the club. Just short of being kicked out. Last to leave, apparently. It's in a shopping mall – closed up. I find an open public toilet and throw water on my face. I black out again and regain consciousness in my apartment. There's vodka and a weed pipe by my side.

I look at my phone. It's blown apart with texts, emails, voicemails from Cuki. I'd dragged him to the club (not something he likes to do – he has a reputation to keep up), then dumped him and lost him in the maze and darkness. Deliberately. He was worried at first, then fuck-you-Jack furious.

I see myself for what I have become. I reach out for a handful of pills to end it all. Luckily, or unluckily, there aren't a handful there. Just a dozen. Enough to nauseate me. I sleep fifteen hours. The madness goes on.

SINGAPORE: HELL

I found myself once again back in Singapore for the necessary visa renewal trip. I'd got the last night flight from Jakarta, planning to spend a short night in the vast wilderness of Singapore airport and then catch the first morning flight back to Jakarta to acquire my visa upon arrival. While I was in the airport, mad fool that I was, instead of stretching out – like hundreds of other waiting passengers – I cruised gay websites. I invited likely guys to come to the airport: the restrooms were very clean and I was very willing. No one accepted the invitation. Nor would I, when sane. Two and a half hours before my plane to Jakarta was due to board, I messaged a kid in Singapore who, I knew from previous visits, was into me.

He was home, thank God. Take a taxi, he said – and bang went all the cash I had in my pocket. So too my trip back to Jakarta and non-refundable ticket. I went to the guy's house.

It was all very domestic and low-key. One-on-one. No party. I explained I was broke. He agreed to buy me a ticket back, and loan me a bit of money to get by. I was good for it, I told him. I really wasn't sure about that. Last-minute flights are expensive: the cheapest was five days on, so I prepared for a short stay till then. The next day my saviour took me to a shop and brought me a clean outfit.

The next morning he went off to work – he was an accountant – leaving me alone in his house. He was happy to have me around. It was all boyfriendish (I slept on the sofa). Alone in the house, and sober, with a long day to kill, I was bored and jumpy. I was in withdrawal, nerves twanging. I toured the usual websites and hooked onto someone who was keen to get high and have sex. I agreed, but only if he could come up with the necessary crystal, ecstasy and G. Oh, and by the way, somewhere to party.

Within a few hours he gets back to me to say he has a hotel room. We meet, have our fun, and then I get greedy for more sex, more drugs, more guys. Before I know it, there's five, coming and going. Guiltily – it's now night – I phone my friend and invite him over. He's furious, disgusted, and rams the phone down on me.

Three blurring nights pass, each in a different hotel room, the guys around constantly changing. I invite over an Indian guy, totally my type, who I've met earlier. My host, the original Asian guy, gets jealous and aggressive. Everyone's nerves are, by now, ragged. I'm wildly bipolar, crystal-overdosed, suffering built-up brain damage. Days and nights have passed in a yo-yoing blur. There's finally a blazing row (about what? Who knows). Everyone except the two of us leaves. (They don't want hotel security to investigate the shouting – there's enough drugs around to land us all in Changi.) I take one more hit of crystal, grab my stuff and leave – raging. It's around four in the morning and I've missed my flight yet again. I phone my friend, who tells me I'm on my own. I call back the guy I left in the hotel. No answer. I find a dark corner and crash. Dead to the world.

I wake up on the pavement. Nine in the morning. My wallet has no money, only a wad of expired, non-refundable airline tickets. Fuck, fuck, fuck. I'm still high as a kite. Off my face with the crystal, ecstasy and G raging in my system, what's left of it. I can't walk, talk, think or piss straight. And I could be in real trouble. In Singapore they have these random street drug tests. The police just stop you (no probable cause required) and put a piece of drug-sensitive paper on your arm. You're positive and it's the station, then prison. It can mean life behind bars, and possibly death. Both Singapore and Indonesia have capital punishment for drug offences. I am offensive. And at this time, 2012, they're coming down on white sex-and-drug tourists.

All I have on me is my Tumi briefcase – from my Branson days. It cost me $1.8K, I recall. I'm thinking hard about money. I've got my phone and computer, thank God. Batteries running low. But lifelines. My clothes haven't been washed for days. I'm beginning to sweat. It's streaming off me. I look as if I've just hauled myself out of a swimming pool. It's not the heat (although that's awful), it's what happens when you're coming down from a binge and don't have any taper-off drugs or a cooling bath to go to.

I look around. I see the hotel and go back in. I've got no

cash or card credit left. I brush past the desk, as if I know where I'm going, but I don't. I've forgotten the room number and even the floor of the party I stormed out of. I bang on a few doors, hopefully. Some of the occupants, who look through the peepholes, will be calling security. Security will mean police arrest. And the next time my loved ones will see me is on *Banged Up Abroad*. I'm still so drugged up I'd have the magic paper zinging ten feet away. Changi, here I come.

I run out of the hotel and its sixty-degree air-con into oven heat. The sun burns me like a white vampire. Something out of *I Am Legend*. I'm coming down with the worst panic and paranoia attack of my life. I need money for a flight back to Jakarta. But in my present condition I'd never make it to the departure lounge or past flight security.

I've got just enough loose change in my pocket for three cartons of fruit juice to rehydrate with. I wander out of the residential tourist areas to somewhere police patrols (that fucking drug-test paper!) are less likely. I find this huge high-rise housing complex. There's a central garden with a large gazebo and lots of benches and flower beds, shaded by the twelve-storey buildings around it. Singapore's the cleanest, tidiest place on the planet. They prosecute you for dropping chewing gum. In London or New York the place would be full of winos. Not here. Just one drugged-up, fucked-up English junkie. Me.

I find shade and sit there, stewing in paranoia, sipping juice. For five hours. I'm making promises to God. Get me out of this, and I'll never use again. I'll be a good person. My phone has enough battery for me to get in touch with the person I know is my last friend in the Far East. Cuki. I reach out to him and he says he'll book me a one-way ticket, collectable at the desk, back to Jakarta. We can work things out there. He doesn't want me to die in the Singapore streets, or in jail. Nor do I.

There's someone in Singapore I know who'll give me enough cash for a taxi to the airport. Not love. Even knowing a convicted drug addict, in my current state, in that country, can get you in trouble. You (me, for example) can talk down your sentence by naming names – they're all on my computer. He'll give me some cash to get me the hell out of Singapore and out his life – with luck, to die somewhere else. We arrange to meet outside a shopping centre. He gives me directions to get there on foot. Easier said than done. I haven't slept or eaten for days. The heat is killing me. I have to stop every two minutes before stumbling on.

We meet on the street outside the mall, say nothing, he gives me an envelope and I walk over the street to the taxi line. I see fleeting reflections of myself in the mall windows. Jesus, what a sight. I could star in that Romero film – what's it called?* The place is crawling with security. They're standing on the pavement, looking at me. There's half a dozen people ahead of me in the taxi line. It's not paranoia. The security guys are really inspecting me, talking to each other. I know the mindset. I've done their job.

Those five minutes waiting for the taxi are an eternity. I'm on the kerb, technically outside the mall. But they could come over in force, arguing I'm a suspected shoplifter, and drag me back. It's what I'd do. They're getting ready to do it,

* John. *Dawn of the Dead.*

I can tell they are – just as I make it to the head of the line.

'Take me to Singapore International!' I shout. 'I'm late.' (I'm not, but I want to get away from that damned mall before they write down the cab licence number.) I have a Chinese driver. He talks. He won't shut the fuck up. He goes into this racist rant about how the Indians are ruining Singapore. I just hem and haw. As if I gave a fuck about the future of Singapore. All of a sudden he looks at me, long and hard, in the rear-view. Then, God help me, he sees for the first time what he's got in the back and starts swearing at me in Cantonese.

He's realised I'm off my face. He's going to drive me straight to the police, I think. They probably pay bounties. But he just jabbers on, in Chinese, getting angrier and angrier, and takes me to the airport. I throw all the money I have at him, pray he doesn't put a call in to the police. 'APB. Suspicious white man. On drugs. Terminal Four.'

I'm regaining some fragments of sense. If those security guys at the mall spotted me, and the taxi driver spotted me, I might as well be carrying a sign saying ARREST ME! I look bad and feel worse. I find a quiet toilet and give myself an all-over. I don't have any razor to scrape my face with. The stubble on my chin is not 'fashionable'. I'm still terrified. I've got to get through passport and security. If they know what they're doing I'm fucked.

I look up at the departure board. Flight delayed three hours. Tiger Airlines, which runs the budget Singapore–Jakarta shuttle, is usually reliable. (I've missed it, and paid double, often enough.) Not today. It's going to be agony, under security and CCTV surveillance, in the airport. But the three hours mean some recovery time, hopefully enough to escape notice at the desks, barriers and security filters. Hopefully. I know enough about security to realise my chances are not great. I'll be high and ugly for hours yet. It's scary.

Singapore International is huge – a global hub. I find a quiet wing with benches where I can stretch out. (Lots of people do that – the flights Singapore caters for are incredibly long. Remember Michael Stipe's 'Departure'.) My guts, meanwhile, are quarrelling about whether they want to vomit or excrete. Is there anything in there? I can't sleep. I don't have a watch. My gold-and-platinum Tag is now on the wrist of a dealer, who knows where. Bastard. I find a power point where I can charge my phone and laptop.

Time passes. I find a toilet and splash water on my face. I practise what I'm going to say at check-in in the mirror, like De Niro at the end of *Raging Bull.* I go to the counter, petrified. Get me through, I'm praying. There's another problem – the entrance visa to Indonesia. But I've got a handle on that. I don't have a cent on me, but I've phoned ever-loyal Cuki. He'll meet me and get the money across the barrier somehow. I'll cross that last bridge when, and if, I get there. Shreds of the drugs are still in my system. I kill time on gay websites. I choose a seat where I can look at guys going into, and coming out of, the restrooms: anyone cruising? Am I mad?

Then, at the last minute, we're told the plane is delayed another five hours. It'll be an early-morning, not late-evening, flight. Sorry, folks. I'm meanwhile keeping my distance from my fellow passengers as best I can. I'm dying.

I haven't eaten for three days. My drug sweat has dried into a pungent stink. I'm getting odd looks and wrinkled nostrils. Can't blame them. My own nostrils aren't that happy.

It's a budget airline, so they don't put us in a hotel. They park us in an empty first-class lounge. There's leftover food and drink, and showers. I force myself to eat and drink and pass on the shower. I'm beyond the help of hot water. I lie out, my trademark panama covering my face. Hoping no one is going to complain to Tiger about the garbage they're carrying.

Next morning the passengers are so angry they're not looking at me any more. Just glaring at the board and the airline employees. It's a short flight, and everyone on board looks like shit now. I'm just a white face in a brown crowd, a bit more stubbled than the others.

After landing I text Cuki. He, incredibly, has slept all night, waiting for me, in the airport short-term car park. He says tell the immigration officer you were robbed, but you've got a friend on the other side of the barrier with money for the visa. It'll work.

Things get better. I see an officer I know because I've 'tipped' (bribed) him a couple of times before to get bumped to the head of the line. I explain. I'll take you through, he says, and bring you back. In arrivals, Cuki is waiting with the necessary sealed envelope. Visa money plus handsome 'tip'. It's straight back and straight out. Saved.

In Cuki's car I cry, uncontrollably. It's a moment of tearful clarity. Cuki cries as well. He remembers me as I was, just a month or two ago. Not this pathetic drivelling wreck. This 'addict'. He drives me to my apartment. Home sweet home. I go to open the door – the key doesn't work. What the fuck?

It dawns on me. The Scotsman's changed the locks. He didn't know I was going out of town and assumed I'd done a runner – and probably sold the key to some burglar or dealer. I haven't paid him a penny. I owe him something over $5K. An impossible amount. Worse, he'll have looked round the flat. Drug paraphernalia (and some weed, which I now desperately need) all over the place. I'd broken crockery, ruined the kitchen floor, garbage everywhere. Tenant from hell. If he's told the management, who have a Xerox of my passport on file, and they've informed the authorities, it's all over with me. Indonesia's line on drugs is as harsh as Singapore's. And the police hate white tourists who came to their country to enjoy what they can't do in their own. Particularly those who can't pay bribes any more.

Cuki, loyal to the end, says I can spend the night at his place. Of course. I pluck up my nerve and phone the Scotsman. At first he's cool. Pay the rent and damages and you'll get the keys, he says. I don't have the money, I say. He goes nuts. He's going to report me. 'I trusted you. You're a drug addict and a thief. You're going to jail.' I freak out. Fear, not anger. Give me three days, I say. Just seventy-two hours. I have one last bit of money. My Empire-CLS retirement fund. Desperate phone calls, they cash it out and wire me $5K (its real worth is twice that). Nick of time. Another bullet dodged. Another safety net gone. I was still scrabbling to make money the studio owed for work I did on *Passion Play*. I'm still waiting.

Did I pay the Scotsman? No. I checked into my favourite hotel and bought a ticket (as economy as I could get it) back home, via Kuala Lumpur. Broken flights are cheaper. I realised, fragments of sanity in a haze of insanity, that I could not get the help I needed in Indonesia. I would have to go back.

Idiot that I am/was, I forgot all my promises to God, and had a last night of P&P. Really the last, I hope. I bought some crystal and invited some boys over.

So ended my six months in Paradise.*

* If I ever win the lottery, I tell myself, I'll buy an island there and live out my life as mellowly as possible and found a hostel for the homeless in Jakarta in my grandmother's name. I love the place – fatal as it nearly was for me.

11: THE THREE Rs: RECOVERY, RELAPSE, REDEMPTION

I arrive at Heathrow, walking dead, weighing 140 pounds. No one's there. Why should they be? I make it to my mother's flat. She opens the door and looks blank. She doesn't recognise me. In the mirror by the door (a fine pier glass, once belonged to my granny), I don't recognise myself. Three months of crystal followed by an intercontinental, economy-class, sleepless flight is no beauty treatment. I feel better after some TLC and the ritual fish and chips. My father comes over and arranges to take me to an AA meeting. A closed gays' meeting. He's only half-qualified, but I'm grateful.

I'd been in Indonesia from January to June 2011. I settled down over the next six months, living in my mother's spare room, using nothing but poppers.* I picked up work where I could, trading on my SIA badge. It was low-paid but plentiful, and around Soho or Vauxhall I was a well-known face. Things were more or less settling down.

ME AND GRAHAM

Flash forward a few years and I'm on the door of Shadow

* Legal alkyl nitrate – a sexual stimulant.

Lounge, eyeing everyone coming in and out. Job of work. In breezes Graham Norton with a friend – one of his team, I later gather. Nothing special. On the way out, after some civilised drink and conversation, his partner goes to coat check and I make my own conversation with the waiting megastar of talk TV. You're listened to on the door.

'I've got a funny story,' I say. Graham's face drops a bit. But he's too polite, by nature, to blank me. 'My name is Jack [big deal] and I'm a good friend of RuPaul [interesting]. I'm that Jack who you mentioned on your American show, with Ru and Macaulay Culkin [dim recollection on his face]. Twenty-two marbles? [Blank, blank – what is this guy talking about?]'

'Yes,' says his friend, who's now back with their coats, 'I remember. *Spunk'd* – "Foreskin Follies". You remember, Graham.'

Intrigue, a little disgust, vague recollection and curiosity are all now visible on that most expressive of faces.

I throw in some detail.

'What did it look like – what does it look like . . . down there?' he says, eyes travelling south. I don't think he wanted a demonstration.

I gave him my business card. He and his guy went smiling out into the Soho night. If he's reading – remember me, Graham.

THE FALL

It's funny, though, if you're an addict like me, how small

things can tip you back into your personal black hole. Before my present – final – sobriety, before the Shadow Lounge, I had made it to six months clean and sober: chips clicking happily on my key ring. But it was a dangerously fragile sobriety. I was walking a tightrope and looking for an excuse to fall off it. I wasn't working a good programme. You can always tell. If the meetings begin to bore you, you're in trouble.

The fall came, as it usually does, from an unexpected direction. I'd made a date with a guy on adam4adam. An Indian – golden-skinned and as good-looking in the flesh as in his website picture (unusual, by the way). Name 'Mick' or something, but my type, that was all that mattered.

He told me he was a forensic psychologist. He might have been bullshitting from too much watching *CSI* or *Bones*. It didn't matter. I wasn't giving him a job interview. It was the second date I'd had in my dry six months. The first had been four months earlier with another young Indian – a baggage handler at Heathrow.

As I say, the London gay world has not the slightest interest in 'relationships'. It took me a while to work that out. I'd played that earlier date pathetically wrong. I'd done dinner in Balans. I was desperate to 'connect' and for us to 'get to know each other'. I, meanwhile, was unloading too much on him. By the time the main course came round he was growing uneasy. At the club later, he excused himself ('I'm so glad to have met you') and was off and away. At least he got a free dinner out of it. All I got was fuck-all.

The six-month date I played cooler. Before doing anything personal, and after dinner (Balans again), this Mick suggested a movie at the Vue Trocadero, the nearest cinema to Old Compton Street. He had a film he wanted to see, *Shame*. It had just come out, January 2012 – terrific reviews. I didn't give a shit about what movie we were going to see. We got two seats in the front row. We were under observation by five hundred people behind us. Enjoy your movie, the person taking your ticket says. The movie was all I would have to 'enjoy' for the next two hours – and I wouldn't.

If you haven't seen *Shame*, it opens with naked Michael Fassbender coming out of the shower with a dangling tool that practically bounces against his ankles. Every eye in the cinema was looking at it. You gasped. Was it, you wondered, prosthetic, like Wahlberg's monster at the end of *Boogie Nights*? No, it couldn't be – it swung and dangled. It was, amazingly, real. Steve McQueen had got the attention of everyone in the audience – women thinking, 'I'd like that inside me, filling my whatnot'; men thinking, well, 'Wow!'

As the plot unfolds, it's a story about the miseries of – what else? – sex addiction. He's the prisoner of that prick; he'll never escape. Watching it, something inside me exploded. I'd come of age in Hollywood but no film ever touched me like this one did. It was so damned accurate. It was as if the film had ripped a scab off an unhealed wound which was spurting like a broken sewer pipe. How, I wondered, had the director, McQueen, found out all this about ME, Jack Sutherland? I was being forced to look at myself and my horrible addiction – like Malcolm McDowell in *A Clockwork Orange*.

I couldn't leave and I couldn't not look. By the end I was convinced the whole audience had forgotten Fassbender's twelve-inch thingy and was looking, pityingly, at paranoid me. I insisted on sitting right through the credits. Not because I wanted to know who the fifth gaffer was, but because I wanted everyone out of that place before I emerged into the bright foyer lights. Shame. That's what I felt.

My 'date' (no longer) went to the toilet, and when he came out I told him I had to go home. By myself. He said nothing, looked at me oddly, and left. He must have felt he'd had a narrow escape, but at least I'd paid for the meal and tickets.

I went to my mother's flat. She was out of town, thank God. I spent a couple of hours just crying, feeling like the piece of shit I was. I vomited. I knew only one thing would help – and it wasn't vodka. And it wasn't marijuana. And it wasn't NA. Only crystal would handle what was going through me. I made the phone call for a pick-up, an hour later, at Holborn station, calling by an ATM on the way. Crystal isn't cheap at that time of night in London. Having done the deal I crossed town to a little head shop in Soho where I bought a lighter, two crystal pipes and a gas fuel can. Along the way I bought some Kamagra and poppers, to sharpen the crystal edge. I was no longer crying – I was a zombie, lurching who knew where. By this time my stuff was ready and waiting at Holborn. At that little alley behind the station the exchange was made. Wordlessly. I remember crying while I prepared the pipe for the inhale that would destroy six months. Then the rush, and release.

Thereafter it was the usual drugs-and-sex spree for days and a spiral down. Two weeks off, three days on. Bumpalong fucking Cassidy. And one film did it.

I pulled myself back together, more or less, with copious amounts of weed, which I eventually tapered off. Then I kicked the alcohol. Bit by bit, I clambered back.

Recovery was difficult. But I had support from parents (God knows why they stuck with me), my larger family, and from the man I love, who stuck by me through some awful times, and whom I have formed a civil union with. Jeison. His, as I said before, is the one tattoo on my body which – God willing – I shall go to my grave with unpatched. If I could I'd tattoo the name on my heart.

I found a couple of groups that really worked for me. One LGBT Crystal, the other in Brixton, where I now live, for all-comers. I have a wonderful sponsor, Eddy, whose sleep I have regularly troubled with phone calls and sporadic crises. I am, at the time of writing this, coming up to two years. Twelve more to go to beat my own personal record. If I do it, it will be one day at a time – starting with tomorrow.

I'll leave it there.

EPILOGUE/DRUGALOG

I'm an addict. I have to accept it if I ever want to get beyond it. I've been an addict ever since, aged nine, I glugged a bottle of cheapissimo alcopop* with the neighbourhood bad boys, and, after doing a wild monkey act for their amusement, collapsed. Two of them carried me home, leaned me up against the front door, and legged it. Ding-dong ditch, addicts call it. The door opened and I fell flat on the doormat. My parents were first horrified then forgiving. The dangerous thing was – I'd enjoyed it. Aged, I repeat, nine.

In this afterword I'll draw up a checklist of the kinds of drugs I was prescribed and those I abused over the thirty years of life that followed. I'm ashamed of it, but I'll tell it honestly. I can do that, because I'm recovering, and because I've had practice in any number of NA/AA/CA/SA/MA sessions.

I was, when I was 'practising', a discriminating addict. I'd worked out, the hard way, my get-by, get-high intake. As regards scrip (physician prescription), I'd been diagnosed ADHD, bipolar, sex-addicted and pathologically 'angry', at Las Encinas. A dangerous bundle for any human being to wrap around.

* Pink Lady and Thunderbird were their names.

Seroquel – in doses from 200 to 600 mils – has been my chemical crutch. It keeps me from exploding: like those nuclear energy sources, which are forever underwater. I also took Depakote, which blows you up like a blimp. That was for mood, but my mother's bathroom scales persuaded me to drop it after I passed 250 pounds. From time to time I had Strattera for ADHD and anger. You have, if you have my inner madnesses, to mix your own cocktail; one that works for you, but not necessarily for the next guy.

I got these pills, free of charge, from the NHS. (In the US, if you weren't 'covered', bills could run as high $1,800 a month for the drugs I was legally on. I've had to pay that amount between jobs.) There were also some different anger-management and ADHD medications. Most bounced off me without effect.

Once I got the dosages straight, these medicines kept me on the rails and ready for street stuff. My principal drug of abuse was, ever since school days, marijuana. Old faithful. It dissolved my constitutional raging angers. I took it like a housewife taking Valium. Jack's little helper. My tolerance was high enough that I could smoke it (even the strong British skunk, without tobacco, American-style, cigar-fat spliffs or in bongs – coke cans if desperate) without being (too) obviously high. It elevated the Seroquel dullness to mellowness. Recalled my happiest SoCal times – or, at least, deluded me into thinking they were happy.

I haven't touched marijuana for two years now. Not because I don't love the stuff. But I can't control its consequences. That 'gateway' shit the puritans peddle is, for me, true. It opens a door. 'Why the fuck not?' you think. 'This feels good, that will feel better. Stands to reason.' Then, fool that you are, you've kicked the hornet nest again.

Cocaine, like the old song says, doesn't thrill me at all. It gives me no kick, just rhinitis if I sniff it and laryngitis if I smoke it. It stings my snout and does nothing for my penis. Like sniffing sand. I've never done crack. I was put off all that complicated wire and glass and flame stuff. Not to mention the incendiary risks that basted poor Richard Pryor like a Colonel Sanders chicken.

I've smoked, as earlier recorded, PCP just once. As a schoolboy. The preparation is simple. Just soak your Camel in the liquid, wait for it to dry, and puff. It's too mind-blowing for me. I notice that it's popular with African American and Hispanic communities. What little I know of it, a gang drug, and not popular among gays.

LSD and mushrooms I left behind with my school books. They're not grown-up drugs. And you can never be sure how strong the dose is. I've met full-blown psychotics from these drugs who'll never think straight again. Ecstasy wasn't around when I was at school – not generally around, in fact, until I was well into my thirties. I've always liked it – as a sex stimulant, principally. It's pretty tame. No psychosis, but not much kick.

Anabolic steroids and testosterone I've used during my Muscle Mary periods of life (see Chapter 7). They work. Make you feel good, as well. And if you hang out in good gyms, the stuff is readily available, but never guaranteed pure. Side effects, long-term, are not good. Least of all shrivelled testicles. Acne and roid rage are other downsides.

I've never used heroin for the simple reason that, moving

in the company I do, it's never been seriously offered to me. Heroin is not big in the gay communities.* Probably, I think, because it's sexually depressive. Makes you feel good, I'm told. But un-horny and gloomy. Not, in any sense of the word, 'gay'. No one parties on the stuff. I suspect, though, once you're hooked it's the most addictive of them all. I've seen, in the back alleys of Soho, guys injecting between their toes and into their penises. I'm told, when there isn't an injectable vein left, the poor sods will jab the needle into their eyeballs.

In America, if you have a friendly doctor, you can get prescription drugs like Vicodin/OxyContin by the bagful (the co-pays are daunting, though, even on the best health plans). Hillbilly Heroin may have worked in the Appalachians. It did bugger-all for me. Ditto Xanax. These pills didn't even kill the pain when my back was falling apart (nor, by the way, did Oramorph, institutionally approved morphine, in less than near-lethal and hugely constipating dosages). I gave away the packs showered on me by my HMO to whoever wanted them. I was surprised how many of my friends did want them.

My one experience with so-called 'legal highs' is painful. In my later years in LA I used to hang out and smoke weed with a bunch of straight Hispanics who went regularly down to Mexico. We'd smoke a lot and talk a lot. One of them told me, with a misty look in his eyes, about this drug called salvia, which was like the peyote the Indians and 1960s hippies

* There are, as this chapter will make clear, gay and straight drug preferences, as well as old and young preferences.

were into.* It had given him the trippiest high he'd ever had, he said. I registered the fact, without much interest.

A couple of years later, in London, I discovered that salvia is Britain's 'Number One Legal High'. What the hell, I bought a pack, along with few other legal highs, off the internet. With some excitement I opened the sachet up. It looks like ground-up pepper. I stuck a pinch in a crystal pipe, lit up, and puffed cautiously. Nothing. I stuck a little in a glass marijuana pipe and did the same. Still nothing. Ground-up pepper would have delivered a better high. I stuffed more in and took a gigantic puff.

The effect was instant. And bizarre – a full-on out-of-body experience. I saw myself, six feet beneath myself, sitting on the sofa rocking in what looked like agony or ecstasy. So far, so good. But I was also suffocating. I was watching from a distance while feeling, down on the sofa, my lungs bursting. I had three minutes of consciousness and ten minutes of life (probably brain-damaged from anoxia) left. It got terrifying. Finally, with a gigantic effort, I drew in the biggest, raspingest breath I've ever drawn in my life. Out of body or near death? Both. I was back in the land of the living. It was the worst drug experience I've ever had in my life; and I've had plenty. I threw the salvia and all the other little packets away. Fuck 'legal'. From now on, only illegal or prescribed.

Temazepam ('tams') is, I've discovered, quite big in Soho. I've taken them from time to time, as doctor-prescribed sleeping pills. (Oval in shape, one of their street

* *John*. And Aldous Huxley, viz the hippy holy text *The Doors of Perception*.

names is 'rugby balls' – who says junkies don't have a sense of humour?) They work. I've never injected them. I've seen what they do. Your arms and legs turn black and drop off. If I'd been straight I suspect I might well have been into crack and heroin, Vicodin and temazepam. But my nature took me down different chemical pathways.

Ketamine – the horse tranquilliser – is big in London clubs. Particularly gay clubs. Jonathan Hellyer, in his show *The Dame Edna Experience* at the Royal Vauxhall Tavern (where I occasionally did security), liked to begin his routine with a barrage of K jokes. The glazed eyes of the crowd confirmed that he knew his audience. (They took the stuff, I hasten to add, outside the place and my watch.)

My using partner at this period (around 2010), Nathan, was hooked on K. I took it a few times, but it never really worked for me. Neither did mephedrone – meow-meow, as it's called. I might as well, to be honest, have been taking Pro Plus.

Same with amphetamines, which have never worked for me. Straight uppers have never upped me. Methamphetamine is something else.

I have strange patterns of resistance and tolerance. By the twenty-first century, I was getting to know them well and work round them. The one time that K did work for me is worth an anecdote.

It was in a public sauna. I was with Nathan and my for-the-night chemsex partner. I had a stash of crystal. Nathan, as usual, was loaded with enough K to tranquillise a herd of horses and still have a good time himself. He also had some mephedrone.

There we were, three of us, in a cubicle. Ready for action. I had several sniffs of Nathan's stuff – the usual no effect beyond stinging nostrils. Nathan, ever resourceful, then mixed K and MM into one bag, shook it up, and gave me and my partner for the night a 'bump'. That's what you do when there's no surface to lay a line. You put a little heap on a key.

This unfamiliar chem-mix worked on me. I felt drunk, but perhaps a little too drunk. I didn't like losing total control this way. Thanks, Nathan. I staggered off to the dry sauna to sober up. I was beginning to feel dangerously drug-fucked. Bad. It got quickly worse. A lot worse. I recall walking down the corridor, screaming Nathan's name. Then I collapsed. Nathan dragged me onto a bench. Then, damn him, went off to continue his bonking. First things first.

I was freaked out. Utterly. Raving and weeping. Then, as the drugs continued to hit me, I entered what is called the K-hole. Hell. I was now lying, on my back, conscious and wholly paralysed. My brain, eyes and ears were working perfectly. Too well, if anything. My body and mouth were in paralysis. It was locked-in syndrome. I remembered, all too clearly, reading recently about some kids who'd overdone mephedrone and ended up drooling vegetables. I'm going to live in this coffin, my body, for the rest of my life, I thought.

The terror was beyond words. And, dammit, these were drugs I'd never really wanted to take. I only did it as a kind of bathhouse favour to Nathan. And where the fuck was he? Shagging the night away. 'Has he had a stroke?' I heard someone say. Others were high-tailing it out of the place. The last thing you want is to answer ambulance and police questions with a towel round your middle and a tumescent penis peeking through.

It lasted an hour and a half, until sensation began returning – first, believe it or not, to my little finger. That was my last experiment with those two poisons. The long-term effects of them, as I've observed and been told at meetings, are worse than even heroin. K, I'm told, eats holes in your bladder – having finished perforating your brain.

I finally found what would be, for the remainder of my drug career (a year), my drug cocktail of choice. A mix of GHB and crystal jokingly called G&T. It was, along with with marijuana, ecstasy and small vodka chasers, exactly what worked for me. For me and crystal, see the San Francisco disaster. I was using it, and had a reliable supply stream. (It can be incredibly expensive, I found, in London.) I'd always stayed away from GHB, although I'd often been offered it a number of times. One of its legitimate uses, I believe, is as a heavy-duty degreasing agent, particularly useful on car-wheel rims (who says drugs aren't glamorous?).

It's highly corrosive. Think of the drool of the monster in *Alien*. You swallow it from glass containers (not plastic – the stuff eats through plastic in seconds. And stomach liner?). You swallow it mixed with Coca-Cola, or some other soda. By itself it tastes beyond foul – like rim-cleaner, you might say.

Dosage is critically important. Half a mil will give the beginner a high. Four mils will kill him. (Women, I think, would no more think of drinking G than nail varnish.) Four mils will, to be honest, kill most anyone. This is not a drug for the careless. Or the nervous.

The first night I took G makes for an interesting story. And, I hope, a warning.

In London, during this wild 2010 period, a Latin chemsex date invited me, after we'd got to know each other past the first hook-up, to his place across the river. An unusual friendly act. Normally it was slam, bang, never see you again, where's the money. He was Latin. We hit it off, in a matey way.

He lived on the South Bank with his ex-husband, now a flatmate, an older English guy. It all sounded civilised. I had an Addison Lee account and drove over (sober and not carrying anything), found the place and waited an age to be buzzed in. He's high, I thought. Just as I was about to leave, the door opened. I went up to the flat to be welcomed in by a totally naked middle-aged white guy. He was totally drug-fucked. I assumed it was the ex-husband-current-flatmate. I am not into elderly white guys.

I was stone-cold sober and I had two choices. Bugger off or get high. I went in before making my mind up. What met me (by now gobsmacked) was, I calculate, nine guys, all naked, white, and older than me. And all off their nuts. I was pulled into the kitchen, passing my chemsex mate in the bedroom with four guys round him like lions round their prey. I'd been expecting one-on-one but suddenly I found myself the star attraction of a geriatric P&P. Now I understood why I'd been invited. To swell the crowd.

A crystal meth pipe was shoved in my mouth. Freshly loaded. I gulped some heavy hits out of sheer nervousness. But it wasn't enough. I was so out of my element (P&P was not something I ever enjoyed) that I still felt sober.

At which point the guy who had opened the door for me offered me G.

Momentous. I'd up to now religiously avoided the stuff, but so embarrassed was I that I decided to try it. 'Enjoy,' he said – a 'G&T' (G&Tina, i.e. crystal). The first time I'd heard the joke. The combination, he said, would 'relax' me. He gave me a two-mil measure. Dangerous as fuck for a first-time user.

I gulped the brew down. Ten minutes later I was hit with a feeling I can only describe as 'animal-horny'. A rhinoceros on Viagra with two horns. I'll keep the details of the next part blank. You want to fill the blank in (who the hell would?), call up wildgayorgy.com or whatever. But the feeling was unfathomable. And it went on all night. When the party was closing down, next morning, me and my friendly fat white doorman went to another all-day party. I was there thirty-six hours.

G&T, thereafter, was my tipple. Until, a few months later, I changed my life, for the last time, as I hope. I pass stalls selling crystal pipes every day in Brixton market. Dinky little things. The sad sacks you see buying them, digging in their pockets for the pennies left there, are not advertisements for the drug. What's always struck me as odd is that everywhere you go in the US you see before and after posters about crystal. Not, for some reason, in the UK.

It's a killer. It fucked my teeth – I still have eight grand's worth of work to do on them. (Don't ask where the money for this book is going.) Stick that message on the pipes, like they stick the surgeon general's warning on cigarette packs in America. 'Is this worth your teeth?'

I'll finish with a word or two about one of the stranger aspects of crystal. Like the word 'chemsex' itself, sex, for me, was – during my bad years – inextricably linked to drugs. I have a high libido, I've never had any performance problems. I've never needed Viagra or Cialis or Kamagra except to sharpen the edge of whatever drug I happened to be using. Icing on the cake.

My sex drive drove me first to multiple, excitingly irresponsible, anonymous encounters in public or nondescript places. Cottaging, as it's oddly called in Britain, although there was nothing cosy about what I liked. I was increasingly reckless – that, of course, added to the sex-addiction high. Adrenaline was, in these episodes, as important to me as crystal. You get the adrenaline high from danger.

The drive evolved (I'm not alone here, check out Grindr.com) to a fascination with role play and scenarios. It began, as best I can put a date on it, around the time I was diagnosed bipolar. It was quite simple to begin with. I liked to walk in, supposedly surprising two guys doing it (after some tantalising voyeurism) and 'intrude', 'interrupt', 'join in'. When I had a house of my own, it could get quite elaborate, with a lot of preparatory to and froing on the net.

In a funny kind of way I was like an MTV director. I did indeed (at home) photograph a few of these encounters. The screenplay was always the same – me, the intruder. Often I'd do it in a state of simulated surprise and fury. 'What!! In my House!!' Then I'd join in. Sounds stupid, I know. But what kind of sex, if you stand back and take a good look, isn't stupid? It's a problem that faces every pornography shoot.

One of the effects of crystal I've mentioned above is that,

after you've got into the habit of taking it, straightforward sex no longer has any point or thrill to it. You've somehow left it behind. I read somewhere it's a brain and receptor thing.

The kind of sex I came to need, in my using years, became laser-narrow. I could either have NSA ('no strings attached') or increasingly ritualised role play. Preferably the second, but, if push came to shove, the first. This is how the ritual went – the 'plot', so to speak. I walk into a dark room. There's an unknown person waiting for me – dressed only in white briefs. He's on his knees. There's no talking. Tomb-like silence. If he so much as says 'Hi', it's all over and goodbye. They take my cock out and do what I've come for. When it's over, I leave, not a word having been said. Summary: no lights, no talking, no touching, suck and goodbye. I never did a repeat with the same guy. The whole thing laced with crystal.

Drugs really fuck you up. They contort you and take away everything natural in your life. I hate them.

So that is my user profile. Every day now puts it, and the madness that goes with drugs, another day in the past. Thank God, thank my parents, thank NA. My advice? If your doctor prescribes a drug, get a second opinion before you use it. They'll sometimes give you scrip just to get you out of the surgery. Particularly if they sense you're a problem user. My advice on non-medicinal drugs? Don't. And, if you do, Stop. And if you can't stop, do as little harm to your loved ones before the drugs kill you. They will. Quickly, if your loved ones are lucky. If there's anything here that you think glamorises drugs and using, ignore it.

RU: REUNITED

The preceding narrative was two years ago. I've put my life together. Like Humpty Dumpty, it won't be what it was. But I can honestly claim to be recovering.

NA/LGBT has helped. My family, friends, sponsor and partner have helped more. It's hard but good things happen and that strengthens you. One of the other best things happened about a year ago. I have a friend, Chrissy Darling (drag artist), who's a great fan of RuPaul. We talked about him, which brought back a load of memories. Some great moments in my life, some (particularly the last Vegas disaster) painful.

That was a Friday. The next day, Saturday, a strange number flashed up on my phone. It was Ru. He'd been at a meditation meeting and thinking of me. He'd riffled through the scores of numbers he had for me, and – 'Bingo!' It was the first of dozens of old numbers he had on his phone. Kismet.

I told him everything in an hours-long phone conversation.

'How fucking strange is that?' I said. 'Just last night, you were so in my thoughts. I was on the edge of reaching out to you.'

It was a gift of God. I'd so missed him.

CV: JACK OF ALL TRADES (ALL JOB OFFERS WELCOME)

Profile

Retrained and certified in 2010 as a Close Protection Operative, Level Three, with Longmoor Security. A determined, versatile, discreet and well-presented professional with a wealth of experience gained from careers in the high-end sector of the chauffeured transportation and personal protection industry.

Career

2010–2016: Sutherland Specialist Security – Close Protection / Head of Security

Working freelance: Personal Bodyguard, Head of Security, Door Supervisor, Artist Liaison and Security Guard

2009–2010: Mickey Rourke – Close Protection / Personal Assistant / Chauffeur

Working for Mickey Rourke during the making of the film *Passion Play*, staring Megan Fox, Bill Murray and Mickey Rourke. Four months' preparation in New York and two months on location in New Mexico.

2007–2009: Virgin Limousines – Vice President / Dir. of Business Development

Was initially recruited as the Director of Business

Development to strengthen the existing operations and grow market share in their San Francisco location. Was then promoted to Vice President by Sir Richard Branson and the Board of Directors. I was then responsible for opening two new locations, the first inside the Fairmont Hotel in San Jose and the second in Los Angeles.

2006–2007: RideWell Transportation – Vice President Sales & Marketing

Recruited to grow the reputation and brand of this leading high-end chauffeured transportation company.

2006: Empire-CLS Chauffeured Services – Senior VP Sales & Marketing

Promoted to create and drive the company's global sales and marketing strategy. Was responsible for both the San Francisco and Los Angeles locations, which entailed commuting to both locations.

2005–2006: CLS Worldwide Chauffeured Services – General Manager

Promoted to restructure and integrate newly-acquired CLS Worldwide into Empire International, and head the continuous development and operational management of the company.

2004–2005: CLS Worldwide Chauffeured Services – Director of Sales & Marketing

Recruited by Doug Trussler (Bison Capital) and Charlie Horky (former founder of CLS Worldwide) to rebuild and nurture relationships with existing accounts, and develop new business.

2002–2004: Dav-El Chauffeured Transportation – Operations Manager / General Manager

Managed the HR, Accounting, Reservations, Dispatch and Fleet Departments, providing services to high-profile clients in the entertainment and business sectors: Sony Pictures, Universal Pictures, Bank of America, Fleet Bank, and Morgan Stanley.

1997–2002: Budget on Sunset / T&T Limo – Special Projects Manager / General Manager

Hired as the Special Projects Manager to work on various projects and then promoted to General Manager. Budget on Sunset was a high-end car rental serving the entertainment industry. When I started we had one location and we then grew to four locations, which I oversaw. T&T Limo was the sister company of Budget on Sunset – I was a part-owner as I opened the company from the ground up for the primary owner, Tony Phelps.

1996–1997: Joe Blasco Cosmetics – Special Projects Manager

Hired as the Special Projects Manager to work on various projects and then primarily involved in restructuring and reorganising the Cosmetics Division within the Joe Blasco family. I worked alongside Mr Blasco and spent my time between the Los Angeles head office and the Orlando manufacturing plant.

1995–1996: REM, *Monster* World Tour – Personal Assistant / Close Protection

Hired as the Personal Assistant to Michael Stipe, lead singer of the band REM. This year-long world tour included:

Australia, New Zealand, Europe, Asia, Tel Aviv, Canada and the USA.

1993–1995: Film and TV Production

Started working on music videos as a Production Assistant and Artist Liaison. Then started to work on commercials, TV shows and feature films. I held various positions during this time, such as: Locations Manager, Transportation Manager, Production Coordinator, Assistant Director and Second Assistant Director. Worked with such renowned directors as Danny Boyle, Mark Romanek and Gore Verbinski.

1992–1993: Southwestern Academy – Administration

After graduating from Southwestern Academy as the Salutatorian and Student Body President, I was hired by the Administration Department to work in the Accounting and Admissions Department.

1990–1992: Planned Parenthood – Peer Counsellor

Worked as a Counsellor with teenagers in Pasadena, South Pasadena, and San Marino. Trained in sex education, and contraception and AIDS awareness, I conducted group lectures and one-on-one support to teenagers.

1985–1990: Volunteer / Work Experience – Jack of All Trades

I have always loved to work and started working for free just to get the experience. Over these years, I did the following: Saddlers' Hardware (UK), Market Seller (UK), Farm Hand (UK), Coffee Shop (LA), Old People's Home (LA), Horse Groom and Horse Exerciser (LA).

Qualifications and Training

2013: Level 2 Certificate in Door Supervision

2013: Physical Intervention Training: Restrictive Interventions (Maybo)

2010: Hostile Environment Close Protection training with the Longmoor Group, resulting in Level 3 Certificate in Protective Security (Bucks New University)

2010: First Aid at Work Certificate

2010: Oxygen Therapy & Use of an AED Certificate

2010: Close Quarter Combat Certificate

2010: Tactical firearms training with the Longmoor Group in Slovenia, covering: use of cover, advance to contact and drills (both IBG and CP team). Small arms used were the Glock 17, AK-47, MP5 and MP5K.

2010: SIA Close Protection (Door Supervisor / Conflict Management)

2002–2004: Attended three separate new-hire customer service training for the Ritz Carlton Hotel

2002–2005: Attended two separate new-hire customer service training for the Four Seasons Hotel

1992: Graduated with Honours from Southwestern Academy, Los Angeles

ACKNOWLEDGEMENTS

First and most important are what I call my Guardian Angels. Those without whom I know I would not be here today. I am not a lucky person and have never had much luck. So the fact that my years of using and abusing my body, combined with my previous life choices, have left me with no major consequences can only be considered by me to be a **miracle** and a **gift**. Today I am not willing to play Russian roulette yet again with the precious and valued life that I have, by using one more time. I am here today and not dead or facing a long or life sentence in some jail, and my health has not been affected.

Powers Greater Than Me!

My Higher Power (God)

My Guardian Angels Above

❖ John Watt (Papa) ❖ Isabella Watt (Granny) ❖

❖ Yvonne Reynolds ❖ Frank Talamantes (BJ) ❖

My Rocks

Mary Guilland Sutherland (Mum)

John Andrew Sutherland (Dad)

Jeison Valencia (Paquito)

I would like to thank each and every one of following people below. They have each played a major part in helping me through the challenging times in my life and they have contributed to making me the man that I am.

Thank you from the bottom of the heart for the part that you have played!

Edith Emenike, Jamie Charles, Matt Waterhouse, Mitchell Pardington, Bilé Dirir-Guled, Jamie Page, Dani Gibbison, Ciara Walsh, David Mason, The Margarete Centre, Intuitive Recovery, George Richardson, Jason Dickie, Jakub J Ar, Cuki Darmawan, Mawan Hatman, Max Salerno, Chrissy Darling, Chris Amos, Gary Devonshire, Dr Christian Jessen, Daniel Agoston, Nathan Barry, Anastasia Makarenko, Mickey Rourke, Javier Chavez, Trung Lee, Albert Vasquez-Cartagena, Reza Partovi, Patrick Carnes, Charlie Horky, Joey Henriques, Robert Davila, Arthur Belmontes, Patrick Cooney, Ryan Miller, Scott Solombrino, Paco Frank Sanchez, Tony Phelps, Luis Zavila, RuPaul Andre Charles, Alex Medina, Joe Blasco, Gene La Pietra, Freddie Barrios, Noah Mariano, Rod Rave, Ron Martinez, Dayne Peavy, Louie Ochoa, Byron Torrento, Carlos Harveaux, David Heredia, Martin Medrano, Luka Postmyr, Cornel Sorian, Nikolas Nikolaou, Javier Castillero, Michael Stipe, Line Postmyr, David Unger, Corina Conti, Rhea Rupert, Jason Garrett, Sandra Djohan, Genc Gizer, Sarah Correia, Adia Millet, Crystal Rodriguez, Mark Hamilton, Natasha Marcy, Nicholas Glenn, Leland Mothershead, Kennith Veronda, Lynn Yekiazarian, Aaron Fricke, Peter Gabriel, Michael Ferry, Jeana Herbst, Lyla Marquez, Pamela Marquez, Jennifer Iida Underhill, Job Carder, Morningstar

Harmon, Michael Fisher, Jeff Langley, Janie Morgan, Anna Lewis, Jasiek Watt, George Watt, John Watt, Eva Watt, David Johnston, Sarah Upton, Penny Upton, Frank Mills, Ben Reynolds, Sandy Watt, Oliver Watt, Hugh Watt

P.S.

I would also like to personally thank Lee Brackstone and his entire team at Faber & Faber for believing in both my father and me and for fighting for this project.

Lastly

This project would not have been possible with out my truly amazing and talented father. It has always been a dream of mine to write a book together. (Not sure this is what he expected.) He has stood by me continuously through my entire life, giving me nothing but unconditional love and support right from day one. I could not have asked for a better father. I would not be here today or be the man I am without him by my side.

Thank you, Dad. I love you!

SECRETARIAL AFTERWORD: JOHN SUTHERLAND

I started out intending to be a listening device, nothing more. I failed. My (writerly) voice mixes, as will be clear, with Jack's spoken voice. And there's a third person in the mix. Raymond Chandler – God help me. That master of LA noir, and his 'cadence', as he called the Chandlerian voice, has always been, for me, the perfect tone for the place Jack called home all those years. The fibre, though, is Jack, through and through. Any stylistic finish is mine. Discreet, I hope. At some points, I admit, it's ventriloquist's dummy. At other points – his afterword, for example – it's Jack's unvarnished voice and timbre.

Did we, people who've read the manuscript ask, 'bond'. Yes, and no. My genuine feel is uneasy. You shouldn't, in parent–child relations, know 'everything' – at least, not after infancy. Changing a grown man's nappies is no work for a father. You can't buddy-bond across generations. I understand that better now. Depression, Jack's ailment, is, I think, contagious. At times, particularly in the later, grimmer, sections, I've felt so low I've seriously considered talking to my doctor. If I was still drinking I would have been dead drunk around page 230.

Frankly, I like Jack a little less and love him as much as ever – more, even – having listened to hundreds of hours of what most parents, for their own peace of mind, should be spared.

What he feels about me he can tell you himself. Or not. On the whole I'd prefer not.

*THE LAST WORD: HE DO THE LAPD IN DIFFERENT VOICES**

OCTOBER 2010: LONDON

I had been up for a Party and Play session with a couple who lived in a lavish penthouse near Hyde Park. One of the partners was just my type: Latino, late twenties, hot body and stunning face, with just the right goods going on with his package and perky bubble butt. The other partner could not have been further from my type: early fifties, out of shape and circumcised. However, the one thing he did have was an endless supply of G&T, not to mention all the necessary side dishes needed to complete the menu – the only reason I had agreed to join them after hours of holding out for a more appealing offer. And importantly, everything was free of charge, which was perfect, as I had fuck-all in my wallet and a negative balance in all three of my bank accounts. If I was lucky I maybe had enough coppers to buy a large latte. No flavoured syrup, though, and what fucking good would that coffee have done to take the edge off? The only price for joining them was my dignity, my pride and, of course, my Viagra-hardened dick to be used equally on both.

The older guy was very white English with an incredibly

* *John*. The following is entirely Jack's own words.

upper-class accent that alone would normally cause me to instantly lose the stiffest of chemical erections. Nothing against the upper class or their accent, but they just did not complement the dirty, sleazy type of action I required after the chems had rushed through my body and got me proper on it. Every time he would speak, it was like a slap in the face or a quick sniff of smelling salts bringing me back into reality, which was precisely what I was trying to escape from. It felt like I was about to shag a member of the Royal Family, which is not right in any way.

They had invited me to join them for the usual bareback chem play on at least forty occasions over the past few months, and I had always politely declined without mentioning the real reason why – that I was not into old, white, fat and cut. I had only agreed to go on this occasion because I was so desperate for a fix. I had just spent over six hours hunting on every known gay website, desperately seeking any free chem fun that I could join within a twenty-five-mile radius of central London. The longer I tried, the more intense the feeling of sobriety – reality was creeping up and hitting me HARD. Towards the end, it felt like leaving a warm house to walk into the bone-chilling wind of Chicago in the deepest of winter. It was 00:15 when I gave up. I was so desperate for any drugs that I asked them to send an Addison Lee on their account to pick me up from Holborn.

As I walked into their flat, the first thing that caught my eye was the pipe, laid out alongside the other requisites on the massive glass dining-room table. Large bag of Tina? Check. Large bottle of G? Check. Several packs of Viagra? Check. Several bottles of poppers? Check. Large bottle of lube?

Check. Not a condom in sight? Check. All the ingredients necessary for a shag session with someone that no amount of money would normally have convinced me to sleep with. I had once, in my early twenties, been offered a considerable sum – $18,000, to be exact – for a night of just walking around in various underwear, wanking while being watched by a wealthy client who used to rent high-end cars from me. He would be smoking cocaine and directing me what to do – no touching involved, I was promised. I declined. At that point my pride had no number attached to it.

After getting the introduction and bullshit formalities out of the way, I asked for a hit on the pipe – all within two minutes of walking in the door. I had not even taken my coat off. Initially, the older partner was controlling and lighting the pipe for me. They were both drug-fucked and gagging for fresh meat. The hot Latin guy kept trying to get into my pants while I was hitting the pipe. I could tell he was on it good, but I could not bring myself to look at the older guy. I just kept my eyes focused on the glass table. After a few mediocre hits, I said that I needed to hit the pipe – my way to relax and get on the same level as them. The older guy finally gave me the pipe and I jumped into the driver's seat going 150 m.p.h., hitting it like there was no tomorrow. Huge puffs of white smoke blew from my mouth like massive peaceful clouds – the type you can only see from an aeroplane window. In between puffs, I asked them to prepare me a strong shot of G, just under 2.5 millilitres. I clearly remember feeling sick to my stomach for how I was about to lower myself. This was the first time I had been willing to do ANYTHING to get some Tina running through my body. The American term 'strawberry' came to mind – a female sellin' pussy for crack. It was truly one of the worst and most degrading feelings I have ever experienced. And unfortunately it was not to be the first and last time, as I promised myself. It was the beginning of the long period of my life's lowest point. The door had been opened wide and could not be shut.

Within a matter of fifteen to twenty minutes, the overwhelming rush of the T and the G combined hit me like a steam train. I stripped off naked, and my disgust of the older white man had completely gone. I was actually gagging for both, for anyone. I was on it. Bring it on; or, should I say, bring them on.

The session was cut very short, about five and a half hours after we started the Sodom and Gomorrah play. The couple had already been up for two days and the Latin guy was way too high and getting very messy. I had just taken another strong two-mil shot of G when the white guy told me very abruptly that I had to leave. He was trying to look after his partner while pushing me out the flat as quickly as possible. No Addison Lee offered on my trip home. I remember being so fucked – I don't know how I managed to get dressed or make it down the stairs.

It was still dark outside and lightly raining. Luckily it was early and there were no other people on the street. I had to wait about thirty minutes on the front step of the building as the G had hit me too hard to move. Finally, I composed myself enough to start the trip home. I didn't have money for a taxi and was in no condition to do the bus thing, so I decided to walk to Holborn. It felt like for ever and I am sure I was going round in circles because I was so fucked. I eventually made it home in full daylight, feeling very sober and extremely guilty. I took my so-called sleeping pill – a powerful combination of vodka, copious amounts of the strongest herbal cannabis and three to four times my normal dose of Seroquel – and after three or four hours I eventually drifted off.

I awoke very slowly from a troubled sleep, feeling like an eighty-five-year-old man who's had a life full of proper hard graft. I was lying in a damp and soggy bed with an outline of my entire body stained in salty-coloured sweat on the red sheets. It looked eerily like a murder scene. My confused head struggled to grasp the harsh world of reality from the state of heavy self-medication required to get at least a few hours of rest, when my bipolar brain properly shuts down and goes blank.

I finally managed to get out of bed, but while my mind was working my speech and body were desperately trying to catch up. Once I felt more or less alive, the heavy-hitting comedown from the drugs combined with the reality check of what I had lowered myself to became unbearable. An ever-familiar guilt slowly climbed through me, starting from my toes – the realisation of who I am, and how I have let down my loved ones and family. I am shit, I am worthless, I am a nobody, I should be dead. Like a champagne bottle shaken for hours until it violently explodes, I burst into uncontrollable tears, barely able to get a breath in between the sobbing. I looked up at the ceiling and begged God to stop this life sentence of mental torture. This was the start of long and painful time in my life. It truly felt like a divine punishment for all of the bad things I had done, all the pain and suffering I had caused, all the selfishness I had functioned on for years, all the people I had let down by not being there for them. I would wake up daily and once the reality of life had hit, the tears would come. I would beg God to save me and take my breath away in my sleep. This was hell.

5 OCTOBER 2015: DAIOS COVE LUXURY RESORT & VILLAS, CRETE, GREECE

Today I am twenty-eight months sober from drugs and alcohol, something that thirty months ago I would have thought completely and utterly impossible. It's the longest I have been sober in the last twelve years of my chronic-relapsing life. I never managed more then nine months before. Today I sit here feeling completely calm, and at peace. The overwhelming feelings that run through my body and mind are the polar opposite of the feelings I had for so many years before getting sober. I have a genuine feeling of pure happiness and contentment for the life I have chosen. In all my years, and especially when I was stereotypically successful, I was never truly happy. Today I am a relatively uncomplicated man who does not need the materialistic trappings I once fought and worked so hard to have. I can appreciate such things in reflection, but I now know that in themselves they do not provide happiness. This feeling I have today of absolute contentment comes from within and is driven by the simple things in life: family, loved ones and friends, and also just being happy with who you are and the way you live. These and my fellow addicts in recovery, combined with a strong set of moral principles, give me more than any amount of money or possessions can ever bring.

Today I can honestly say that it's not the old Jack I have back, but a completely different person who in some way resembles the old Jack – maybe a distant cousin, or something. The new and drastically improved version, you could say. I am not saying I am fixed, or cured, or anywhere close to perfect. But today I try just to do the right thing on a daily basis, and when I get things wrong – which I do, and will continue to do, a lot – I am able to look inwards and identify what went wrong. I can then make the necessary amends, learn from the mistake and move on as hopefully a better person. Today I have the greatest gift possible: I have control of my life back, and I am able to live it being present on a daily basis. I am no longer stuck in the deadly and terribly painful life of active addiction.

I am writing this from the balcony of a beautiful beachside Villa 211, at the amazing Daios Cove Luxury Resort & Villas in Agios Nikolaos. This special trip is to treat my life partner, Jeison, and myself in celebration of our three-year wedding anniversary, his birthday and my two years of sobriety. This ultra-luxurious resort is the type of place I would only have had the pleasure of staying at while I was accompanying an A-list celebrity, carrying their bags and working through the entire trip to ensure that their holiday was utterly perfect from start to finish. Today it's my day. It's my holiday. It's my hard-earned trip to enjoy with my partner. The view to the crystal-blue ocean is the one of best sights I have ever set my eyes on, and the resort is by far in the top three I have had the privilege of staying in. Yet I am under no illusion that without all the hard work I have put into rebuilding my life, slowly, one brick at a time, this treat would never be possible. Every penny that went into this trip was earned by me during my new life in sobriety. Money does not bring you happiness but it does allow you to create memories and experiences of happy times. Today I can sit back and enjoy the view, the resort and the time spent with my amazingly loving and special life partner. This gift to us is priceless and one that I will treasure for ever.

MY SEXUALITY

My sexuality has always been, and still is, something that I, like many LGBTQ people, struggle to come to terms with. I first turned to drugs and alcohol as a boy to escape the fact that I was gay and feeling 'less than'. I have thought about not going through with this book project because of fears of coming out as gay publicly. I am – or was until this was published – still in the closet professionally. I have to this point always been in control of choosing whom I come out to.

I was able to build up a suit of armour that came from my professional success. For years, many people knew I was gay in my industry but the question was never asked. When my sexuality was made public and joked and laughed about, I reverted to the weak fourteen-year-old boy who wanted to end his life rather than live gay. My suit of armour melted. The addict in me took control during this period.

My addiction took possession of me for fourteen long years. Being gay is like being adopted: only those that are can fully understand what it's like.

It's important, I believe, to send the message that not all LGBTQ people are strong or confident in their sexuality and many take their lives rather than live with who they are. Everyone's sexuality should be private. Sexuality must not define us or play any part in our professional careers.

HOW I DID IT, THIS TIME!

Let me say first of all that obtaining sobriety, and the path that an individual takes to acquire a life of sobriety, is always going to be unique for each and every person. My belief is that it is similar to a snowflake. Each and every one is different, but beautiful in its own way. I don't think there is a right or a wrong way to win back a life from active addiction. As long as the end result – beating the cycle of addiction – is accomplished on a daily basis, that's all that matters. For me it's important that, as an addict in recovery, I do not judge others on their programme, their journey of sobriety and recovery path.

The way I see addiction is simple. There are two types. The first is when someone becomes addicted to a substance or a behaviour to cope with a certain time or experience. This is being addicted but not necessarily an addict. For example, if a person is responsible for accidently taking someone's life, they might turn to drugs and/or alcohol to deal with the feelings of guilt. On one of my last two trips to rehab, I met a guy in the outpatient programme. He had been driving home from a party in the late hours of the night, a bit drunk but not wasted. He accidently crashed his car, veering onto the sidewalk and killing a pedestrian. This poor guy had become completely addicted to drugs and alcohol simply to cope with his feelings. He shared on many occasions that prior to this tragedy he was a moderate social drinker and had never taken a drug. He had never shown any type of obsessive, addictive behaviours or tendencies prior to this night. That's not to say that this type of addiction is not bad or that he can even get sobriety back into his life – just that it is a certain type of addiction that is as strong and as life-destroying as the second type of addiction.

The second type is sometimes called a disease. It makes no difference to me what I call it, but what I do know is this is the type that I am. I believe that I was born with this thing, this addictive personality. I think it's something genetic in the wiring deep inside my head. I always have been, and always will be, an addict in every sense of the word. At the end of the day, addiction is addiction whether you are an addict or have become addicted. I think that the only time that this was not present, or at least not active, was when I was a baby. I can look back into my really early childhood years, under the age of six, and I can see where sexual addiction and adrenaline-chasing were clearly evident. I used to be a proper naughty boy just for the rush of it. I was also such a sexually manipulative child, always trying to get my friends, boys or girls, to participate and play with me in a sexual manner. This behaviour too brought with it a rush of naughtiness. It was not learned in any way, it was just inherent in my DNA.

Most people who are addicts have cross-addictions, like food or sex or gambling. There are endless forms of addiction that the average person – or 'normies', as we call them – would not think to classify as addiction. For me, it started with adrenaline-chasing and sex. Then it changed into drugs and alcohol. Then it went back to adrenaline-type jobs and driving at crazy high speeds to get the rush. Then it went into work, and that was when I became extremely successful at everything I put my mind to. Then the sex addiction came back with a vengeance. Then it was sex, drugs and alcohol for years on end. Now that I am sober again, it's gone into food, and some minor sexual issues have recently started to become apparent. I am now starting to address them. I am prepared for spending my life fighting back against active addiction in various forms. The addict in you will never leave you and will always try to regain control of you any way that it can – and if you allow it!

What worked for me this time around was very different from my first stretch of fourteen years, and my other attempts at sobriety. In hindsight, the first fourteen years were not really being sober; it was more like abstaining from using. I was still a very sick and unwell person deep inside. Things got worse when I cut all ties with the twelve-step programme and lost touch with my sober friends and my then sponsor. Part of me doubted that I was really an addict. Was it just that my parents panicked, seeing my teenage experimentation with substances? Did they possibly see signs of my father in my behaviour, and that fear caused them to send me off to rehab prematurely? Then, after spending a month on the inpatient ward, was I simply brainwashed into believing I was an addict? I think these doubts were why I allowed myself to have that initial first relapse after maintaining sobriety for fourteen long years.

Once I started using again, I convinced myself I was not an addict. I believed I was choosing to use and drink, and since I was making a conscious decision I was therefore in control. Addicts are people who are not in control – at least, so I thought. I would tell myself that I could stop if I wanted to, but I did not want to stop, nor did I choose to. Again, under the false assumption that ultimately I was in control. I held on to this belief over the entire decade. When my life would get messy, I simply chose to cut back on the heavy stuff and only allow myself to drink and smoke weed. When life got really bad – but not to the point where I was doing jail time or had wrecked my body permanently – I would manage to abstain from all substances for several months. This would give me enough time to sort my shit out and get back on track. I am a master at rebuilding my life. I can count the number of times I have had to do this on all my fingers and toes on both hands and feet. I was under no illusion about using; I knew that I was far more productive and much more successful in life when I was sober. But I always believed I could use again in a controlled way.

Addicts will try any number of ways to convince themselves that they are in control. It's not uncommon for them to use from Friday evening till 14:00 on Sunday, or maybe they only do hard stuff twice a month. The combinations are endless. I tried every one. I remember that, when I last got nine months sober in London, although I did not admit it to anyone in the NA programme, I had every intention of using G&T

again. The plan was that I would build up my company and earn enough to take two week-long trips a year to Asia to do as many drugs and escorts as money could buy.

The last rock bottom I had was a mental rock bottom and by far the worst and darkest. I had completely lost faith in myself, had convinced myself that I was a true failure, a loser on a grand scale. I had reverted to when I was fourteen and had given up on myself. I believed that all of my previous success was a combination of luck and my gift of the gab from my Irish blood. I truly thought that I talked my way into every job and every opportunity that I had, and that the reason I moved on every few years was because the real me started to show and inevitably failure was the next thing to come. So it made sense to move on before it was clear that I was a fake.

At this time I was working for a security company in their control room in a piece-of-shit building near Blackhorse Road Tube. It was so bad that it was due to be knocked down in the near future, which could not have come sooner, to be honest. I was making under £8 an hour on a zero-hours contract. The job requirements were so basic that one of my colleagues, who shall remain nameless, might well have been the dumbest guy I have ever met. The fact that at one point in my career I had successfully run five multimillion-dollar companies, and now my main function was to patrol this broken-down building and call sleeping security guards every hour just to wake them up, was as low as I could get. I was smoking crystal from the minute I woke up to the minute I took my pills to sleep, every hour or so needing a hit just so that I could numb myself.

My poor partner, Jeison, was forced to keep my drug use a secret from my friends and my family. I was sober when I met him, but within a few months I had started drinking and smoking weed on a daily basis. I then slowly started using crystal again. This repeated story is common and rings true with all addicts. You start on the light stuff in a controlled manner, and guaranteed, eventually you're back on it harder and more intensely than the last time. At first the crystal and G was once or twice a month, and I know Jeison had no clue. But as my addiction grew stronger, it became very clear to him that I was back on it again. Big time. And as the addiction grew, so did my shocking and selfish behaviour. When you're stuck in active addiction, no one matters to you: your child, your sibling, your parent, your lover. Unfortunately, no matter how strong a bond you have, it's never strong enough to stop the addiction. It does not mean that you don't love them; it just means that you're addicted and powerless.

I started to not come home at night, or I would disappear while he was sleeping. I would end up at random sex parties or in the sauna, always to then find thirty missed calls and a hundred text messages from Jeison. It was never the jealous rant or anger, as it would have been from me. It was always complete and genuine fear, panic and intense worry. He wanted to know where was I and was I OK, who was I with and what was the address in case I didn't come home? When I was out Partying and Playing, he would usually keep in touch with me continually via text or WhatsApp. In retrospect, it's clear that he did not sleep much when I was out. He once broke down into tears and said that he could not take it any more, that his overwhelming fear was that I was going to die one night and that he would have to be the one to call my parents. He said that he could not see his life without me, that he needed me. None of this was enough to even suggest to me that I should stop. While in tears, he said that if I could not stop then could I at least stop leaving the house, as this was unbearable for him and he would be in a state of panic and fear while I was gone. He told me that at least if I was at home he would know I was safe and OK and that if anything bad happened he would be there to look after me. This was all so foreign to him – he has still to this day never done any drug and I think he can count the number of times on one hand that he has been drunk. For fuck's sake, he has half a bottle of flavoured cider and he starts to say, 'Oh, babe, I feel it now, big time.' This is a guy who lives for the gym daily and plans his meals around healthy options rather than taste. He has even had a tuna milkshake – I mean, really, who does that?

I eventually, after endless nagging and begging, agreed to his request and started using at home while he was asleep. I would regularly have one or two guys over, using the sitting room downstairs to engage in P&P while he was upstairs. On a few occasions, I would end up with four or five guys round for twelve-hour sessions, again with Jeison being stuck upstairs in the bedroom. I then started to leave the house to join groups. Jeison and I could never make any plans. I would keep him waiting for hours, inventing lame excuses as to why I was running late, but he always knew.

Then he finally started to get angry and said he could not do this any more, that he could not keep my dirty secret any more. He called my mum, saying he needed to see her right away. Jeison and my mum are super-close – she sees him as a son and he sees her as a mum. He finally told her that I was using again. I got a few calls and texts from her but she was not being direct so I just did the usual and did not reply. A few days later, my mum invited Jeison, myself and Jeison's sister round for dinner. I was very late, of course, because I was so stoned on weed just trying to take the edge off the Tina. My mum was very frosty but so far had not mentioned or asked if I was using. About halfway through the dinner, she nonchalantly asked if I was using again. I exploded, screaming, 'Yes, I'm fucking using – how the hell do you think I can deal with all of you and my fucked-up life? Now excuse me as I need to go and get high again as you killed my buzz.' I went to the porter's area in the building to smoke a pipe, then left for the sauna.

I was beyond furious that my partner had betrayed me. I could not fathom how he had done such a thing. I stayed high and away from him with no contact for almost two days. Finally, returning home after finishing all my Tina, I was an absolute mess, wrecked completely to the core. I was so sick (and looked like death warmed up) that I was not able to take a bus or taxi because I kept dry-heaving. I had to walk from Pleasuredrome sauna in Waterloo to Brixton. It took me just under four hours as I was continually having to stop to sit and rest. I went to sleep still furious, not speaking to Jeison. I took my heavy dose of pills and weed and slept for almost sixteen hours. When I woke up I knew that I had finally come to a very serious fork in the road: either to continue down this path of destruction, or to quit and try to get my life back. Although I initially did not want to stop at all – I was not ready to quit – I knew I had to at least try, for fear of losing both Jeison and my mother. I have not smoked Tina or done G since then. I did continue to smoke weed, but only for two weeks before quitting that too.

This turning point was crucial for me. I did not quit for anyone but myself. But having such an amazing loving and caring partner give me a reason to want to try to get my life back. He had stuck by me through the toughest – and what must have been the most painful – time of his life. I knew what we had was special and worth fighting for. So that's just what I did: I fought back hard to break the cycle of active addiction. I went back to NA and got back in touch with David Mason, my key worker at the Margarete Centre, the NHS drug programme for Camden. David had been continually leaving me voicemails, gently trying to get me to come back in. The most important thing, and the first step that I needed to make, was to admit the truth. This was the first time I knew and truly believed that I was and I am an addict.

There is no great secret or complex list of things that have given me this gift of my life back. It's one very elementary fact that has allowed me to be reborn, in some sense, and to live life to its fullest. The fact is that, every day, I admit that I am an addict first and then I make the conscious choice not to pick up or use alcohol or drugs. The rest has simply followed over the last twenty-eight months. This is not a great amount of time in the context of my 502 months alive on this planet to date. I know that, one day at a time, I will continue to grow and improve as the man that I am today.

This is a man that I am proud to be today. The shame and guilt are gone. It's not to say that I have forgotten who I was or what I have done in my past. I take full responsibility for all of my actions and truly do regret so much of my past. But today, through sobriety, I try always to do the right thing and I am conscious of my behaviour and how I can impact upon other people.

Getting sober was a combination of things that I had to do to slowly build back a sobriety foundation, one brick at a time. I started, my way, to do the first three steps of the twelve-step programme on a daily basis:

1. Admit I am powerless over my addiction – that my life has become unmanageable
2. Come to believe that a power greater than myself can restore me to sanity
3. Make a decision to turn my will and my life over to the care of God as I understand God

I was completely powerless in the beginning and I needed to turn my life over to my higher power to help me. I could not stop the drug use, and surrendering to the fact that I was powerless was for the first time a really freeing experience.

I had stopped working so that I could dedicate myself to rebuilding my sober life. I decided that inpatient rehab was not needed, having already had three trips under my belt. I took every option offered to me by the Margarete Centre. It, along with David Mason, truly helped to save my life. I had two key workers: Dave, who was my primary key worker, and a second one who was geared more towards helping rebuild recovering addicts' careers. As I had no career, I signed up for it. I had two psychiatrists and one psychologist, all of whom I saw on a regular basis. I then signed up for a few courses – two of them were really helpful and had a huge impact on me in this early stage of my recovery. The first one I took was Relapse Prevention, and it showed me a different way of looking at maintaining ongoing sobriety. The second one was called Intuitive Recovery. This course was a very different way to look at sobriety. On the first day, I wasn't too sure if it was for me and almost walked out of the class, but I decided to stick it out and that's proven the best decision I ever made for my early recovery. It really gave me, as a lifelong control freak, a different perspective on sobriety and one that has truly given me the strongest foundation, or sobriety bricks. I know I would not be sober today if I did not have the tools I learned from Intuitive Recovery; I highly recommend it. I was able to take the lessons learned from both the twelve-step NA programme and Intuitive Recovery, and combine them to build a rock-solid foundation, one brick at a time.

Today, I start with the Serenity Prayer then I do the first three steps of the twelve-step programme. The steps I say now are slightly different to when I first got sober, as today I am still an addict but I am not powerless over drugs and alcohol, and my life is not unmanageable. It's very simple: today I just don't use, no matter what!

Serenity Prayer: *God grant me the serenity to except the things I cannot change, the courage to change the things I can and the wisdom to know the difference.* I quite often use this one prayer throughout my day when things get challenging.

1. **I** admit that I was powerless over my addiction – that my life **was** unmanageable
2. I believe that a power greater than myself **has** restored me to sanity
3. **I** made a decision to turn my will and my life over to the care of my higher power, asking him to help guide me and direct me into making the correct life decisions that will lead me to a life path of SOBRIETY, SERENITY and SANITY.

I also did what was suggested in the twelve-step programme: I kept coming back. I got the world's most amazing sponsor, Eddy Queens. Getting the right sponsor truly has made such a difference. Eddy has a wonderful, mothering character about her – just what I needed. But she takes no shit and has no problem calling me out on my bullshit. I know that without her I would not have been able to keep my sobriety. She has also given me the strength and confidence to complete and go ahead with this book. I have spent my life in the closet about my sexuality. I am still in some ways ashamed to be gay. While I am very open in an LGBT environment, the people I work with today all think I am straight and married to a woman.

Eddy pointed out to me, on the many times when I thought about quitting this book for fear of judgement for going public with my personal life story, that my primary purpose and reason for this book was to try to help someone still suffering from a life of active addiction, and to carry my story and my message to them. Thank you for that, Eddy! I am proud of my recovery and have no problem sharing that part of my life. Today I am proud to be a recovering addict. I have a strong support network of friends in the NA programme, who I call upon regularly for advice and suggestions about how to cope with challenging situations. I give back by trying to help out other still-suffering addicts. I am slowly but surely working through the twelve steps, and I have recently taken on a sponsee. I try to do the right thing on a daily basis, and I accept each and every day upon waking that I am and will always be an addict, the only difference being that I am one who is recovering at my own speed.

Today I am happy and blessed. I have been given back so much from sobriety: my life partner, who is my best friend, and my mother and father, who are my greatest rocks of support and who have always given me unconditional love and support through all the madness and insanity I have dragged them through. They never gave up on me and for that I will be eternally grateful. One of most amazing gifts sobriety has given me today is the truly special and strong bond and relationship that I have with my mother. This gift alone has made all the hard work and tough struggles I went through in sobriety well worth it, to get here. Today she tells me she is proud of me and she makes it very clear to me how much she appreciates having her son back. This gift is priceless! I have my family, my friends, my own security company, Sutherland Specialist Security, and my professional career in the security industry is starting to take off. The greatest gift of all is that I have my new and improved life back. Life today is not easy, and it will always have its ups and downs, but my shed is packed with so many different tools of sobriety that I should and will always have everything I need at arm's reach to keep me in sobriety. I will continue on a daily basis to be a grateful and truly happy recovering addict.

As I said before, I don't believe there is a right or wrong way to get sober. Just do what you need to do to get it because sober life is great. The above is what worked for me and me only. If you are struggling with any form of active addiction, just know that there is hope, and if you want a new way of life it is possible. I am not the first and I surely won't be the last. Don't be afraid to fight to get your life back – you can do it, trust me. Just reach out for the help and it will be there, from a doctor, family member, lover, or fellow recovering addict. You are not alone in this if you don't want to be!

If anyone is struggling and wants to contact me, please feel free. I have the email below for exactly this reason.

Yours truly,
Jack Sutherland
Recovering Addict

jacksutherland1974@outlook.com